SENSE OF TOUCH

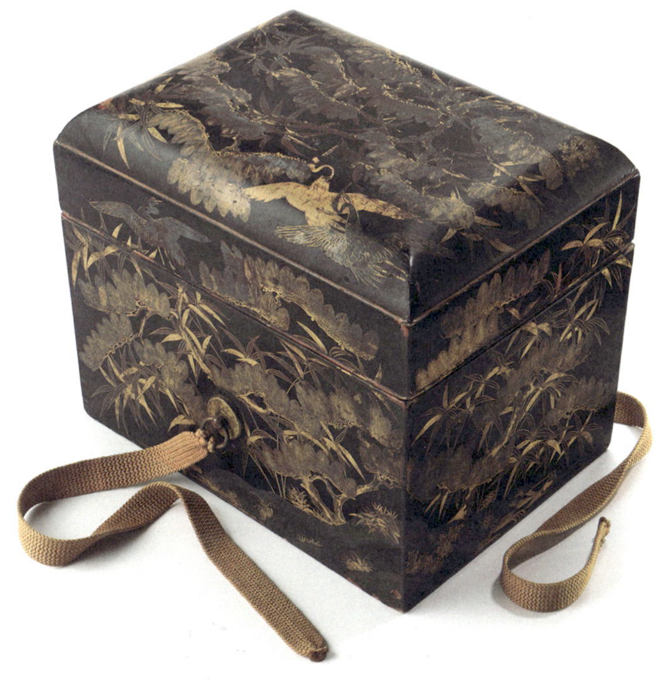

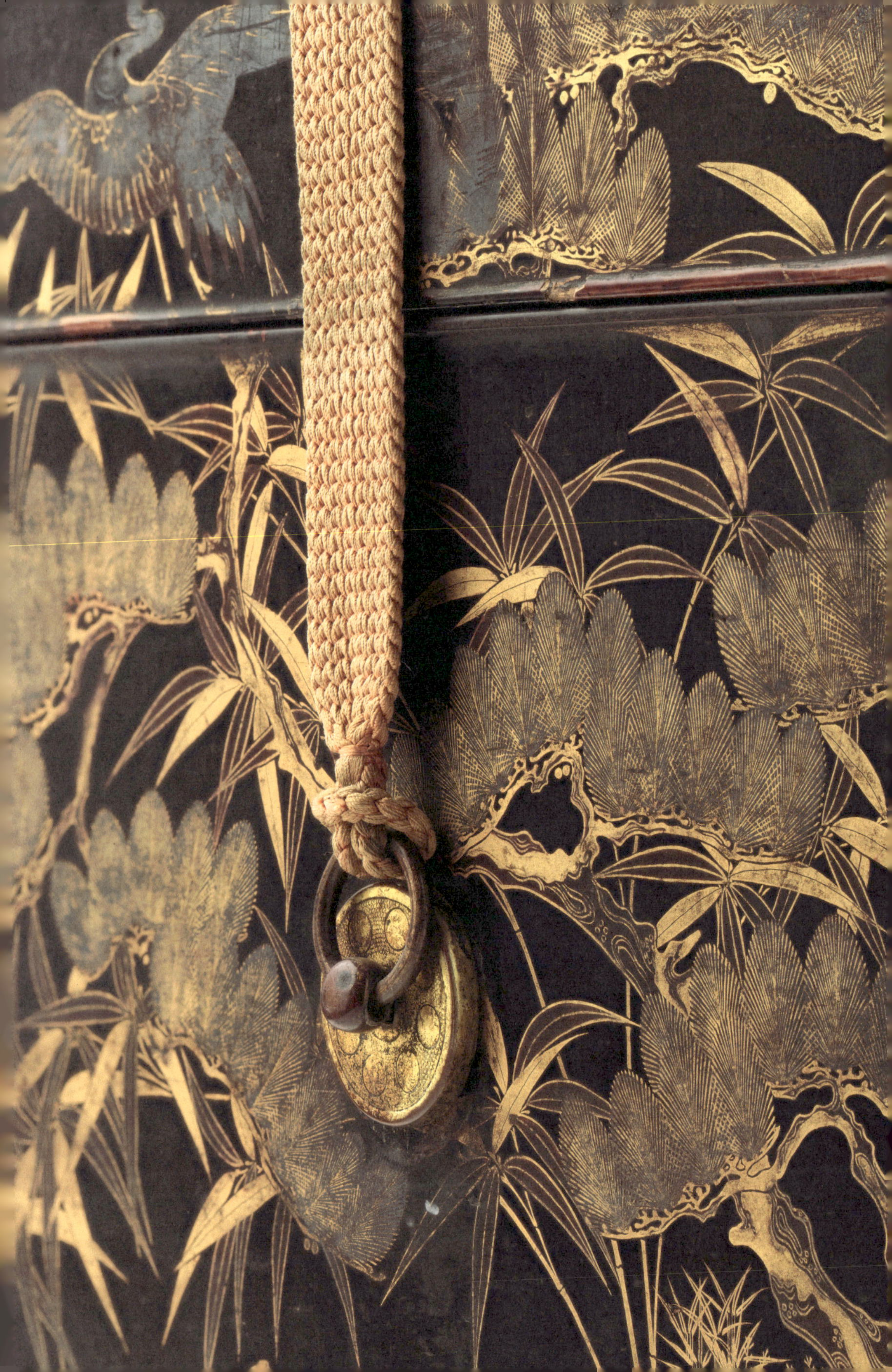

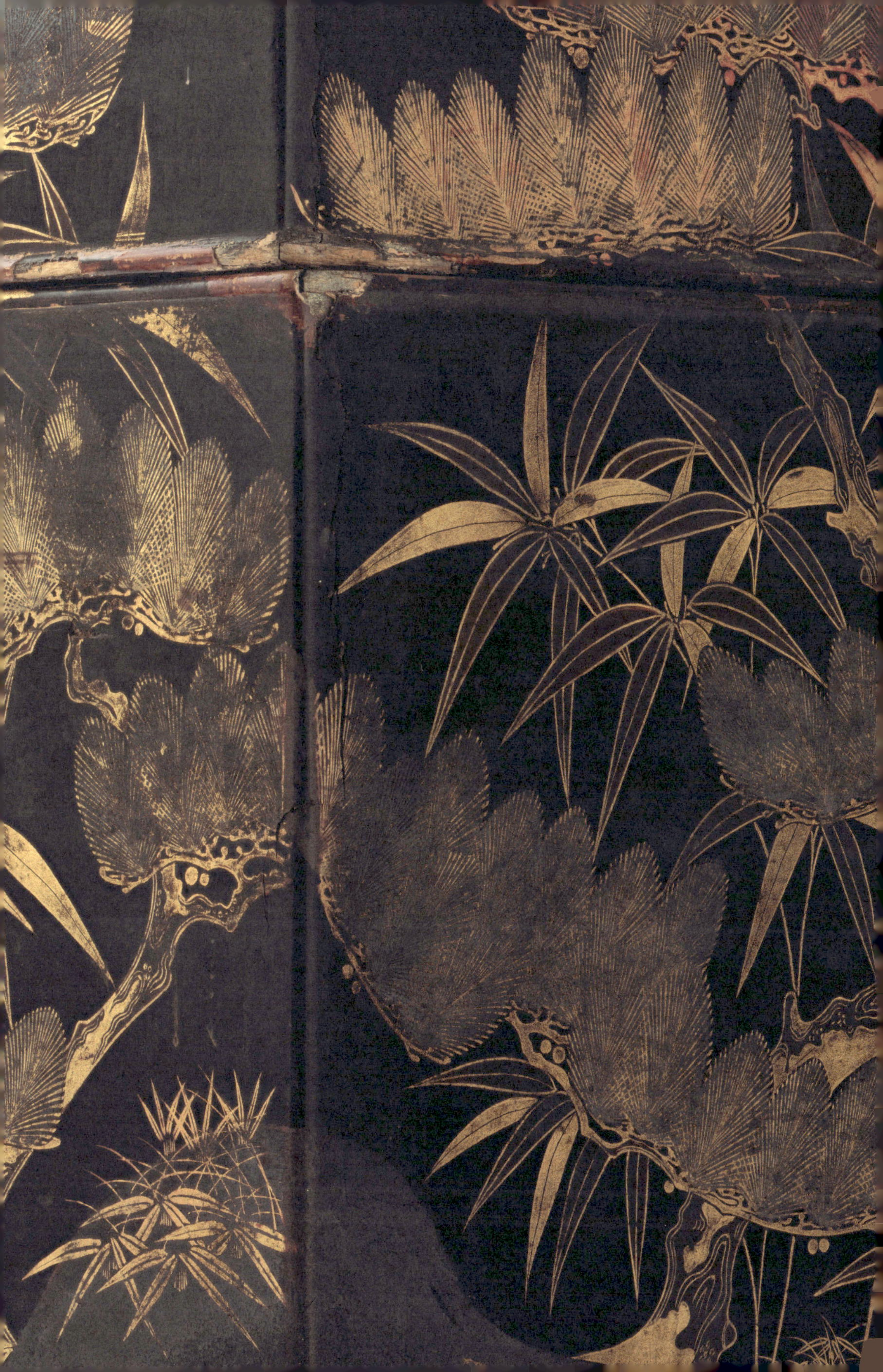

SENSE OF TOUCH

Shokkan and Sensory Exploration in Japanese Art

Edited by **AKIKO TAKESUE**

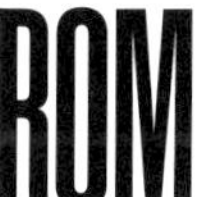

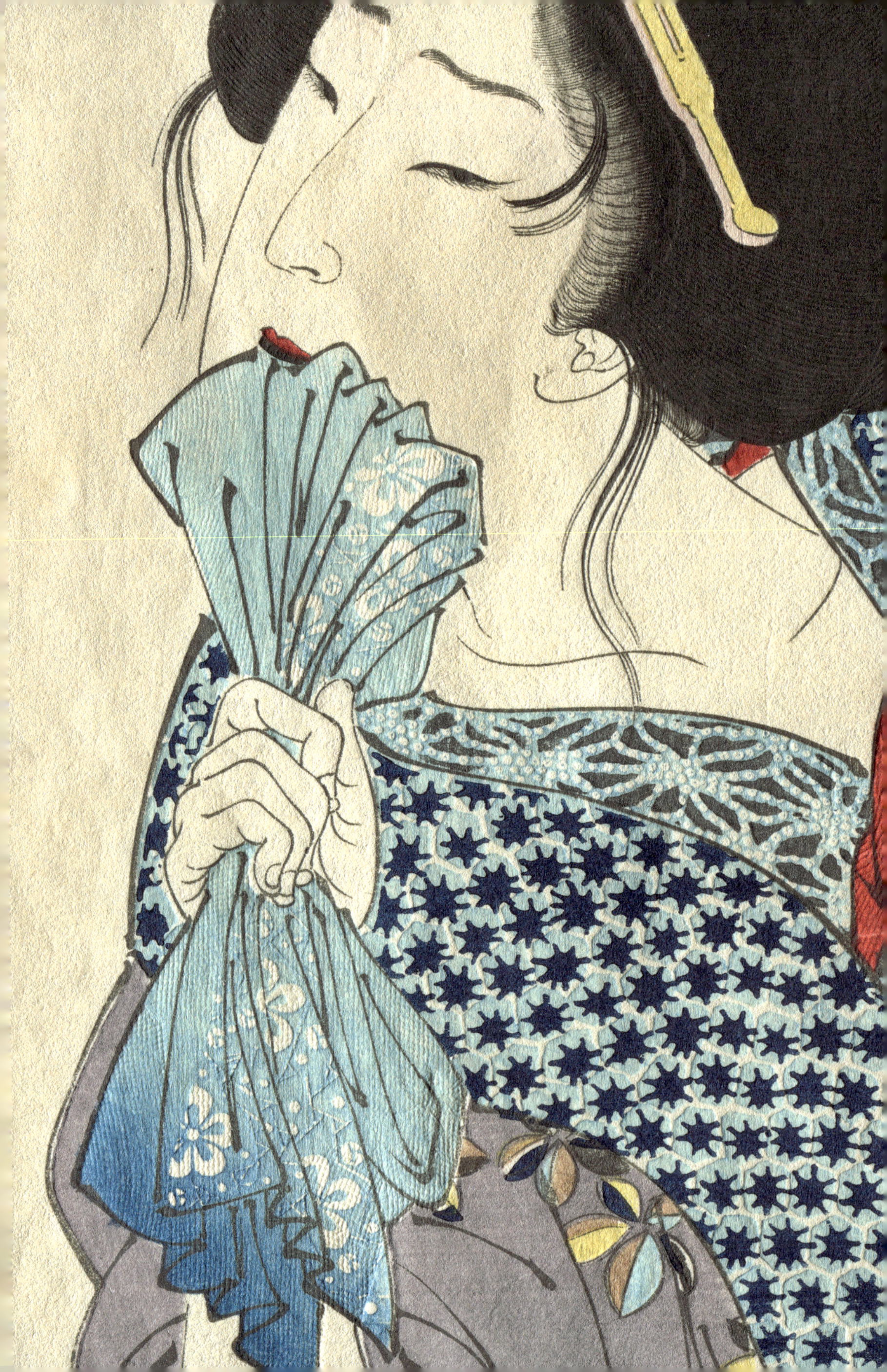

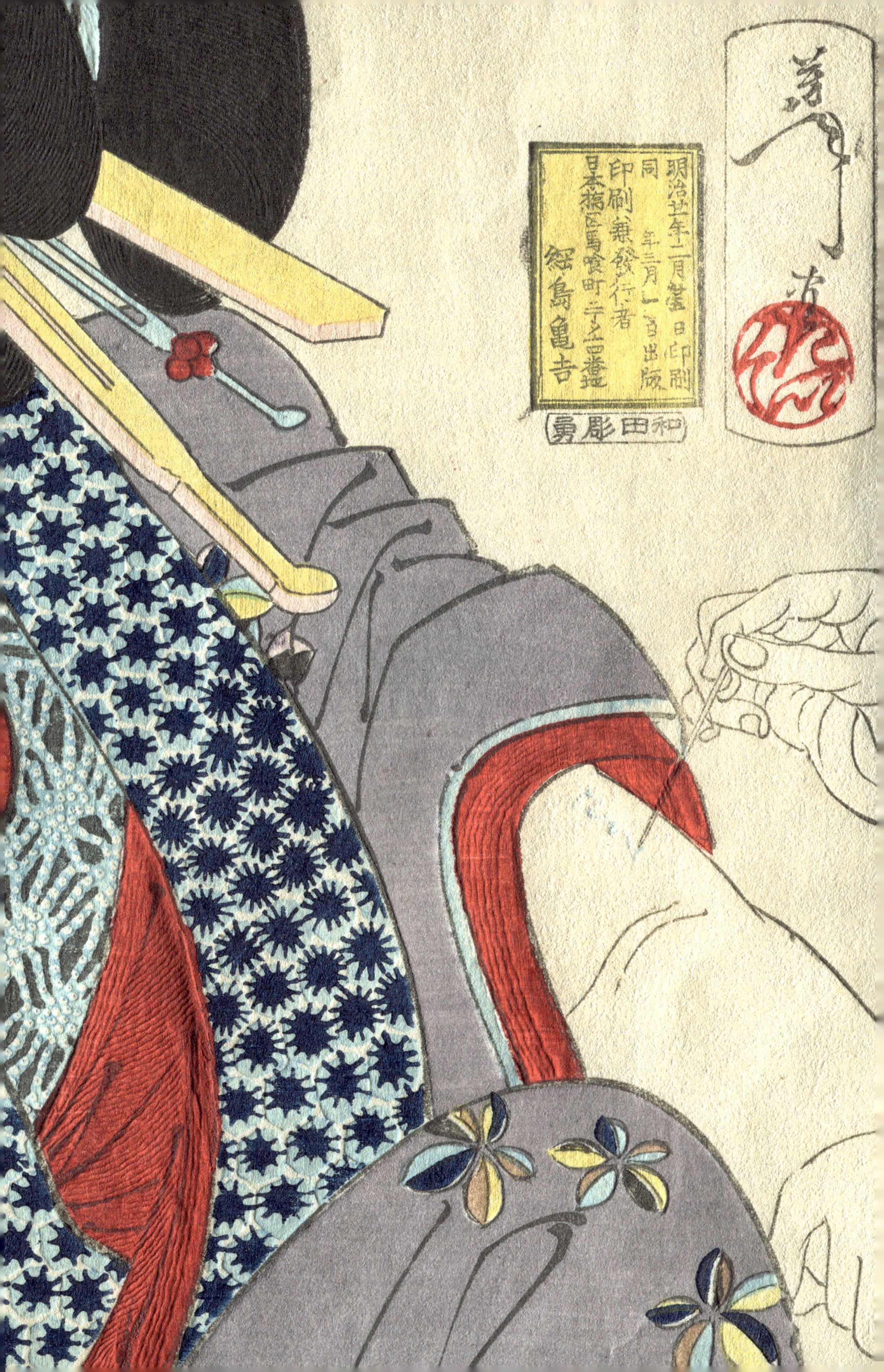

芳年
明治廿一年十一月廿四日印刷
同 年十二月一日出版
印刷兼發行者
日本橋區馬喰町二丁目一番地
綱島亀吉
和田彫勇

Published by the Royal Ontario Museum, with the generous support of the Louise Hawley Stone Charitable Trust.

ROM, 100 Queen's Park, Toronto, Ontario, M5S 2C6
rom.on.ca

Manager, Publishing: Sheeza Sarfraz
Senior Designer: Tara Winterhalt
Communications Coordinator: Monika Tragarz
Copyeditor: Marnie Lamb
Proofreader: Marnie Lamb

Artwork appearing in section breaks
ii–iii: Detail of *Cosmetic Box with Pine Tree, Bamboo, Crane, and Turtle Motifs* on p. 20
vi–viii: Detail of *Looking Painful*, from the series *Thirty-Two Aspects of Women* on p. 30
x–xi: Detail of *Bundle from An Archive of Rememory* on pp. 44–45
xvi–1: Detail of *Netsuke of Shishi Lion* on p.18
52–53: Detail of *Ewer with Matching Basin* on p. 21
72–73: Detail of *Abstract/Expression/Byōbu* on pp. 84–85
90–91: Detail of *Woman's Outer Robe* (uchikake) *with "Pine, Bamboo, and Plum" Design* on p. 25
108–109: Detail of *Woman's Summer Kimono with Design of the Full Moon and Autumn Grasses* on p. 28
128–129: Detail of *Mino Ware, e-Shino–Type Serving Bowl* on p. 99
132–133: Detail (handle) of a sword on p. 9
134–136: Detail of dress and trousers on p. 32

Library and Archives Canada Cataloguing in Publication
Title: *Sense of Touch Shokkan and Sensory Exploration in Japanese Art* / edited by Akiko Takesue.
Names: Takesue, Akiko, editor | Royal Ontario Museum, host institution, publisher.
Description: Catalogue of an exhibition held at the Royal Ontario Museum from April 4, 2026, to September 7, 2026.
Identifiers: Canadiana 20260110426 | ISBN 9780888545367 (softcover)
Subjects: LCSH: Senses and sensation in art—Exhibitions. LCSH: Art, Japanese—Exhibitions. LCGFT: Exhibition catalogs.
Classification: LCC NX650.S47 S46 2026 | DDC 700/.453—dc23

Printed in Canada.
ROM is an agency of the Government of Ontario.

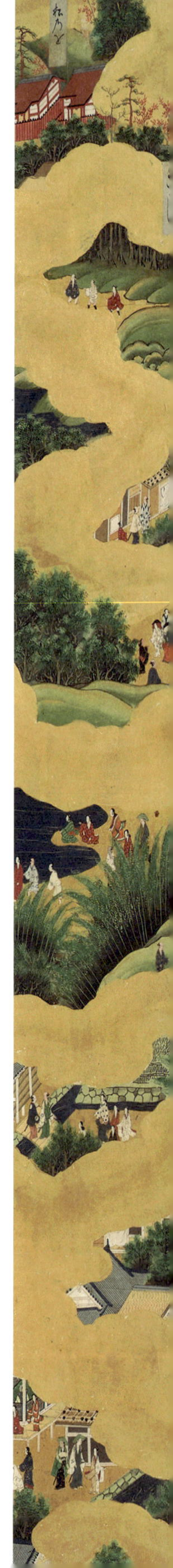

Contents

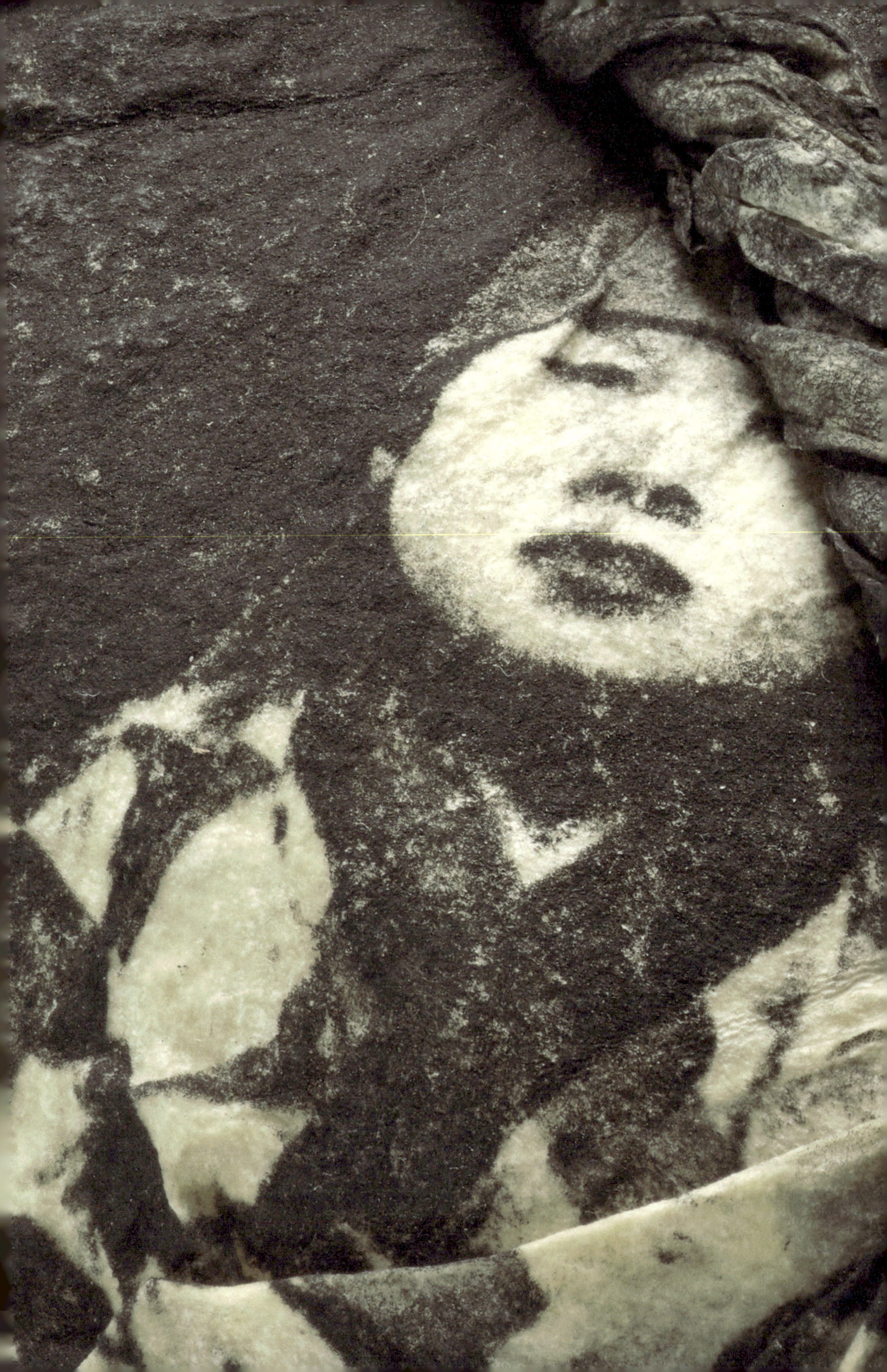

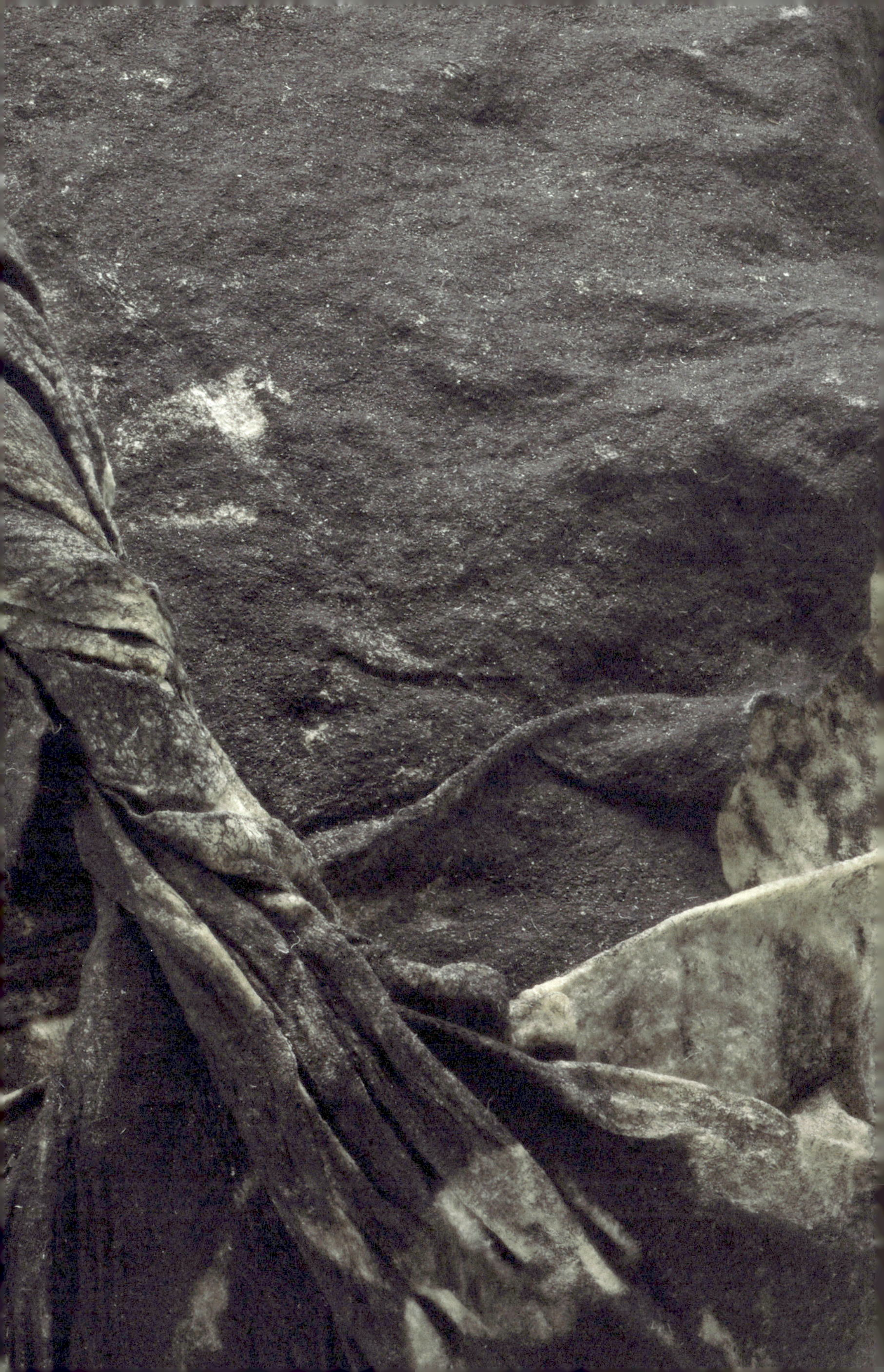

Foreword

A SQUARE TEA BOWL, whose shape holds the touch of its maker and evokes the soothing warmth of tea. A wooden netsuke in the form of a mouse, whose smallness and extraordinary detail invite you to hold it in your palm. Scrolls and folding screens that must be opened by hand to be seen.

These objects, like the dozens of artworks that fill this book and the accompanying exhibition, suggest the diversity of Japanese art today and through the centuries. Importantly, they also expand our understanding of what an experience with art can be. A netsuke shaped like a mouse can invite us to consider not just the way it feels to touch, but also draws attention to the anticipation of that touch. And if we are open to it, exploring these works of art can encourage us to experience the objects we encounter every day in new ways. While the digital and virtual proliferate around us, the art of *shokkan* invites us to slow down and take note of the richness to be found in the sense of touch—whether we have the opportunity to open a handscroll or simply turn the page of a favourite book.

That this single exhibition is so rich with profound ideas and beauty is thanks to the creativity and expertise of its curator, Dr. Akiko Takesue, the Bishop White Committee Associate Curator of Japanese Art & Culture, and her many talented colleagues, some of whom are also featured in this book.

ROM is, as the scholars in these pages rightly note, home to an extraordinary collection of Japanese art, which includes everything from ornately patterned 17th-century silk kimonos to contemporary fabric-wrapped *furoshiki*. It is also a home to an array of diverse experts—conservators, preparators, and exhibition designers—who worked with Dr. Takesue to bring this art out from their cabinets and onto display. Interpretive planners and educators at ROM collaborated with Dr. Takesue to frame the stories in ways that engage and delight. And ROM's publications experts skillfully guided this thoughtful book to a timely completion. I am grateful for their collaborative spirit.

May *Sense of Touch: Shokkan and Sensory Exploration in Japanese Art* be an invitation to change not just the way you think, but the way you feel.

Jennifer Wild
Interim Co-Director & CEO, ROM

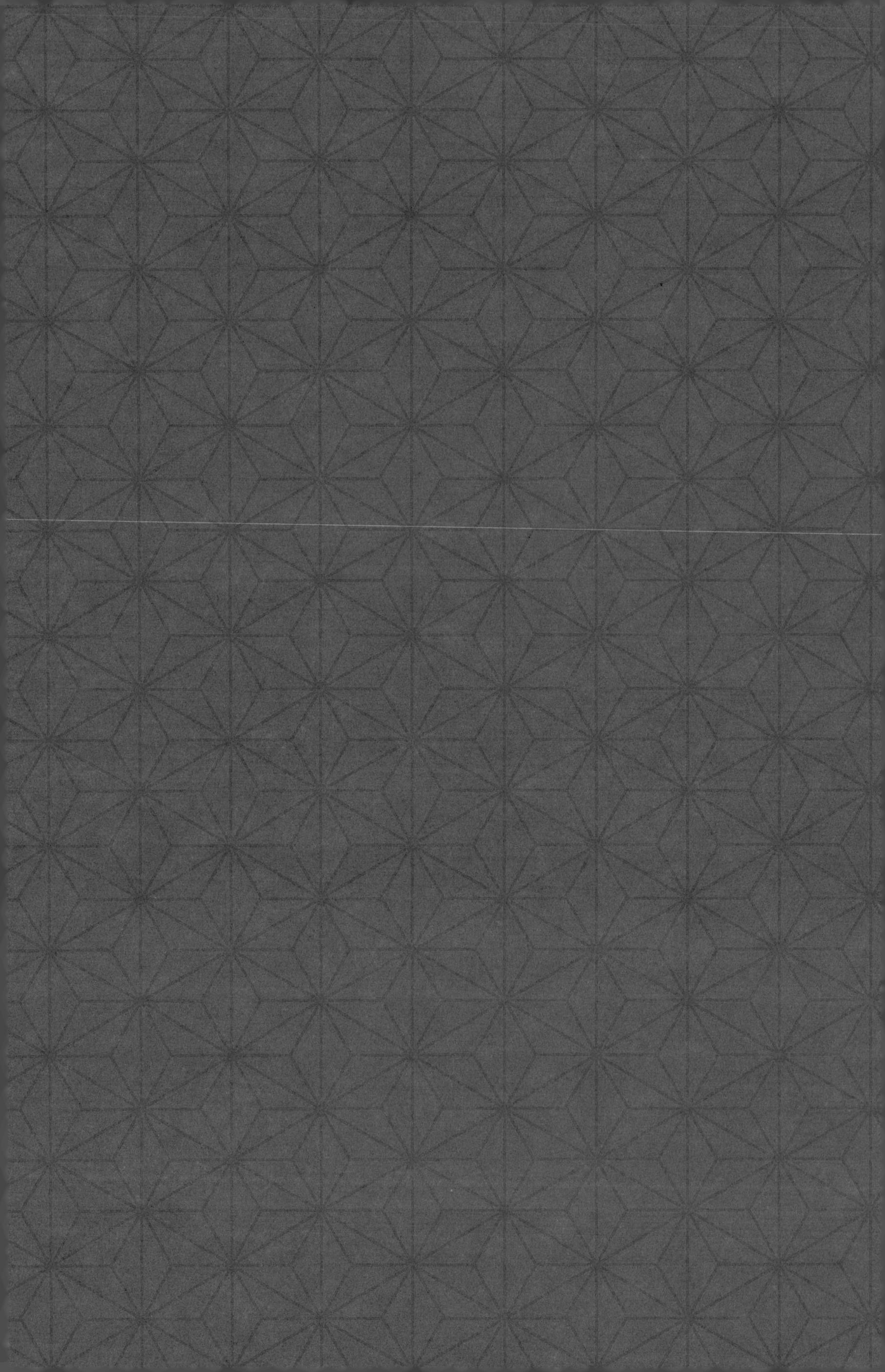

Acknowledgements

THE INITIAL IDEA OF EXPLORING the sense of touch in Japanese art emerged during my PhD research (2010–16) on the Japanese ceramic collection of Sir William C. Van Horne (1843–1915) in Montreal. I discovered that Van Horne kept his over 1,200 pieces in his home office, sharing them only with invited guests rather than displaying them in the public spaces of his grand residence. In his home office, he handled each ceramic individually, examined it closely, and recorded meticulous details in his multi-volume notebooks. As a self-taught painter, he even sketched a thumbnail illustration of every piece. Imagining Van Horne's intimate engagement with these objects, I began to consider how proximity and the act of handling might explain his deep passion for Japanese ceramics.

My interest in tactility in art however did not fully take shape until 2022. While waiting for a delayed flight—to somewhere I can no longer recall—I suddenly realized that the notion of touch could extend beyond ceramics to encompass Japanese art as a whole, where many artworks double as utilitarian objects. I quickly scribbled the thought on a sheet of paper. Now, it is quite remarkable to see how these hastily taken notes have developed into this polished publication, accompanying an exhibition on the same theme.

I am deeply grateful to Dr. Laura Vigo of the Montreal Museum of Fine Arts for her encouragement and invaluable input from the very beginning of the idea. My encounter with *The Deepest Sense* by Dr. Constance Classen provided renewed inspiration and depth to my research, for which I am profoundly thankful.

This publication would not have been possible without the generosity and collaboration of the four contributors, Professor David Howes, artist Kōsuke Ikeda, Dr. Natsu Oyobe, and Professor Kōjirō Hirose, whose immediate and positive responses gave me tremendous encouragement. I would also like to express my appreciation to translator Brian Bergstrom for his consistently excellent work.

Finally, I thank many of my colleagues at the Royal Ontario Museum for their support of both the publication and the exhibition. While I cannot name everyone here, I wish to acknowledge in particular Sheeza Sarfraz and Tara Winterhalt for their dedication and support in bringing this publication to life.

Akiko Takesue

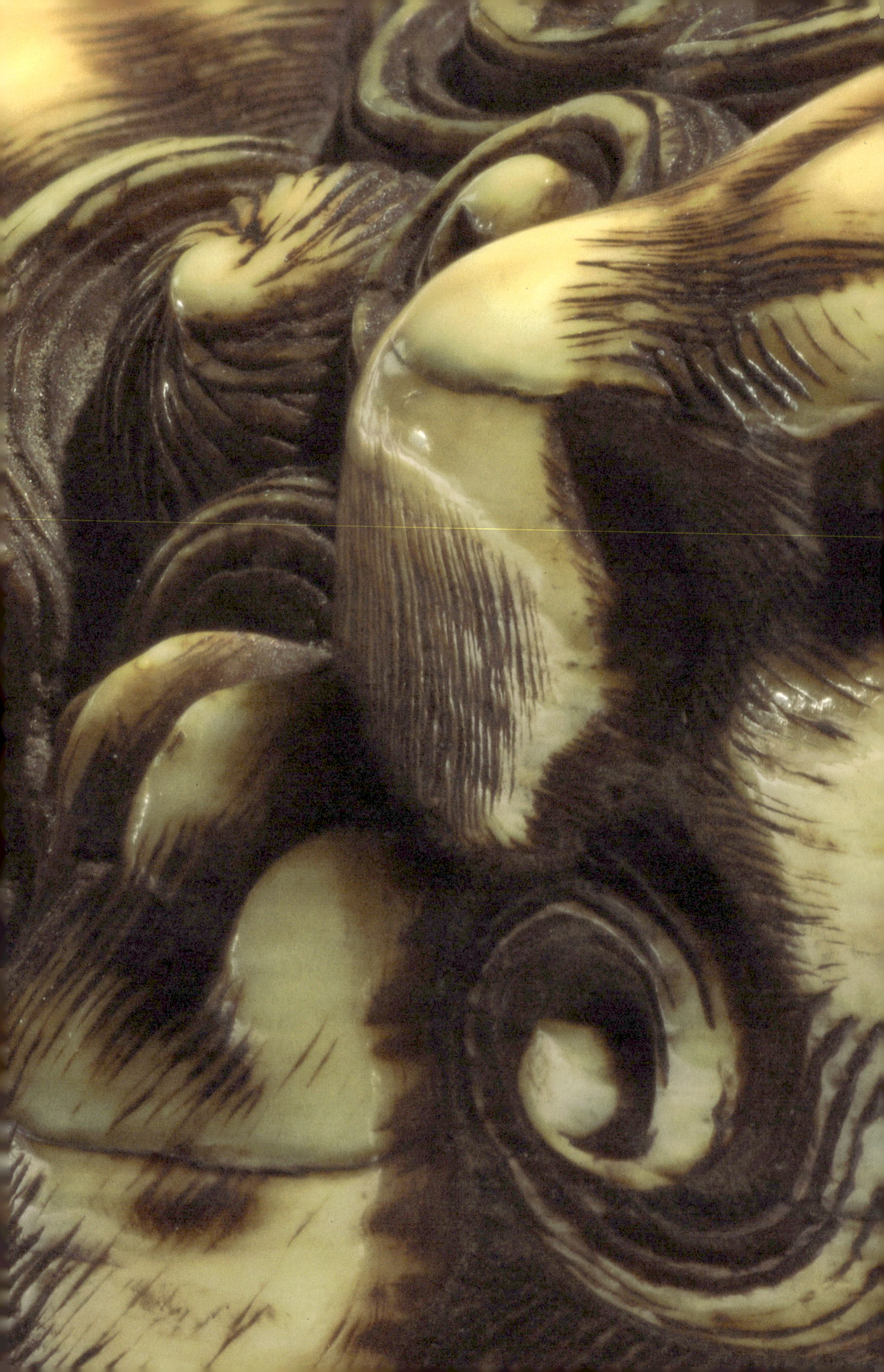

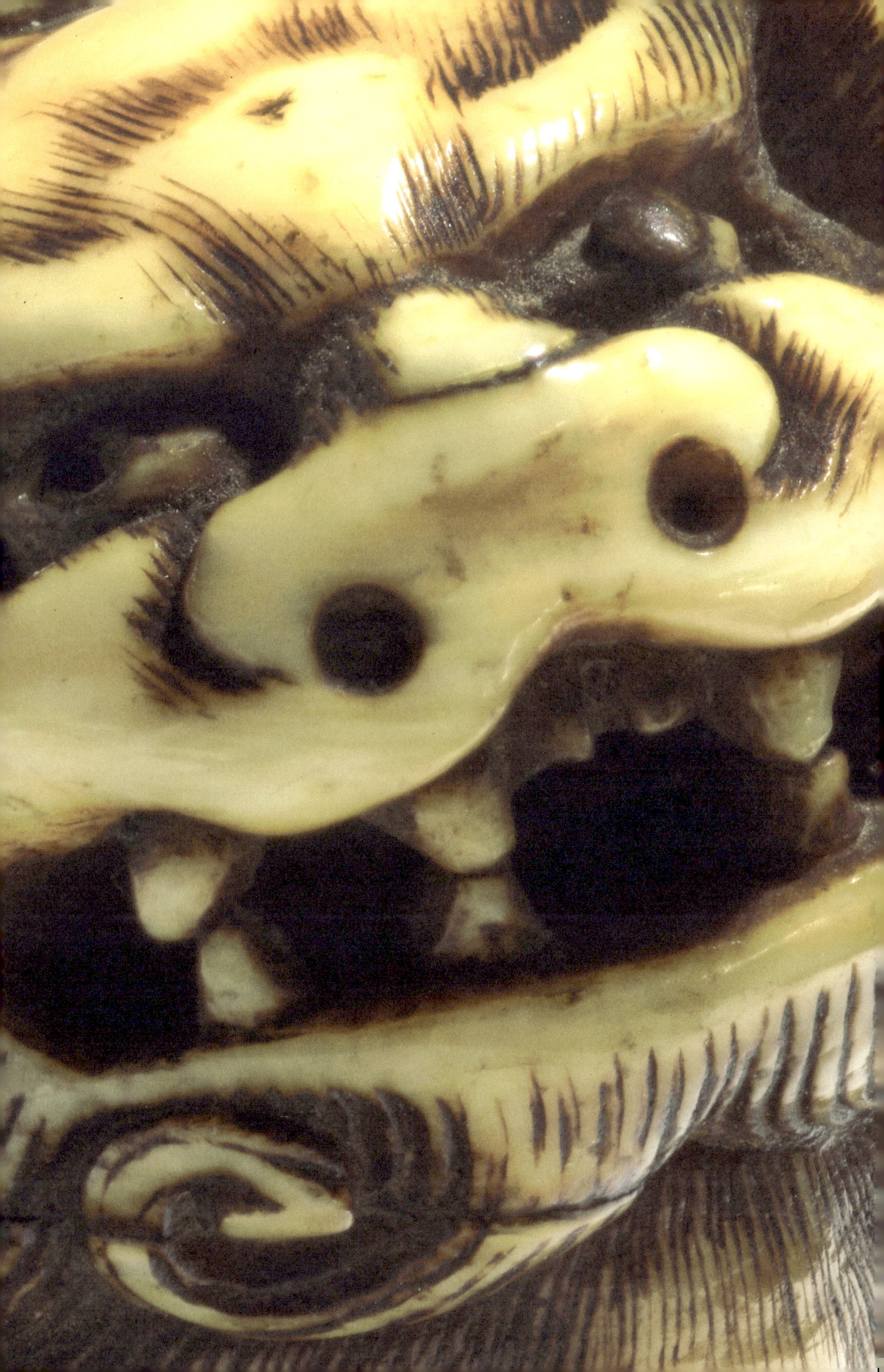

CHAPTER ONE

Re-Interpreting Japanese Art through Shokkan

AKIKO TAKESUE

There is more to touch than "meets the hands."

— JACOB HORNICK, 1992

The five senses are not so much that they have in common with each other, but that they are almost entirely united in the sense of touch.

— KŌTARŌ TAKAMURA, 1928

SHOKKAN, OR THE SENSE OF TOUCH, is a critical component in the creation, appreciation, and circulation of Japanese art. Yet the importance of shokkan is often taken for granted. It has never been explicitly analyzed as something that penetrates many aspects of Japanese art beyond discussions like "Japan is a country of handmade objects," or "the true beauty of tea utensils cannot be understood without holding them in your hands." This publication and the accompanying exhibition, *Shokkan: Material Encounters in Japanese Art*,[1] are an attempt to broadly examine Japanese art through the concept of shokkan.

Before the role of shokkan is discussed, though, the complexity of the term must be noted. In Japanese, two terms can be translated as "the sense of touch" in English: *shokkaku* and shokkan. The former refers to the haptic physical sensation directly felt by the part of the body touching something. Shokkan, on the other hand, refers to the psychological impression of touch, which is composed of various inputs from other senses, like vision or hearing, as well as from memories

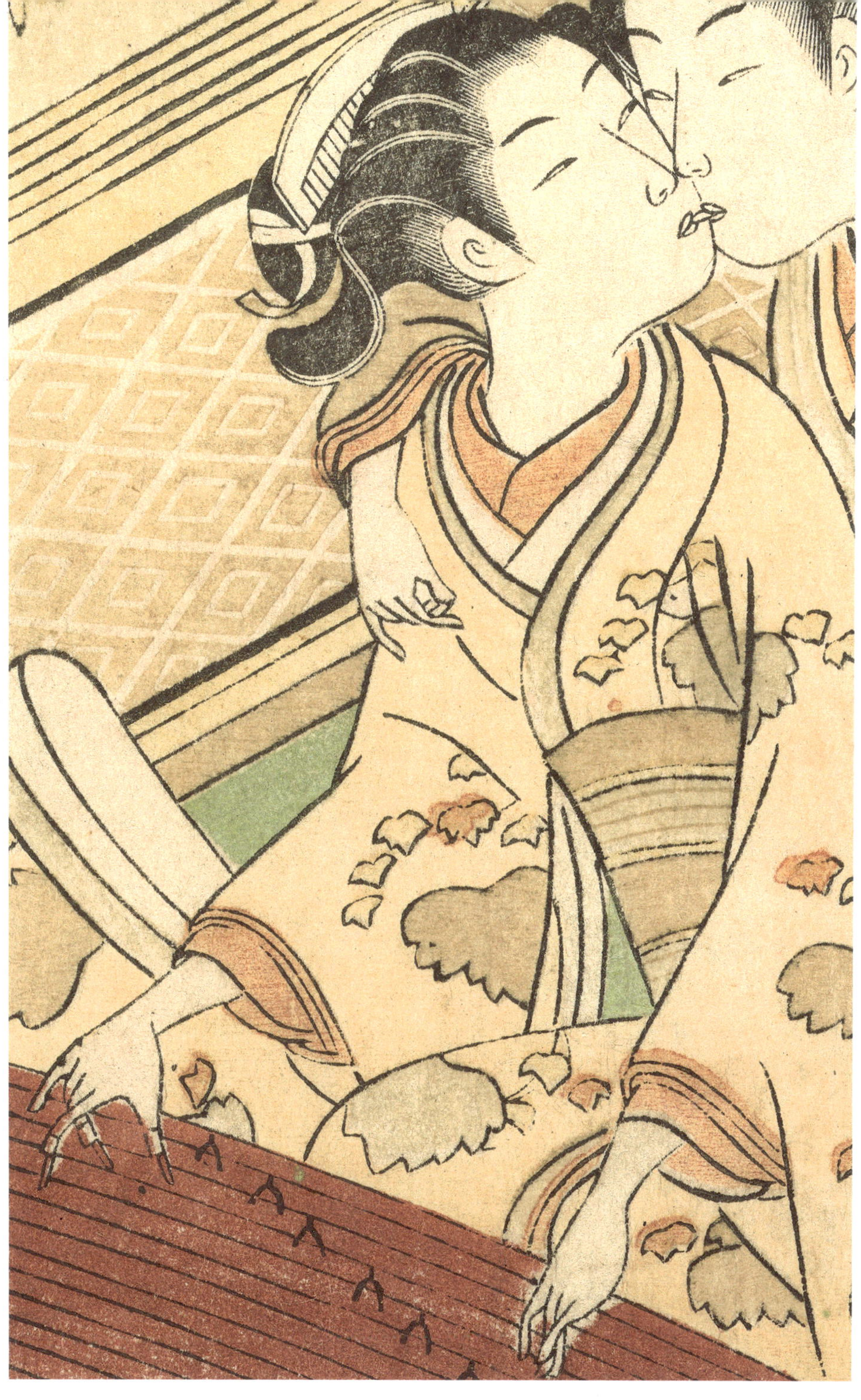

Detail, *Two Lovers: A Wakashu and a Young Woman Kiss*

or words. Masashi Nakatani and his co-authors suggest that shokkan consists of three elements: the object being touched; the part of the body touching the object, along with the nature of that touch; and the resulting subjective tactile experience.[2] This means that, even with the same shokkaku—the same physical sensation—the psychological impression of the touch—the shokkan—varies from person to person according to circumstance. This complex sensory understanding of touch is deeply rooted in Japanese art, where tactility plays an integral role in the creation and appreciation of the object's texture.

The complexity of touch has widely been discussed not only in Japan but around the world. While listing every study of the subject is beyond the scope of this essay, Charles Spense, to name one example, asserts that touch constitutes a genuinely multi-dimensional experience, observing that "an extensive body of research has shown that visual, auditory, and olfactory cues can all modulate people's tactile perception."[3] The understanding of skin as intersensory, proposed by David Howes, challenges "conventional Western understandings of the skin and of touch," which state that senses can be considered separately and that the brain is the sole locus of perception.[4] Jonathan Hay, discussing the "sensuous surface" of Chinese decorative art objects, states that "the object has an excess of affect over perception" and that "[its surface] engages ... the mesoperceptual apparatus of the flesh," which "partly comes into play through handling."[5]

This publication and the accompanying exhibition explore the complexity of touch—of shokkan—in Japanese art from a broader perspective emphasizing the importance of the handmade and the textural, of surface decoration and imagined touch, rather than relying on a simple dichotomy of the touchable versus the untouchable. Taking Japanese art as a case study, this project has the ultimate goal of promoting a new awareness of touch and thus diversifying how we appreciate art of all kinds.

Handmade objects have always been valued and appreciated in Japan, as in many other cultures, especially after the rise of industrialization and mass production in the 20th century. In Japan, a maker's hands are not simply considered tools; rather, hands mediate the relation between an object and a maker's mind or spirit. Muneyoshi Yanagi, the founder of the Japanese *Mingei* folk-art movement, for instance, states that "hands are different from machines in that they are directly connected to the spirit (*kokoro*)" and calls Japan "a country of handwork."[6] Shigemi Inaga asserts that the hand, and by extension the body, mediates objects and the human kokoro; further, the way that the kokoro affects (or is affected by) an object exceeds the powers of language to express.[7]

Making objects by hand surely takes more time and effort than mass production. Yet some potters still insist on producing hand-formed items, such as Raku-type pottery, without using a potter's wheel (Fig. 1.1). Furthermore, Raku ware's firing method, which uses small indoor kilns, is unsuited to large-scale production. Morgan Pitelka explains the relationship between the inefficiency of making Raku tea bowls and their tactility: because the low-temperature firing results in low thermal conductivity, Raku tea bowls are pleasant to hold even when filled with hot tea, and the process involves more handling by the potter, which results in the potter paying more attention to how the bowl feels to the user.[8] Handmade objects are not simply "made by hands" but embody multi-layered tactility, including the direct handling by the maker, the maker's imagination of the user's hands, and the eventual user's actual touch.

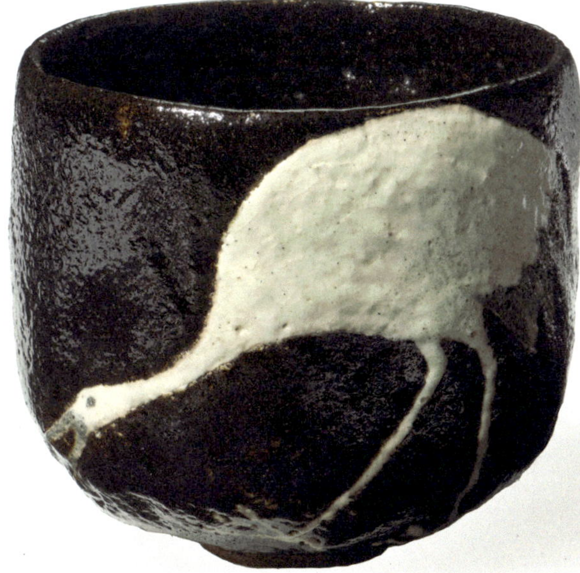

Fig. 1.1
Takahashi Dōhachi III (1811–79)
Black Raku-Type Tea Bowl with Crane and Turtle
Edo period, 1840–79
Stoneware with Raku glaze
9.4 × 10.2 cm
ROM 944.16.4

Given in memory of my grandfather, the late Sir William Van Horne

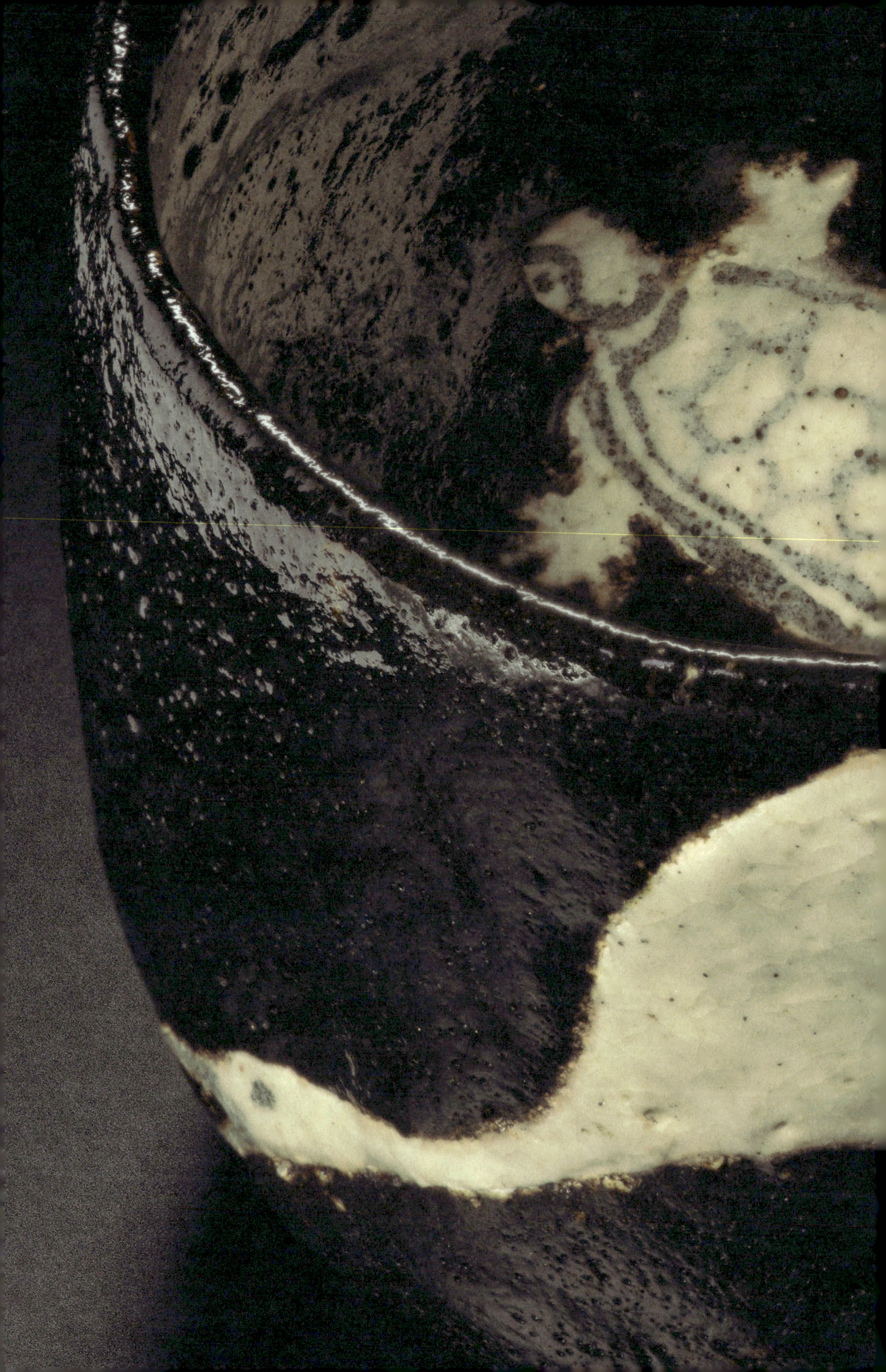

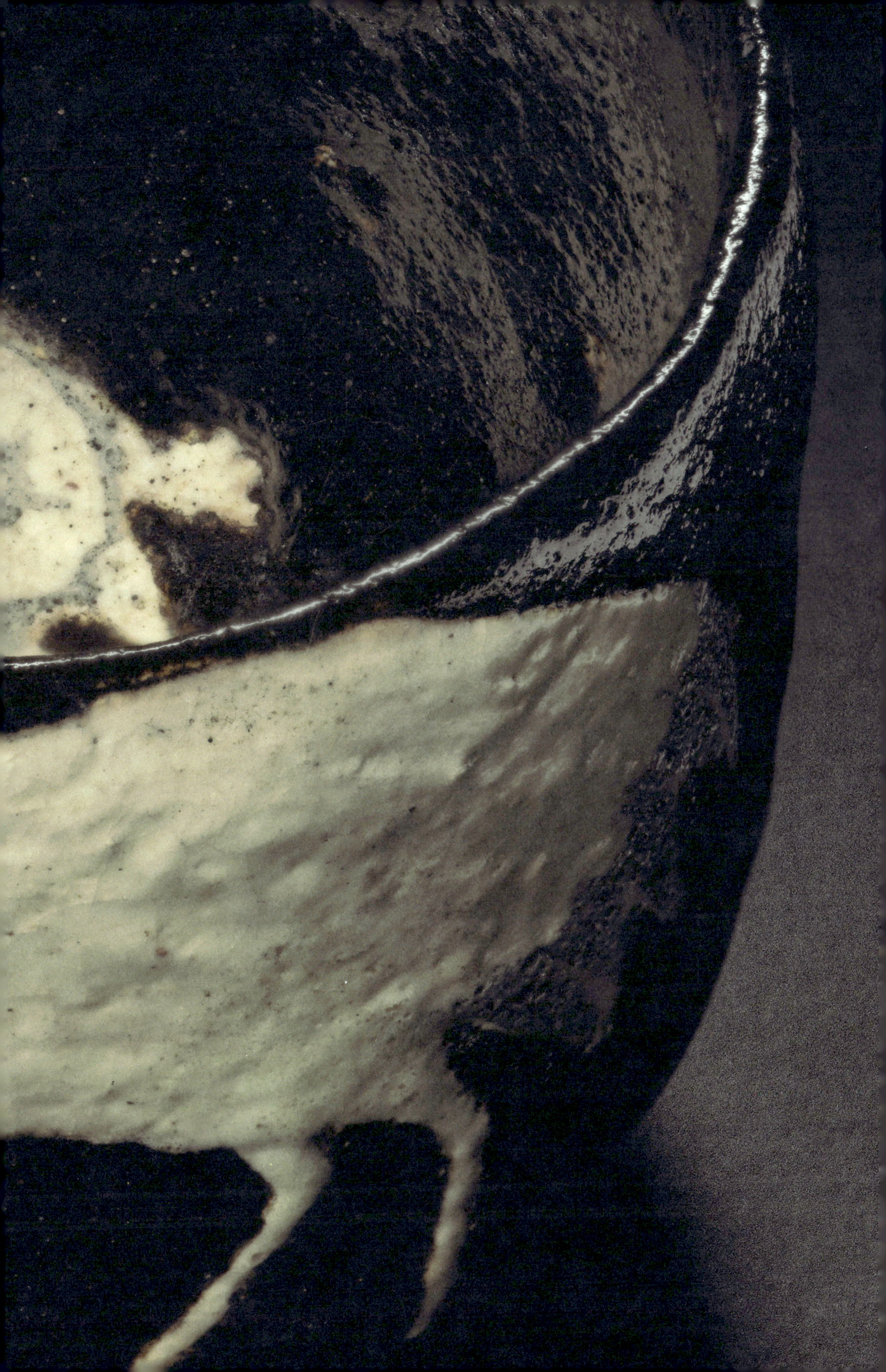

Out of the five senses, only touch and taste involve direct contact with an object. Further, touch is always double-sided: when you touch something, you are simultaneously being touched by it. This directness and double-sidedness make touch unique, personal, and thus multivarious.[9]

The double-sidedness of touch can be found in many Japanese works of art that also serve as utilitarian objects, as they are meant to be handled as part of a user's everyday life. Japanese swords, for example, are appreciated as works of art today, but they were a true weapon before the mid-19th century. The handle of a sword was made to secure a good grip: the wooden core was first covered by textured rayskin, then wrapped with silk cords with a pair of small metal *menuki* inserted underneath. Originally simply functional, the sword fittings developed into intricate ornamentation too that demonstrate the bearer's status and aesthetic (Fig. 1.2 and Fig. 1.3).

In Western culture, oil paintings are created solely for the purpose of visual appreciation and are thus framed and hung on the wall; once mounted, they are rarely moved or replaced. Moreover, their materials are not light sensitive, which means they are hardly handled at all. By contrast, traditional Japanese paintings are constantly handled. Take screen paintings, for example. While they are created to be viewed, they also function as protection from drafts or as room partitions in sparsely furnished Japanese houses (Fig. 1.4). Portable and free-standing, they are frequently changed according to the season and occasion. The light-sensitive materials used in Japanese painting also require frequent replacement and careful storage. As in the case of the makers of Raku tea bowls, the mount makers of Japanese paintings are always aware of these factors and hence pay careful attention to the tactile quality of an object's surface.

Fig. 1.2 (opposite top)
Detail (handle) of a sword
Fittings: Edo period,
late 17th–early 18th century
Various metals
7 × 69 × 8 cm (overall sword)
ROM 910.178.13.A

Fig. 1.3 (opposite bottom)
Pair of Hilt Ornaments (menuki) in Form of Lobster
Edo period, 18th century
Copper, cast and gilded
1.4 × 6.6 cm
ROM 925.29.28-.29

Gift of Mrs. Carlos Buhler

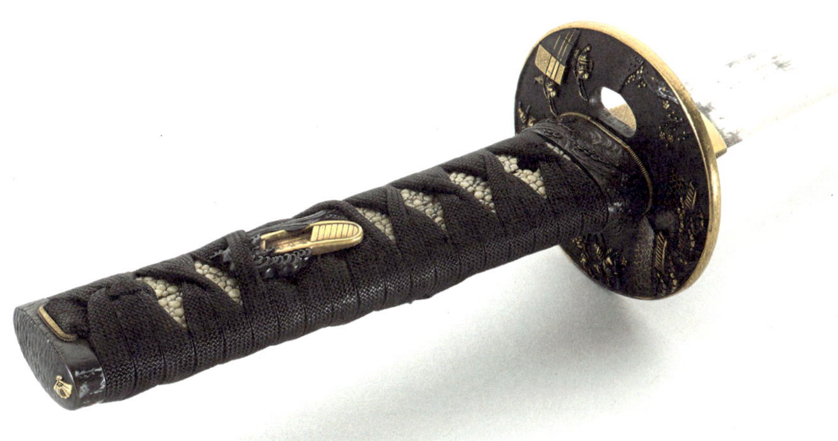

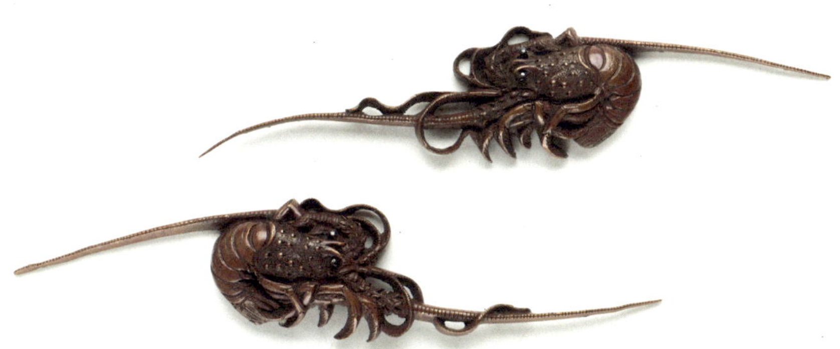

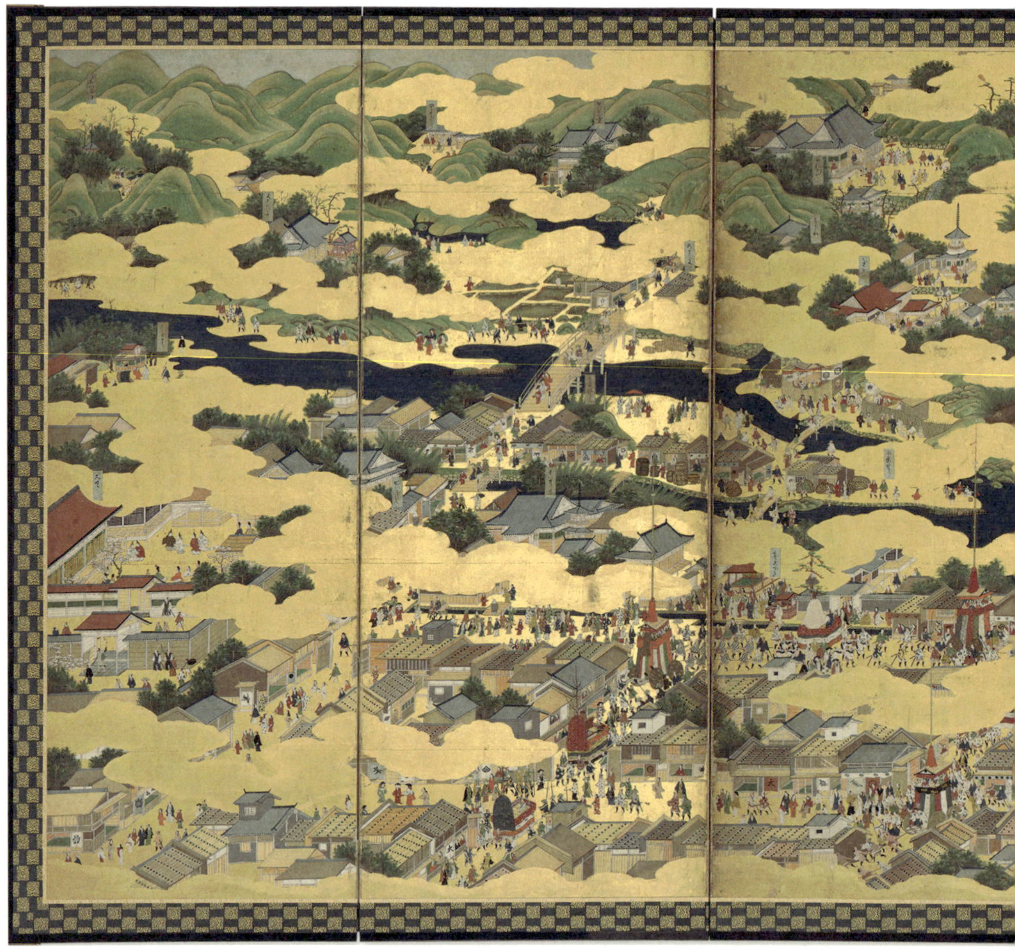

Fig. 1.4
Views of Kyoto and Its Environs (Rakuchū rakugai zu), left screen
Edo period, 1640–60
Pair of six-fold screens;
ink, colour, and gold leaf on paper
168 × 382 cm each
ROM 970.75.1-.2

Gift of Mrs. Percyval Tudor-Hart

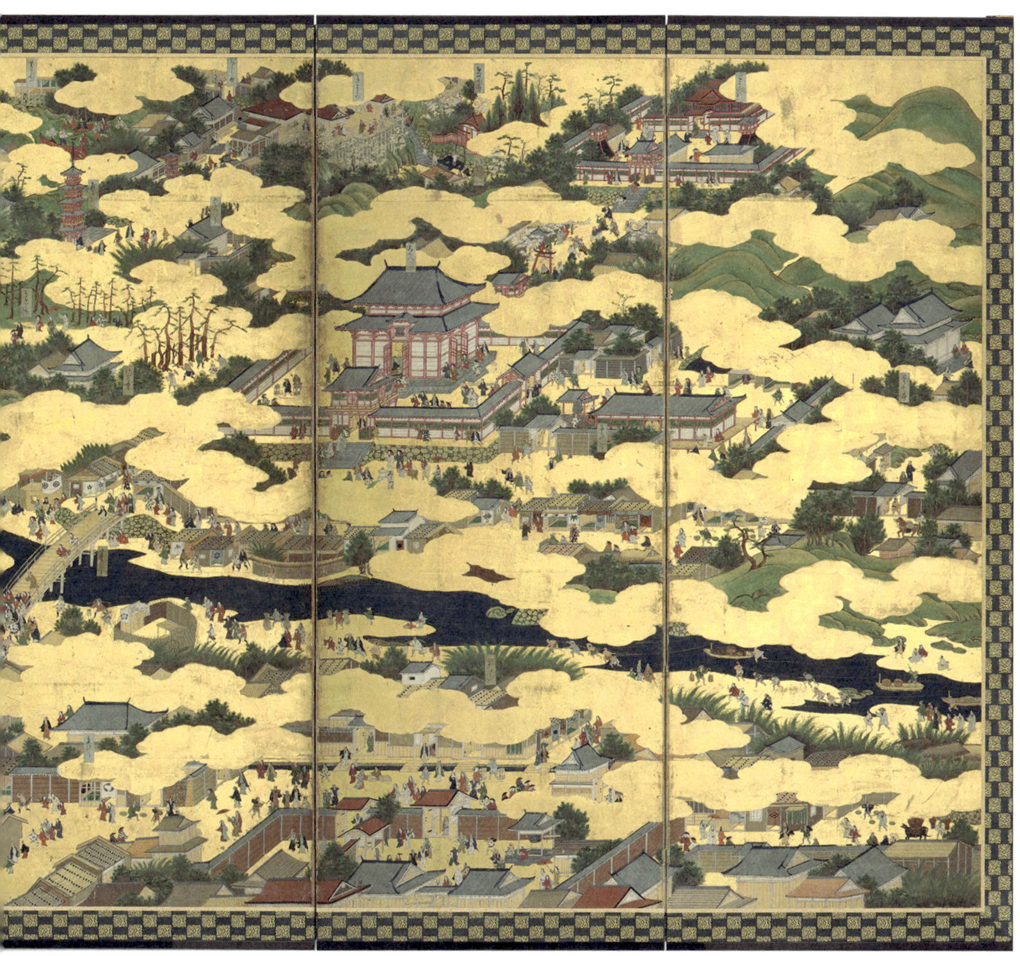

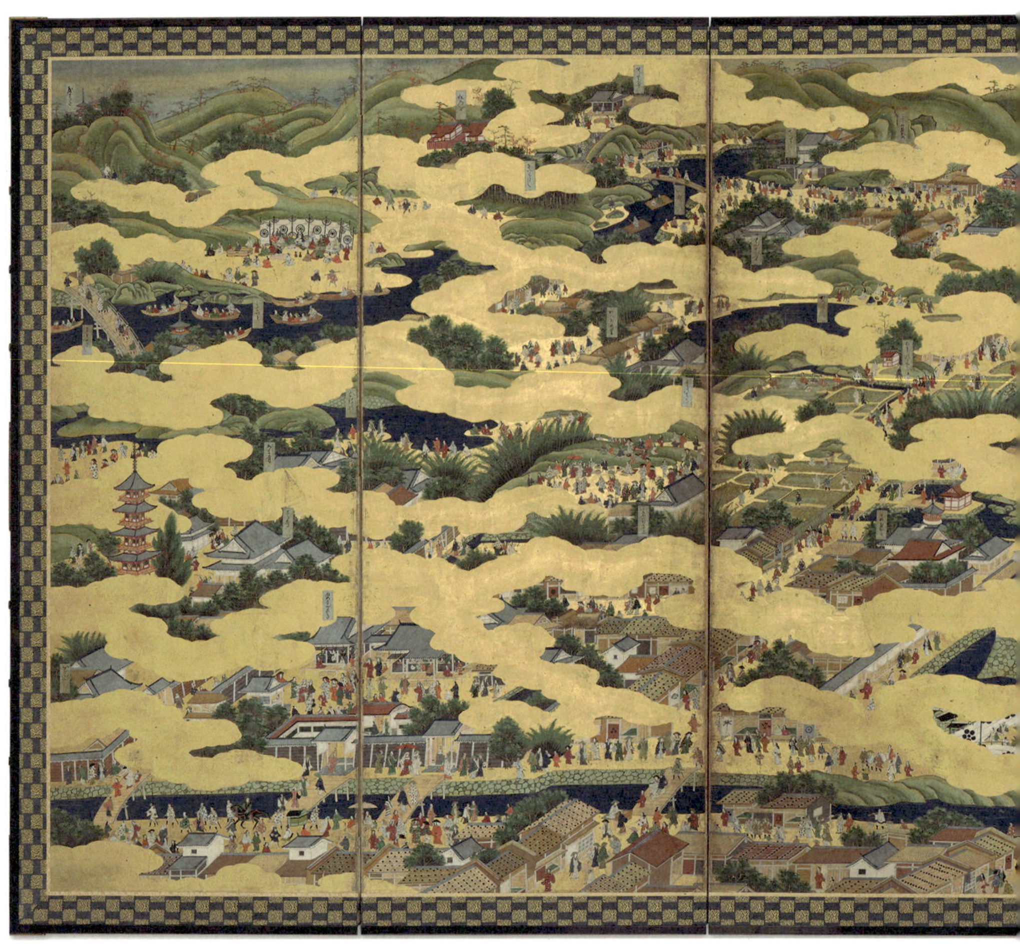

Views of Kyoto and Its Environs (Rakuchū rakugai zu), right screen. Detail on p. 14.

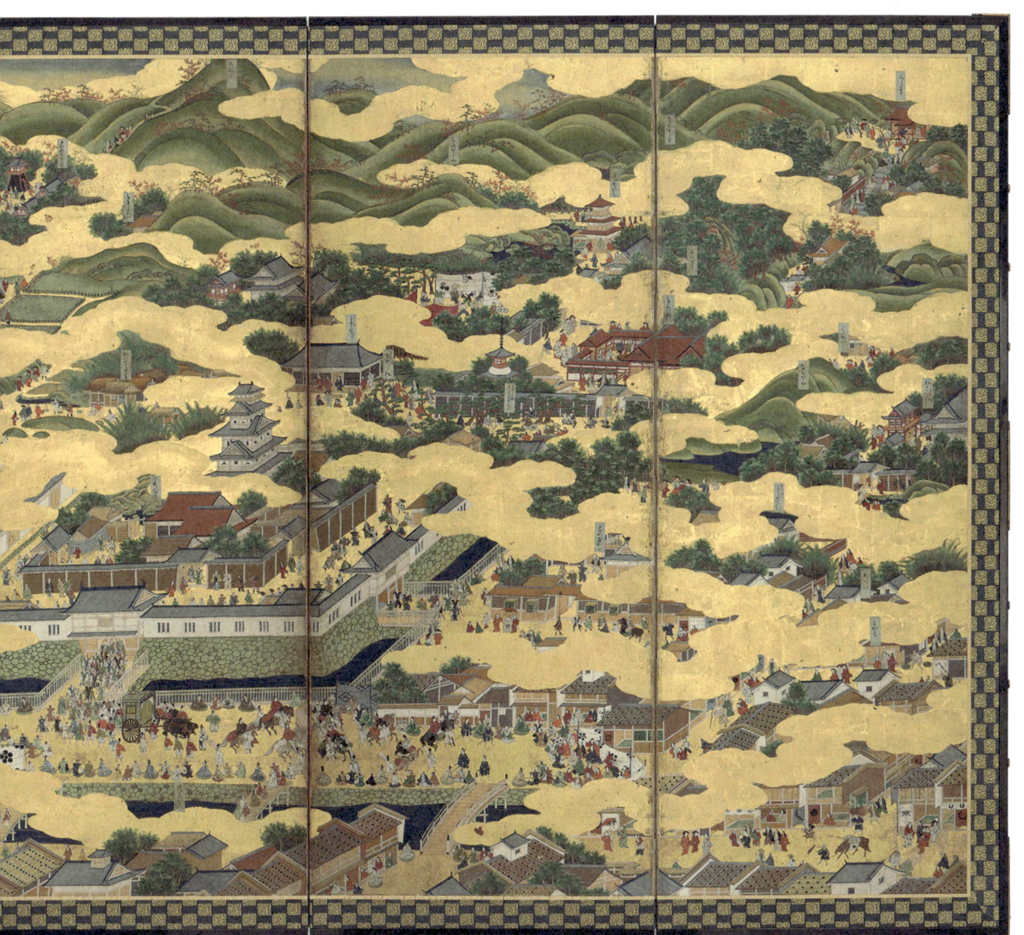

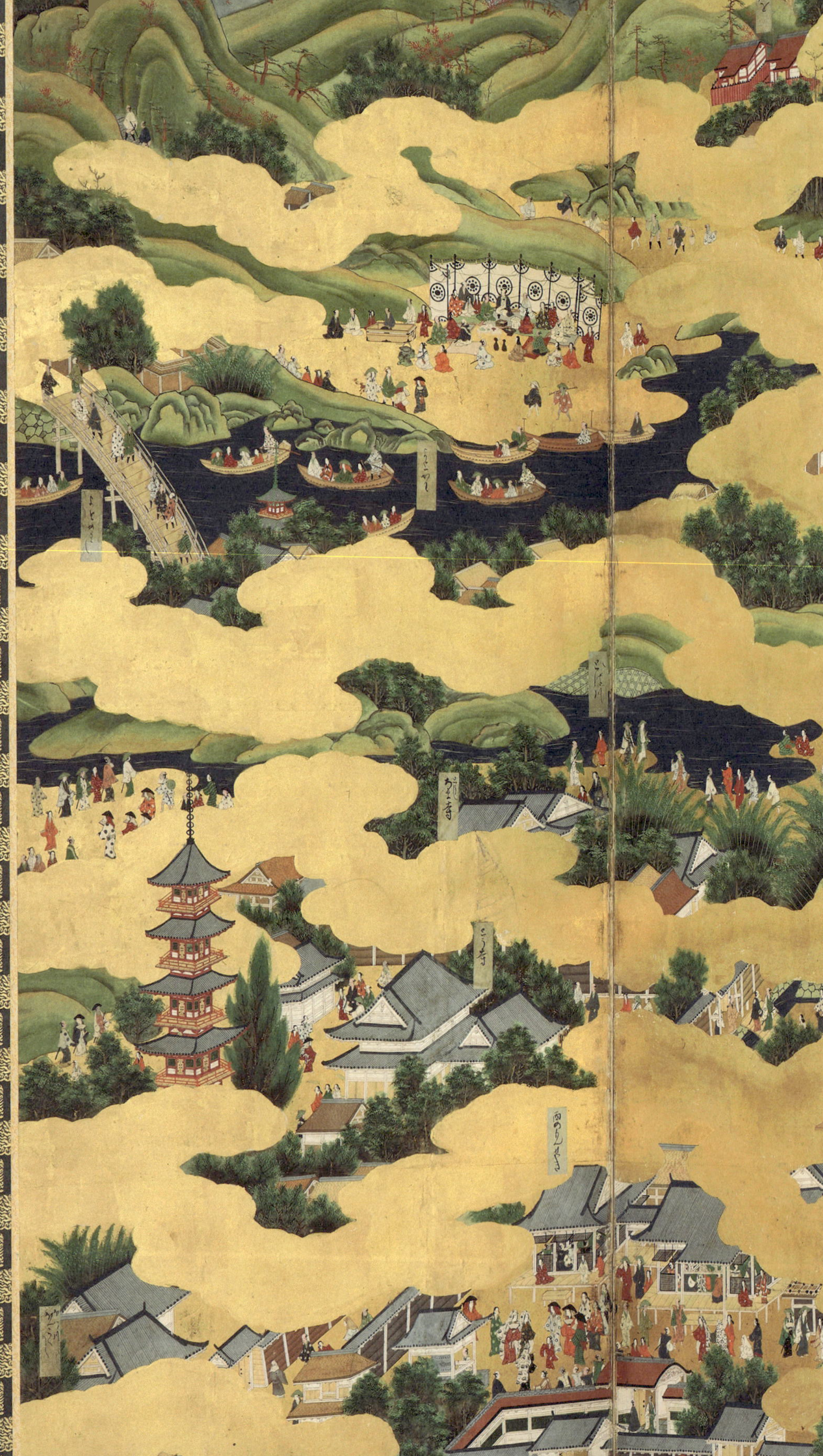

On the subject of folding screens, the contemporary artist Kōsuke Ikeda has further extended his understanding of the screen in today's society to include the partitions used to prevent infection during the COVID-19 pandemic. His folding screen painting *Abstract/Expression/Byōbu*, which is included in the *Shokkan* exhibition, further embodies a multi-layered sense of touch: the artist's brushstrokes (that is, the artist's "touch"); the act of cutting and sticking paper stickers to a screen by hand; and the act of folding and unfolding the screen. Ikeda's essay describing this work and the impetus behind it is included in this volume (pages 74–89).

The other types of Japanese paintings also require frequent handling. Hanging scrolls are displayed during certain periods of season or occasion, and once the period ends, they are replaced and stored away. Viewing a handscroll is an embodied experience: the viewer repeatedly rolls and unrolls the scroll with both hands, revealing a scene as wide as their shoulders at a time (Fig. 1.5).

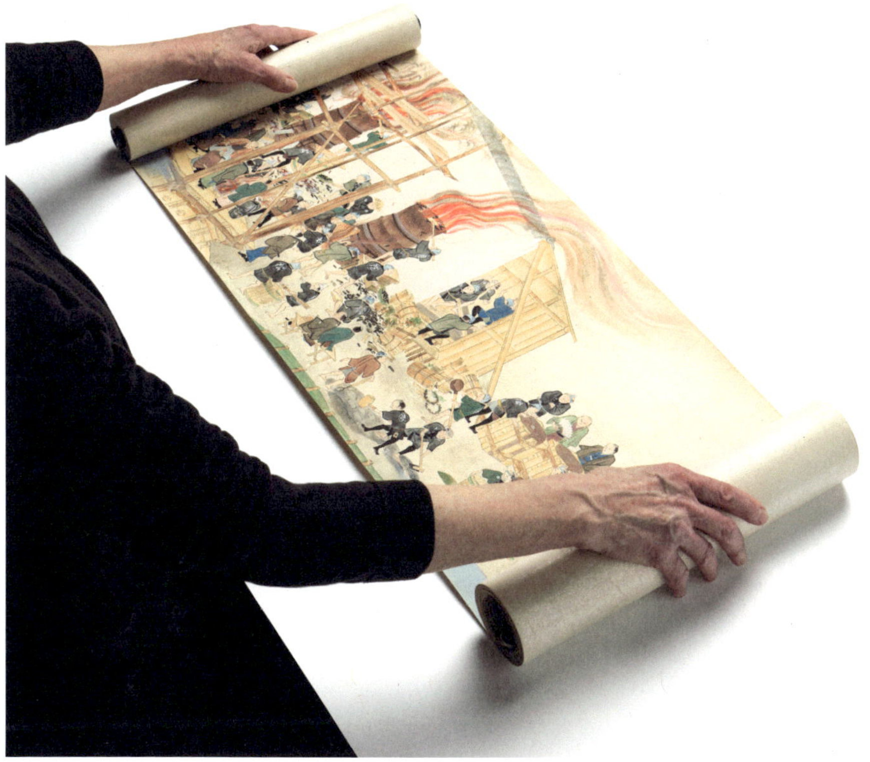

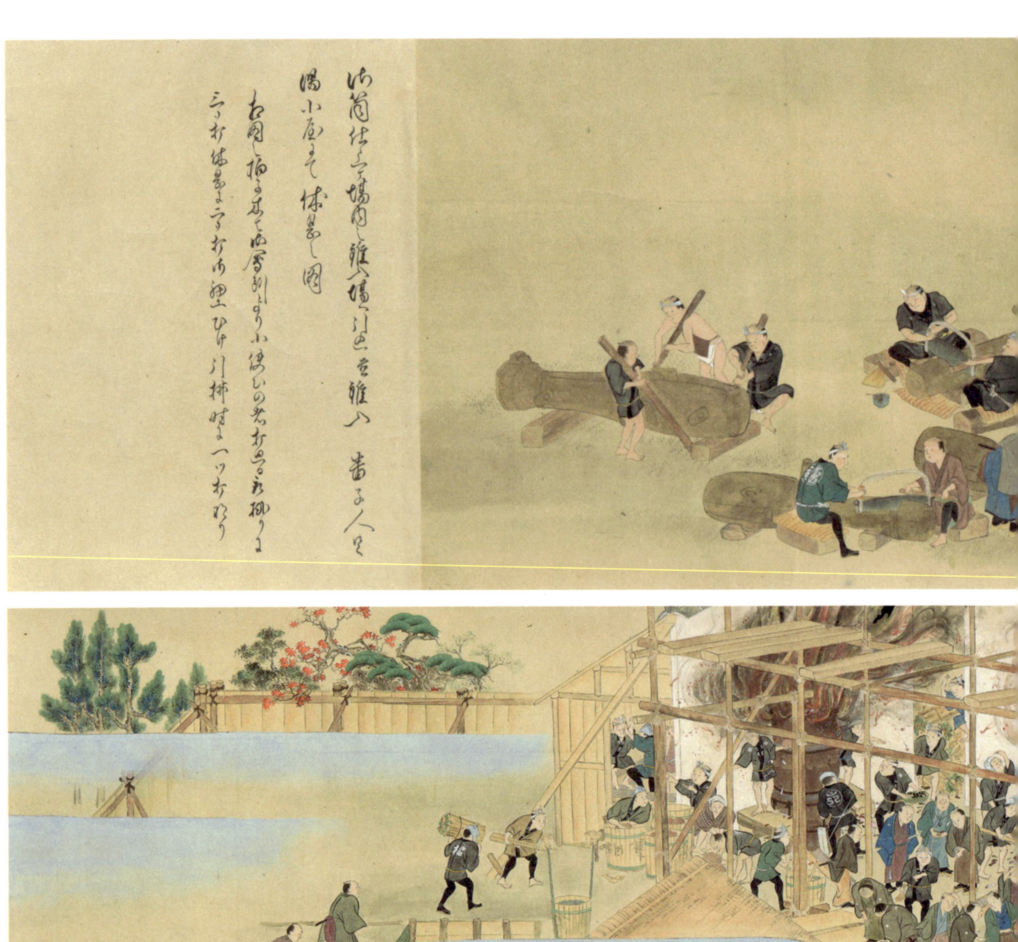

Fig. 1.5
Yamazaki Tomoo (1798–1861)
Cannon Production (details)
Edo period, 1851
Handscroll painting, set of three volumes; ink and colours on paper, silk
34 × 1650 cm each
ROM 998.69.2
Detail on p. 15.

This acquisition was made possible with the generous support of the Louise Hawley Stone Charitable Trust

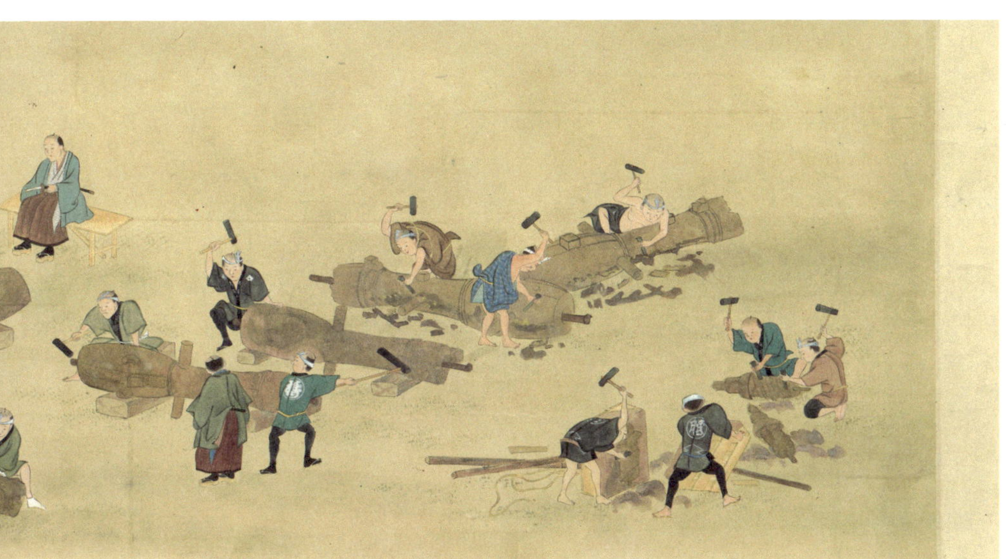

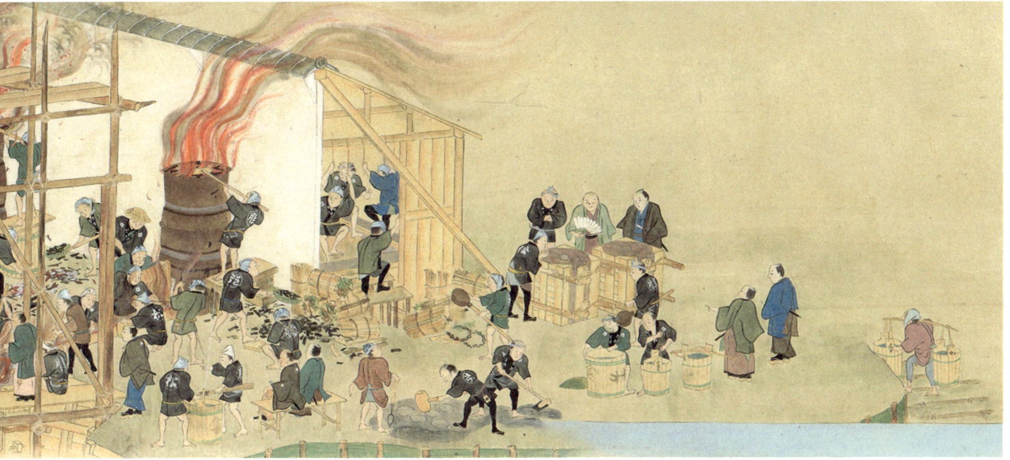

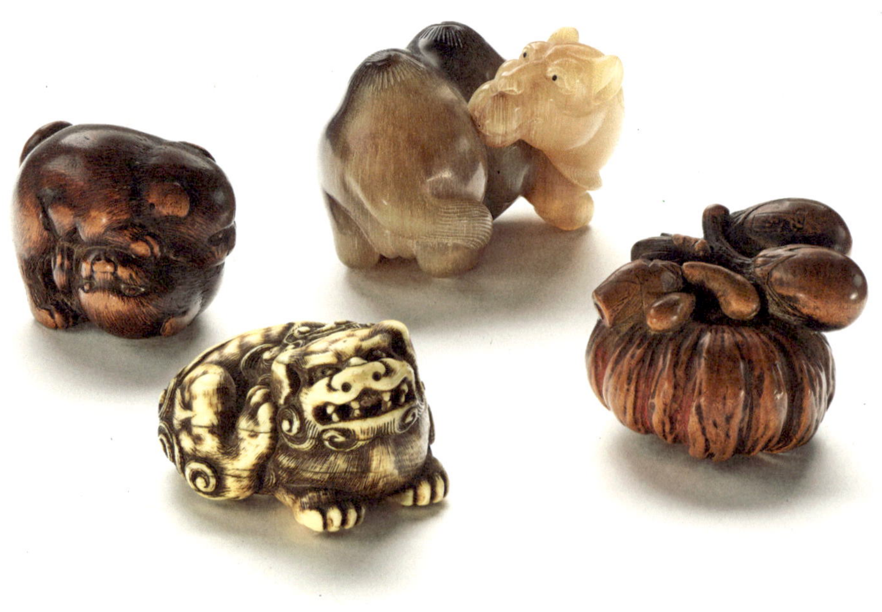

Experiencing the texture of objects via touching them is an essential part of appreciating Japanese art. The patina of a netsuke from long-time use, for example, is a crucial factor in appreciating it: netsuke's beauty partially comes from the human sebum built up through frequent touch (Fig. 1.6). The aesthetic value of a tea bowl too is determined by how it fits in one's palm: its shape, weight, and the texture of its glaze. These examples embody Hannah Thompson's assertion that "beauty is not only about the visual."[10] For the contemporary Shigaraki ceramic artist Yoshiko Takahashi, the texture of the clay and glaze used in her work need to be touched to be appreciated. These aspects of Takahashi's work, along with the tactility of tea utensils, are discussed in Natsu Oyobe's essay in this volume (pages 92–107).

The importance of texture has led the techniques used to decorate the surfaces of objects to become highly developed. One of the best examples of this is *maki-e* lacquer decoration, in which a design is made by sprinkling or spraying wet lacquer with metallic powder, such as gold or silver. This complex decoration technique was developed during the Heian period (794–1185) and has become a representative Japanese lacquering method. The variety within maki-e can be seen in the following pieces from ROM's collection: a cosmetic box from the 16th century exemplifying a simple maki-e technique (Fig. 1.7); a Western-style set of ewer and basin decorated with Japanese motifs in slightly raised maki-e from the 16th century, when Japanese lacquerware was highly prized in the West (Fig. 1.8); and a smoking set from the late 19th century that uses complex designs and materials (Fig. 1.9).

Fig. 1.6 (bottom right)
Tadatoshi (act. late 18th century)
Netsuke in Form of a Pumpkin, Eggplants, and Grasshopper
Edo period, late 18th century
Carved wood
2.5 × 4.2 cm
ROM 909.21.101

(bottom left)
Hidemasa I
(act. early 19th century)
Netsuke of Shishi Lion
Edo period, early 19th century
Ivory
2.5 × 4 cm
ROM 909.21.73

(top left)
Kokei
(act. late 18th century)
Netsuke of Two Puppies
Edo period, late 18th century
Carved wood
2.9 × 3.8 cm
ROM 909.21.78

(top right)
Nakamura Masatoshi
(1915–2001)
Netsuke of Recumbent Camel
Shōwa period, 1975
Rhino horn
3.2 × 5 × 2.7 cm
ROM 996.49.1

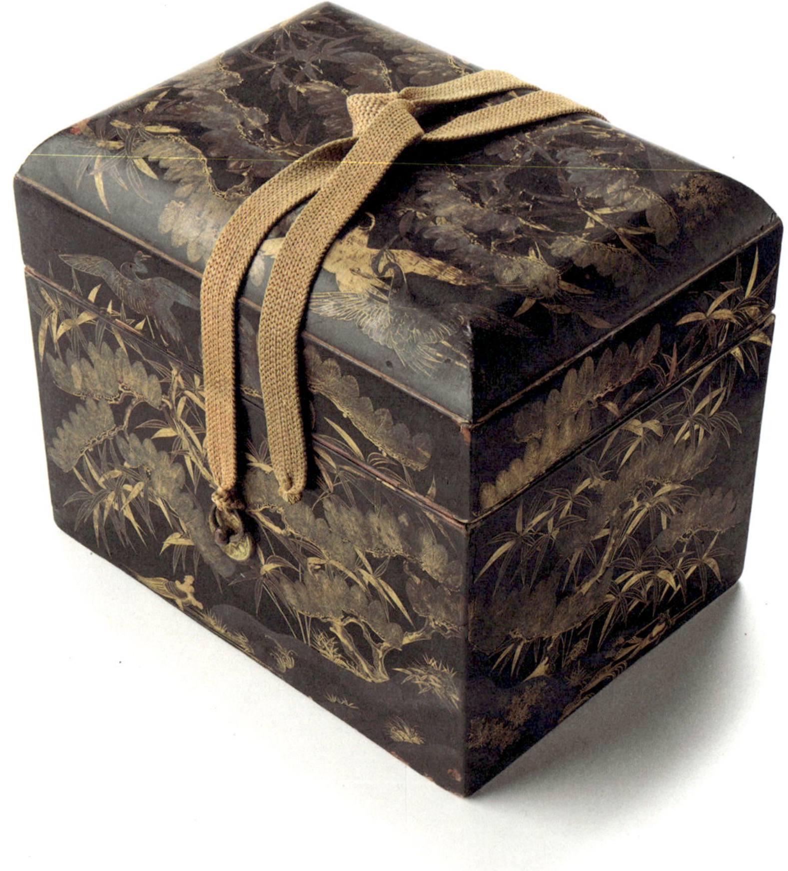

Fig. 1.7
Cosmetic Box with Pine Tree, Bamboo, Crane, and Turtle Motifs
Momoyama period, 1575–1600
Lacquered wood with maki-e decoration and brass fittings
30.4 × 37.5 × 28 cm
ROM 973.149.A-.C

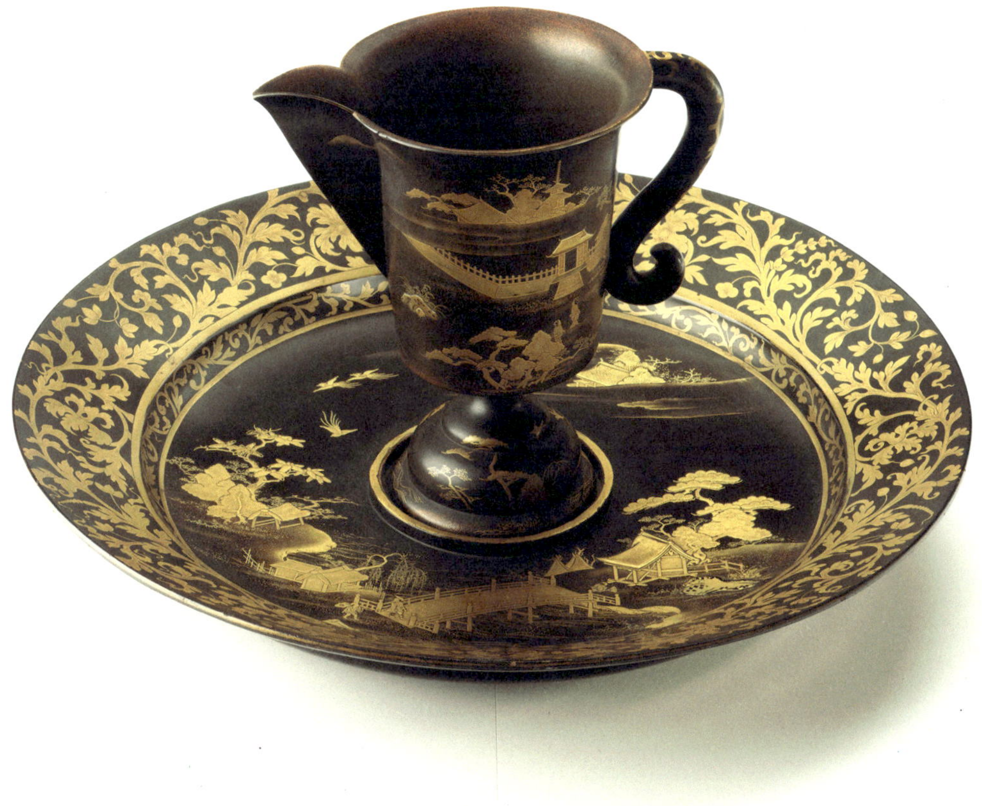

Fig. 1.8
Ewer with Matching Basin
Edo period, early 18th century
Lacquered wood with maki-e decoration
Ewer: 25 × 25 cm;
basin: 8 × 52.5 cm
ROM 997.49.1.1

Bequest of Professor Ronald Smith

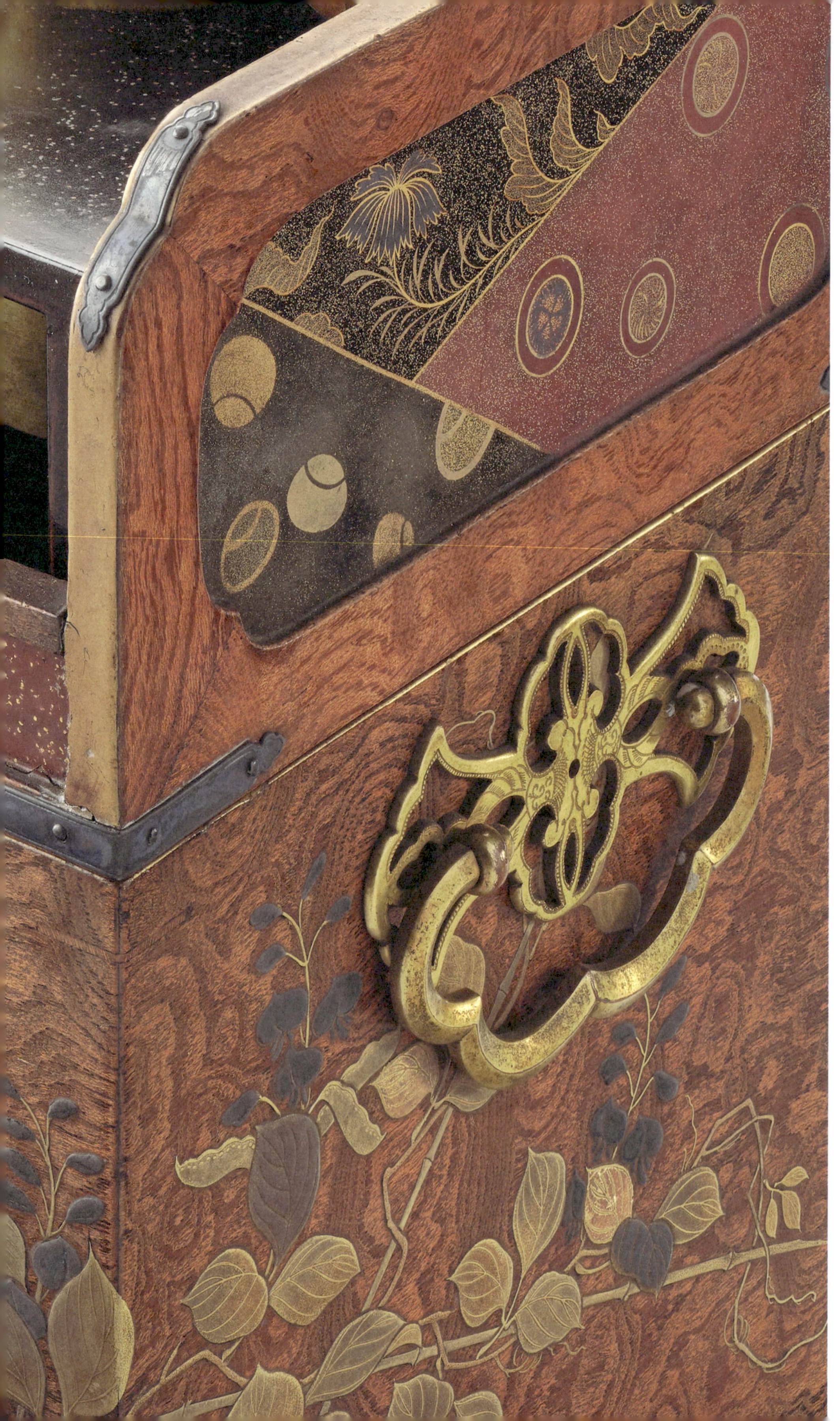

Fig. 1.9
Smoking Set Drawer
Meiji period, late 19th century
Lacquered wood with maki-e
decoration and brass containers
26.2 × 15.5 × 25.2 cm
ROM 930.25.1.A-.I

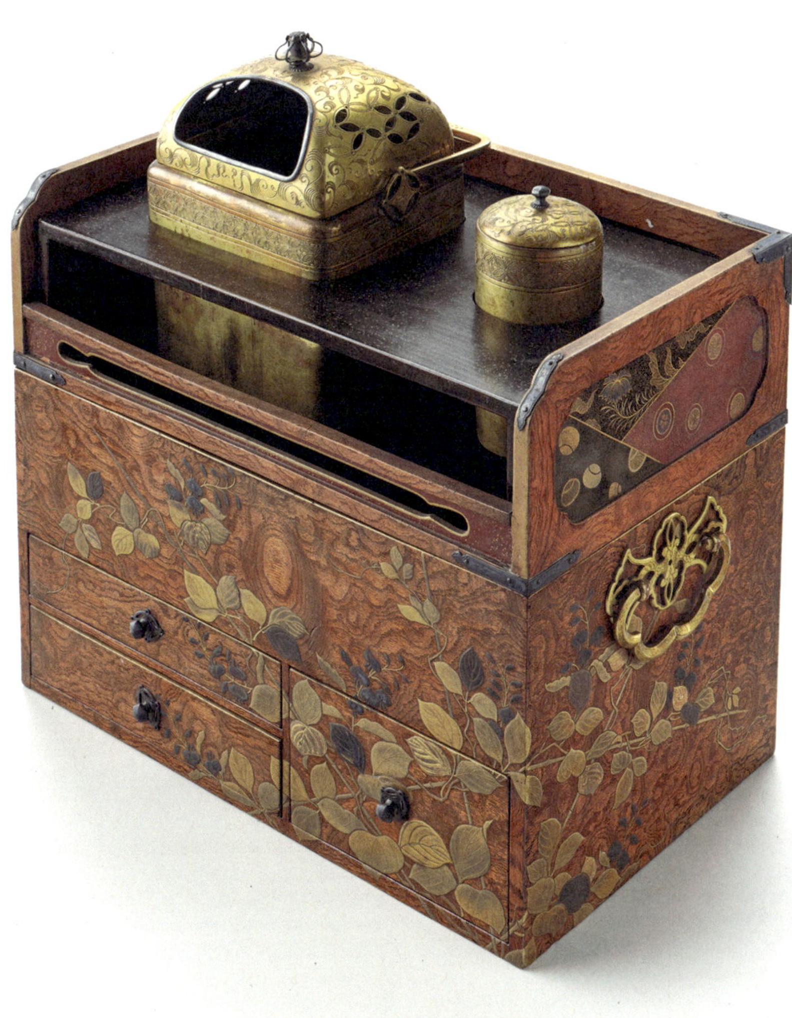

The textured surface of kimono, featuring embroidery and tie-dyeing, called *shibori-zome*, provides another example (Fig. 1.10). The process of shibori dyeing includes multiple labour-intensive techniques, such as stitching elaborate patterns with cotton threads, which are then tightly gathered, or tying many small areas to make a pattern. The tied areas are left undyed, creating patterns as well as distinctive 3-D qualities when the threads are removed (Fig. 1.11). Such intricate textures remind one that a single kimono may have gone through multiple artisans' hands before touching the wearer's skin.

Among countless varieties of fabrics, translucent gauze is used for the summer kimono to keep the wearer cool (Fig. 1.12). Although its fabric is thin, the example shown here has woven patterns that create a distinctive texture. It also features resist-dyed motifs of the full moon and autumn grasses at its hem, not only providing a sense of the literal coolness of the fall but also demonstrating the sophisticated taste of the wearer, who is getting ahead with the season.

The attention to the detailed texture of kimono is represented even in 2-D woodblock prints, as seen in this print (Fig. 1.13). Lit with raking light, it clearly reveals the textured patterns on the woman's kimono and the towel in her hand. This 3-D effect is created by a technique called *nunome-zuri*, or textile-weave printing, in which the weave designs of fabrics are embossed on the paper.

A more recent example of a distinct texture of textile might be found in the world-renowned permanently pleated garments innovated by Issey Miyake (Fig. 1.14). Intended as simple, everyday wear, the pleated garments accommodate any body types and movements, providing the wearer with a sense of individuality and freedom in daily life. The unique feeling of pleats on skin may represent the ultimate form of shokkan.

Fig. 1.10
Woman's Outer Robe (uchikake) *with "Pine, Bamboo, and Plum" Design*
Edo period, first half of the 18th century
Silk rinzu damask with shibori resist-dyeing and embroidery, padded with cotton wadding
Height 182.5 cm
ROM 949.49

Gift of Louise Hawley Stone

Fig. 1.11 (pp. 26–27)
Detail of the uchikake in Fig. 1.10 showing shibori tie-dye

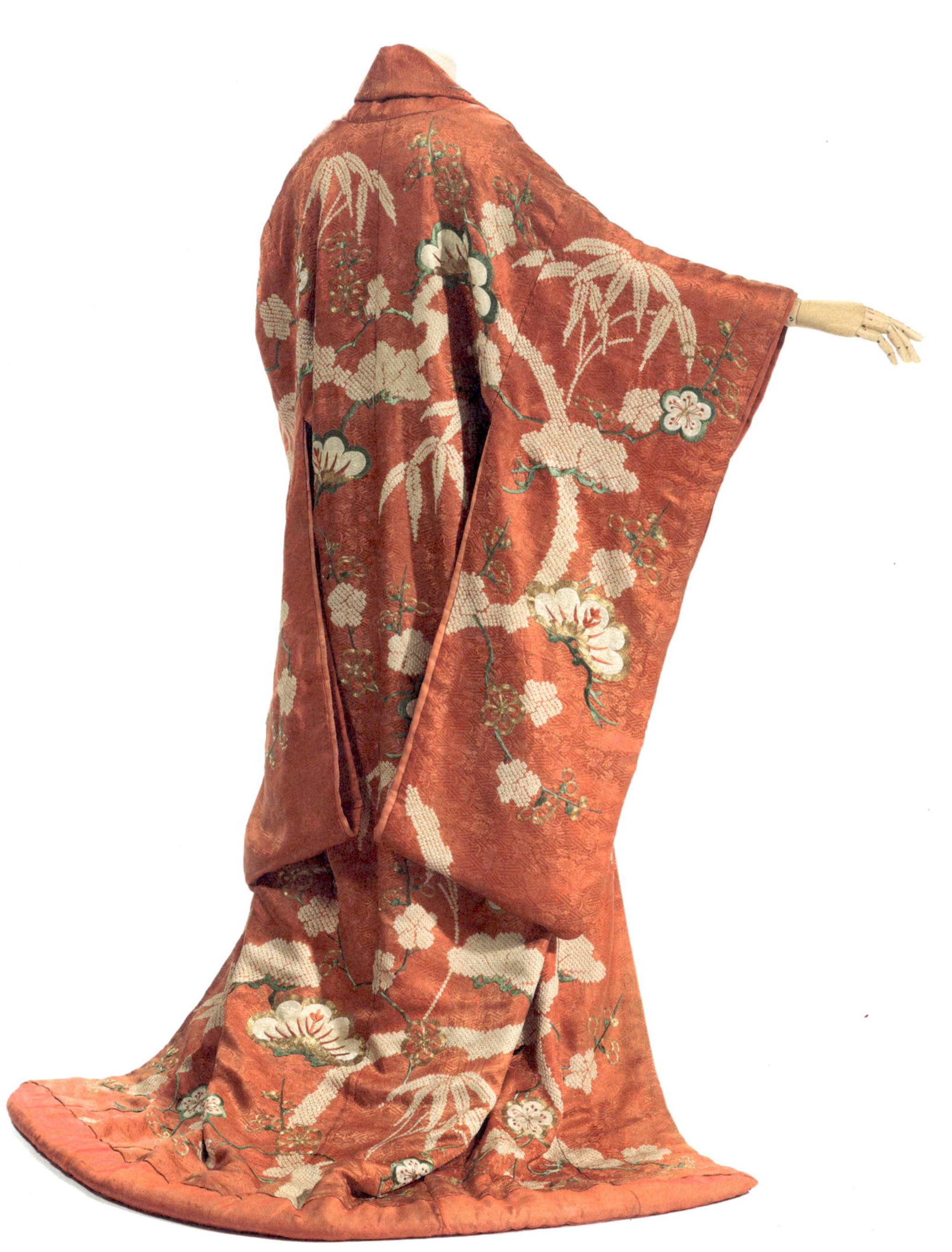

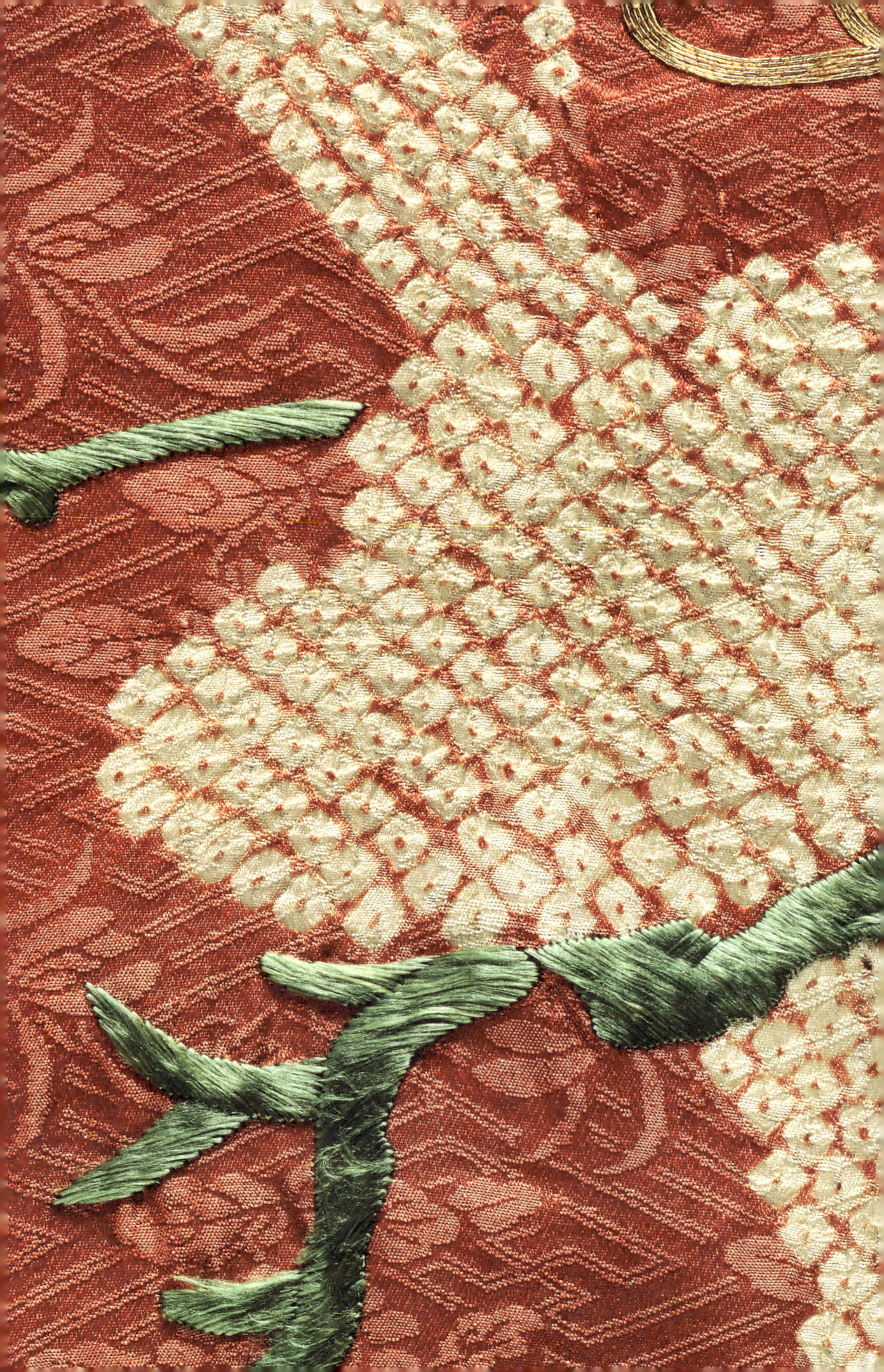

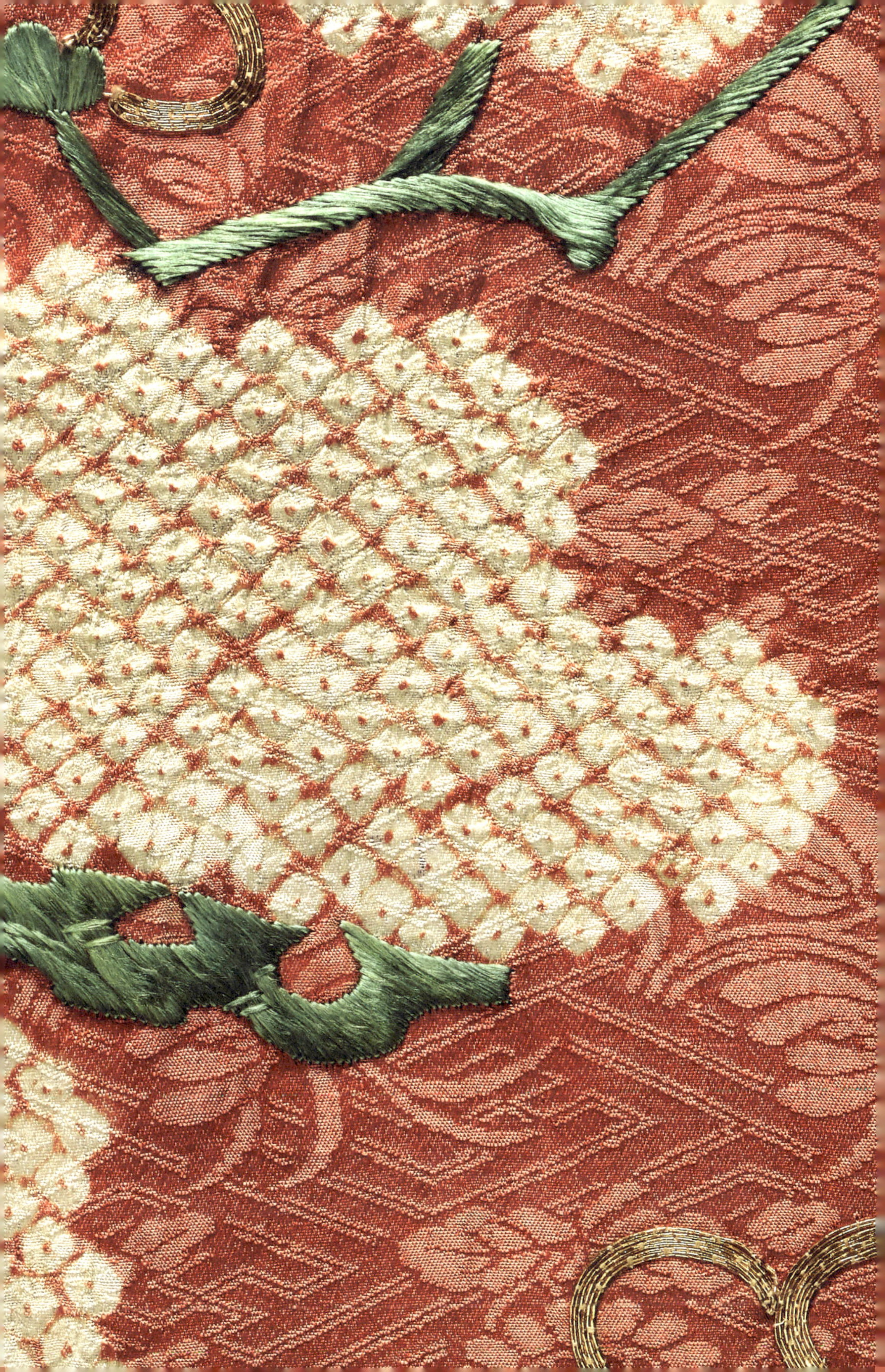

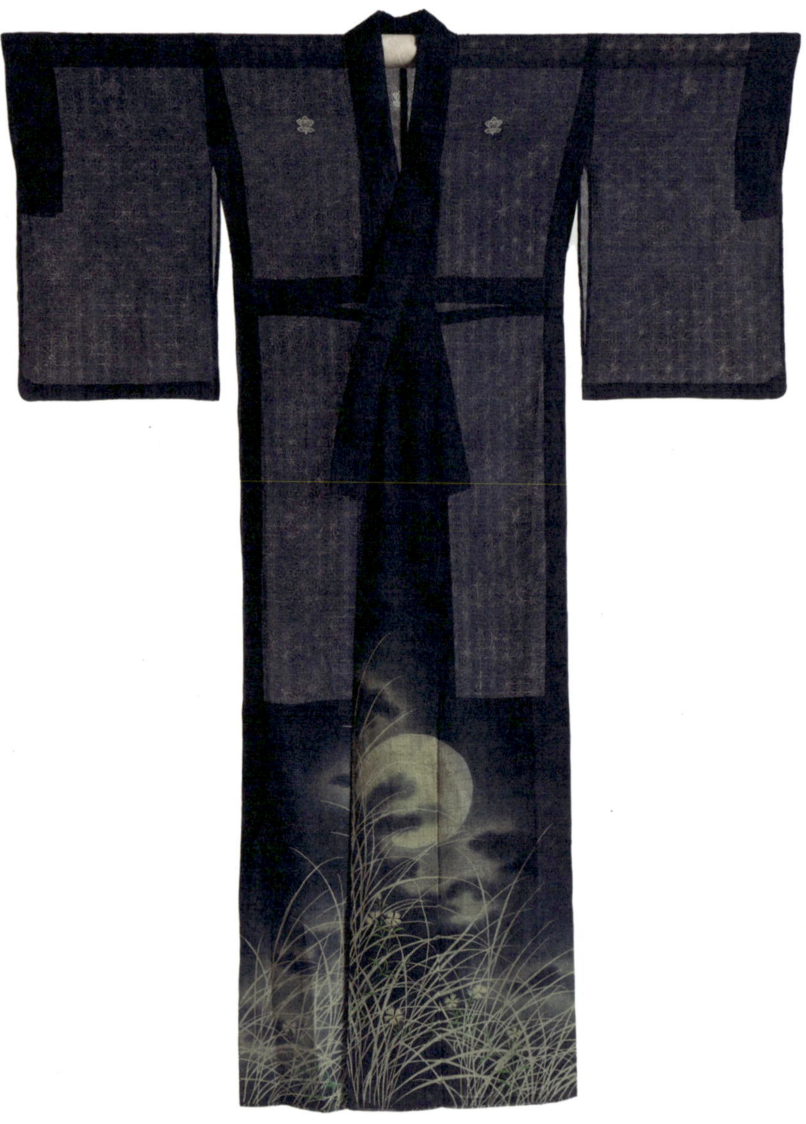

Fig. 1.12
Woman's Summer Kimono with Design of the Full Moon and Autumn Grasses
Shōwa period, 1929
Patterned gauze, painted and resist-dyed
168.5 × 124 cm
ROM 962.67.26

Gift of Miss Adelaide Lash Miller

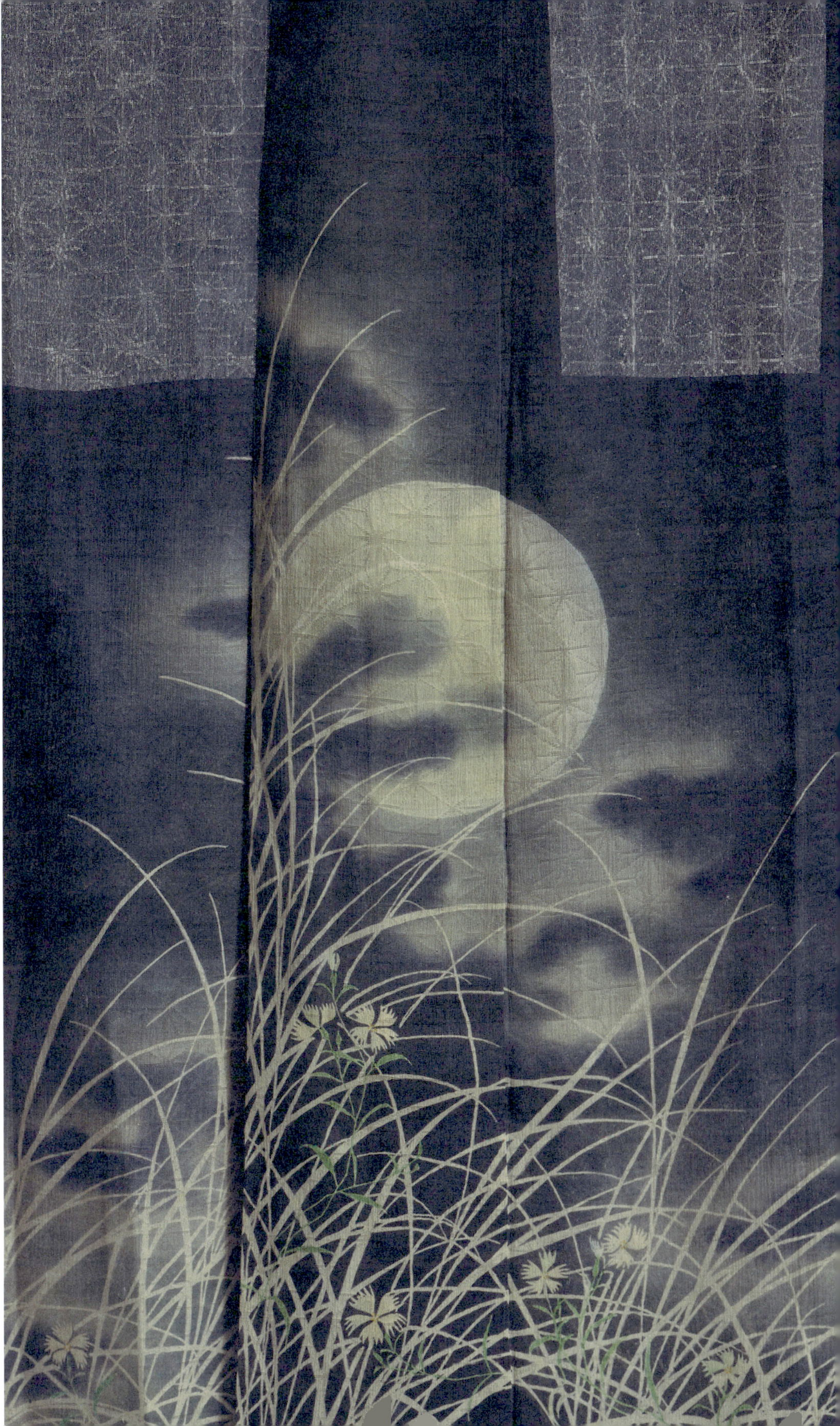

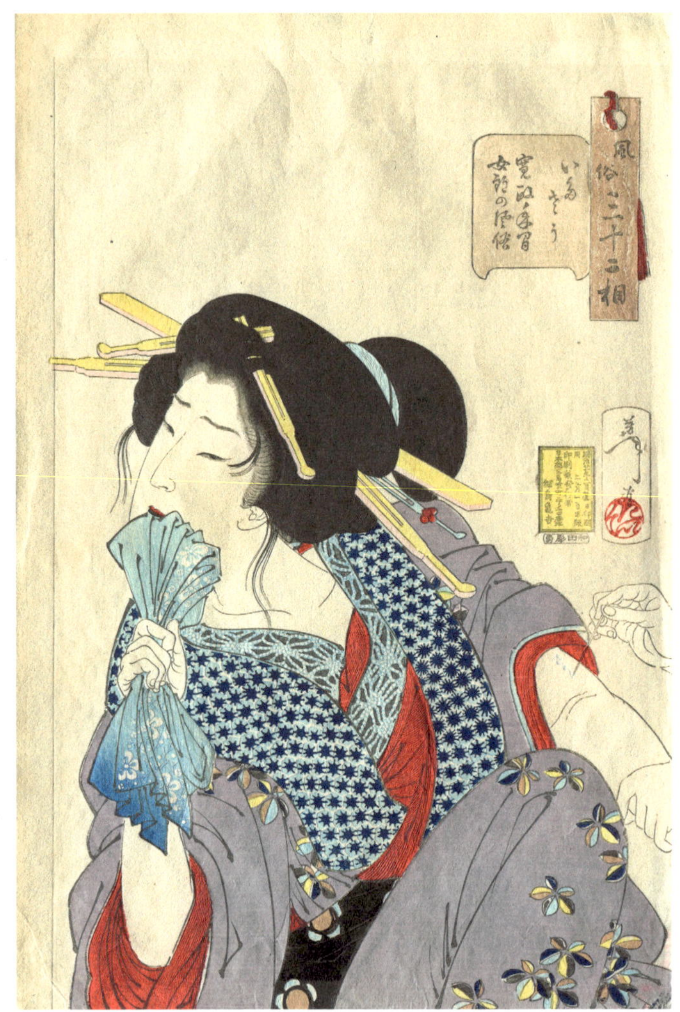

Fig. 1.13
Tsukioka Yoshitoshi (1839–92)
Looking Painful, from the series
Thirty-Two Aspects of Women
Meiji period, 1888
Woodblock print
37.4 × 25.6 cm
ROM 2016.10.2

This acquisition was made possible
with the generous support of the
Louise Hawley Stone Charitable Trust

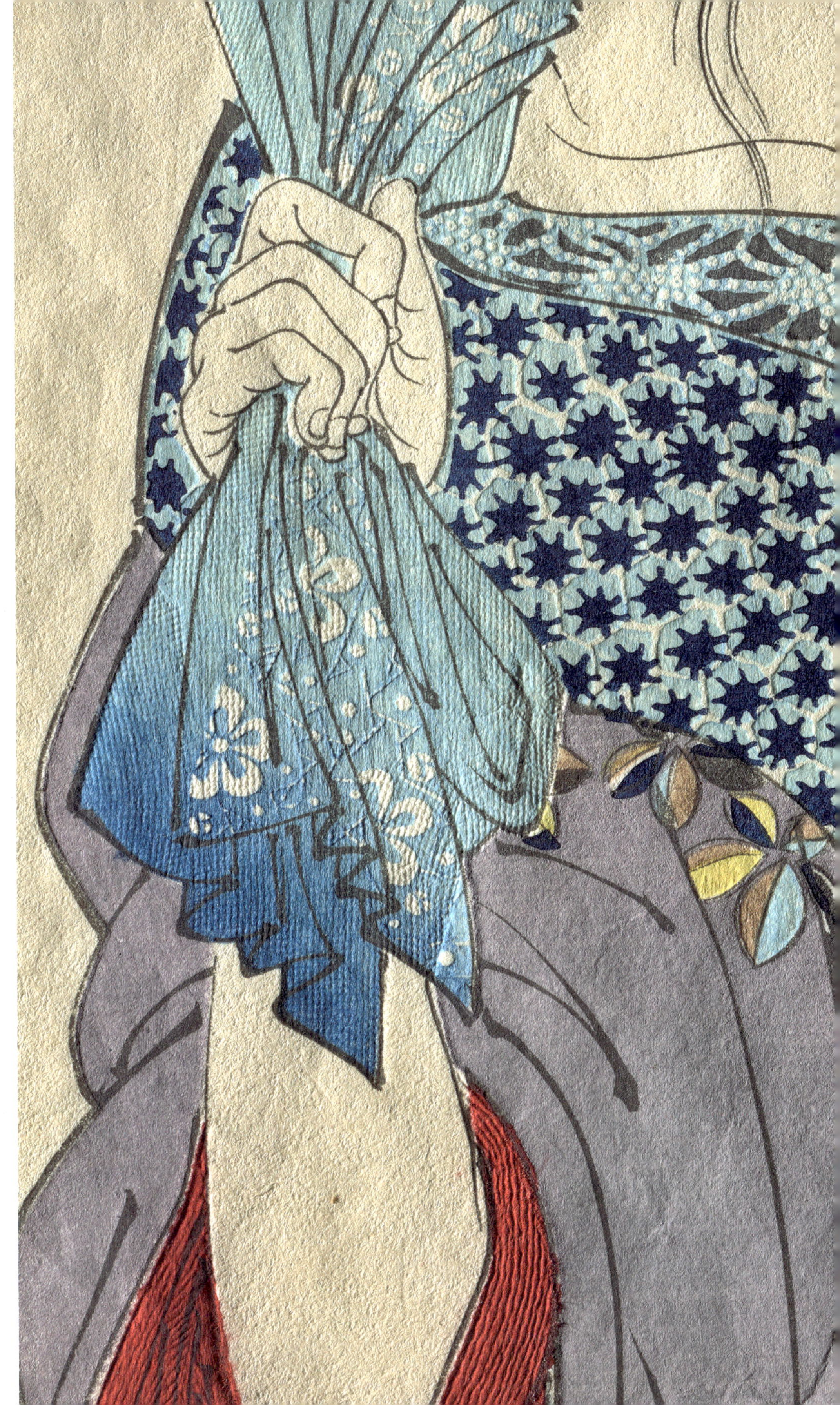

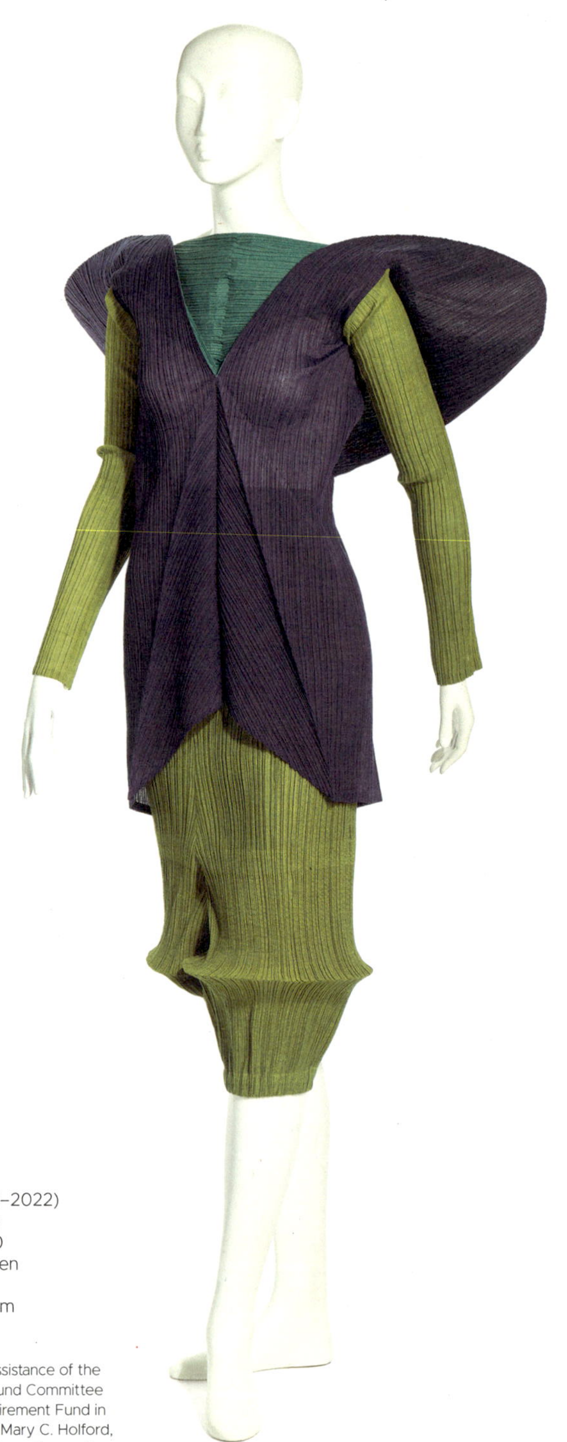

Fig. 1.14
Issey Miyake (1938–2022)
Dress and trousers
Heisei period, 1990
Polyester (fibre), linen
Dress: 77 × 86 cm;
trousers: 67 × 49 cm
ROM 990.62.1.1-.2

Purchased with the assistance of the Textile Endowment Fund Committee and the Director's Retirement Fund in acknowledgement of Mary C. Holford, Costume Curator, on her retirement

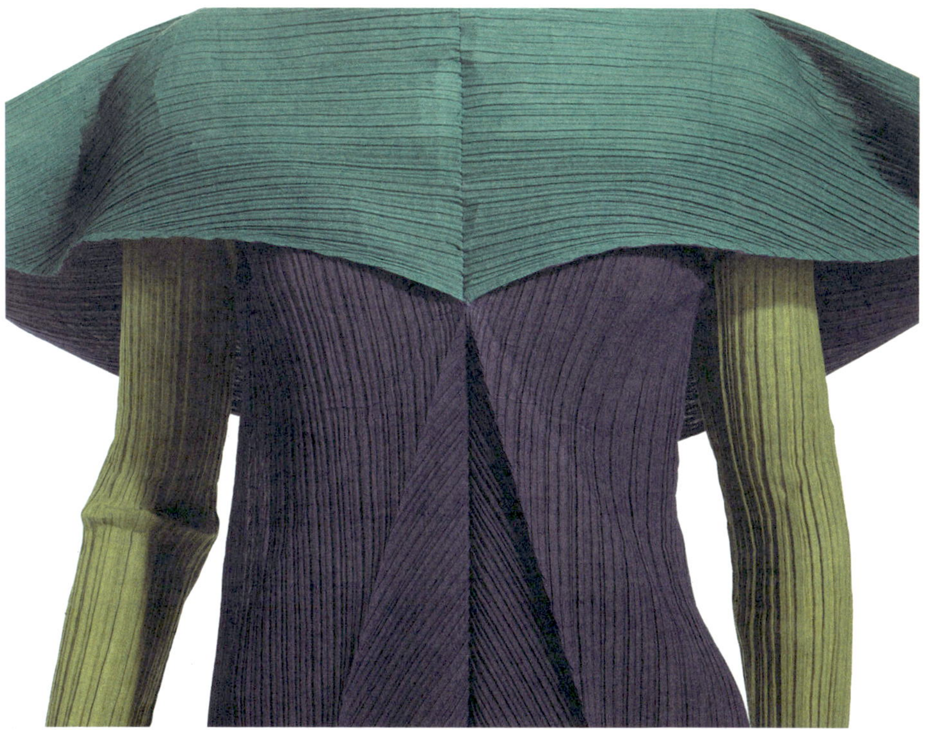

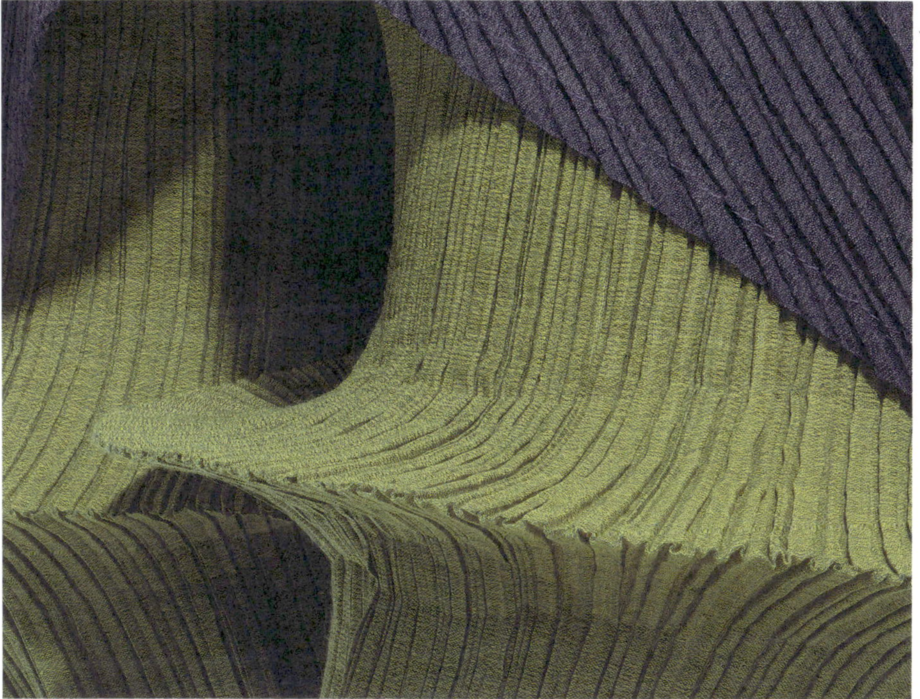

The sense of touch also seems to have played an important role in the global circulation of Japanese objects from the mid-19th to the early 20th centuries. During the "craze for things Japanese" in the West at that time, small objects that could be held in one's hands, such as netsuke, incense boxes, and tea bowls, were avidly collected. Since they were small and relatively inexpensive, they often became the subject of a collector's obsession, leading to the amassing of large collections of similar small objects.

For example, the American Canadian businessman Sir William C. Van Horne (1843–1915) of Montreal collected over 1,200 Japanese ceramic objects, including tea bowls, sake bottles, sake cups, and other small objects at the turn of the 20th century (Fig. 1.15). The purpose of his collection was not primarily visual display, though: he kept them in his home office, where only invited guests had access (Fig. 1.16); he examined the objects by holding them in his hands; and he sometimes drew intricate watercolours of individual pieces (Fig. 17). Obviously, Van Horne's relationship with the objects was a close, tactile one.

Similarly, French politician Georges Clemenceau (1841–1929) was obsessed with collecting Japanese incense containers (*kōgō*). He amassed over 2,000 of them, mainly ceramic (Fig. 1.18). Most were small enough to be held in one's palm, and according to a photo of his office, he had several kōgō on his desk at all times (Fig. 1.19). The fact that these Japanese objects were kept within close proximity to these collectors' daily lives, as well as the sheer size of their collections, demonstrates how eagerly and intimately collectors engaged with their objects.

Fig. 1.15
Tokkuri Sake Bottle
Early Imari type, Arita ware
Edo period, 1650s
Porcelain, underglaze blue with transparent and iron brown glazes
26.3 × 13.5 cm
ROM 909.22.81

Gift of Sir William C. Van Horne

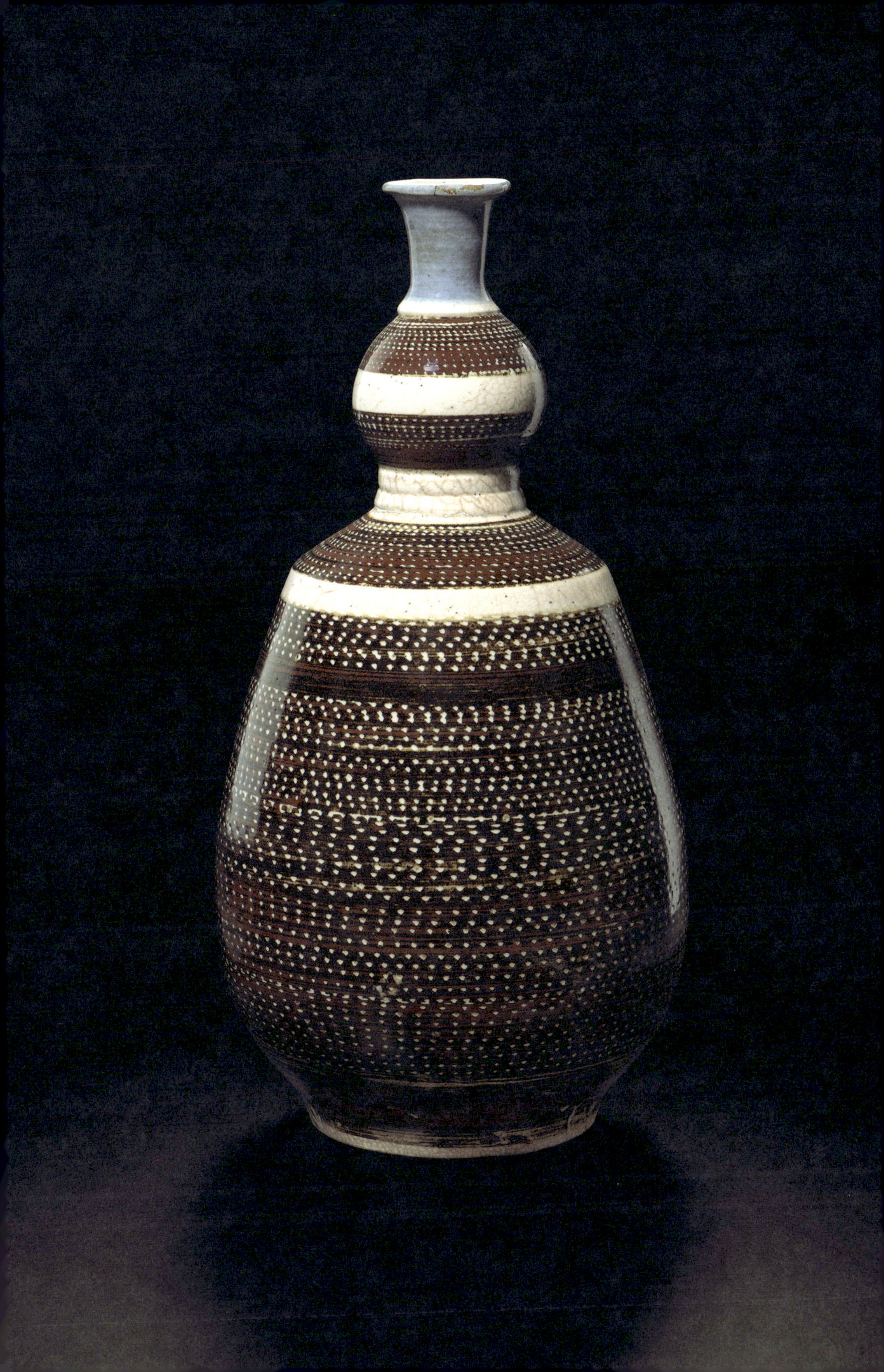

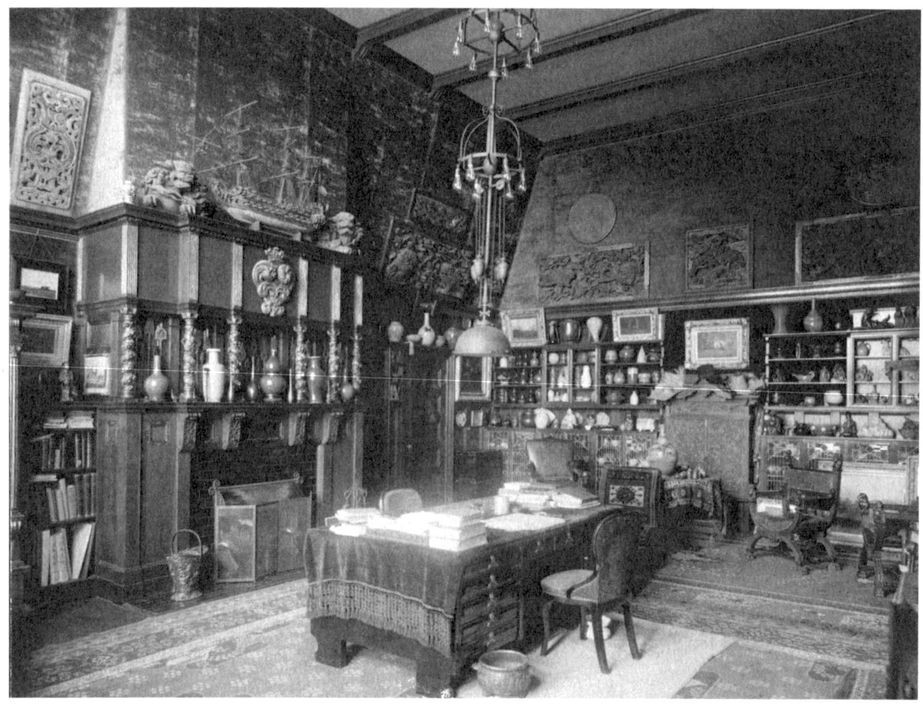

Fig. 1.16
Interior of Van Horne's Residence (Office), not dated, photographer unknown.

Photo: Courtesy of Library and Archives Canada, Ottawa. e003641851-v6.

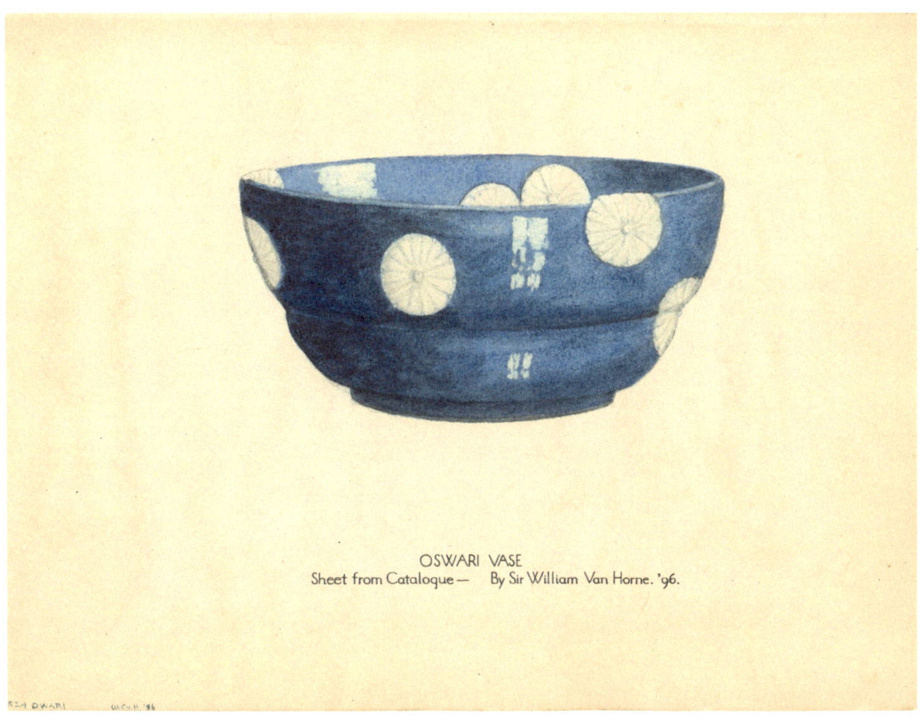

Fig. 1.17
William C. Van Horne
(1843–1915)
Drawing of a Japanese Ceramic Bowl
1896
Watercolour on paper
28.5 × 38.5 cm
ROM 946x97.6

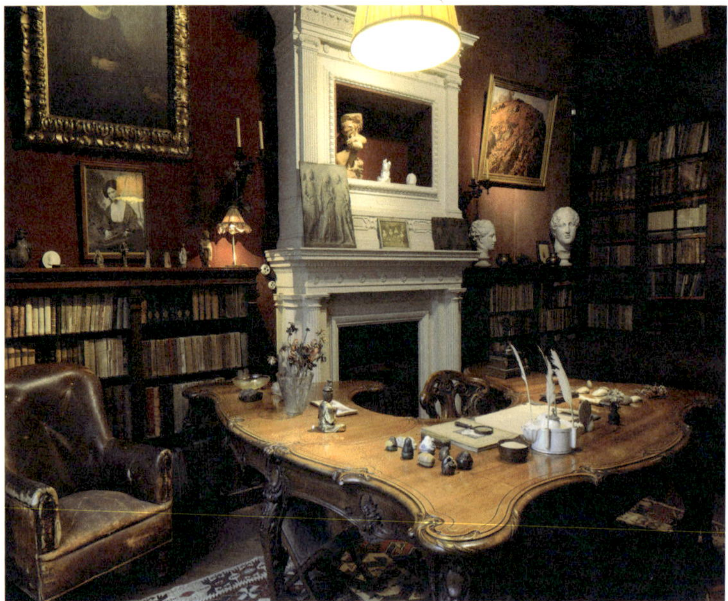

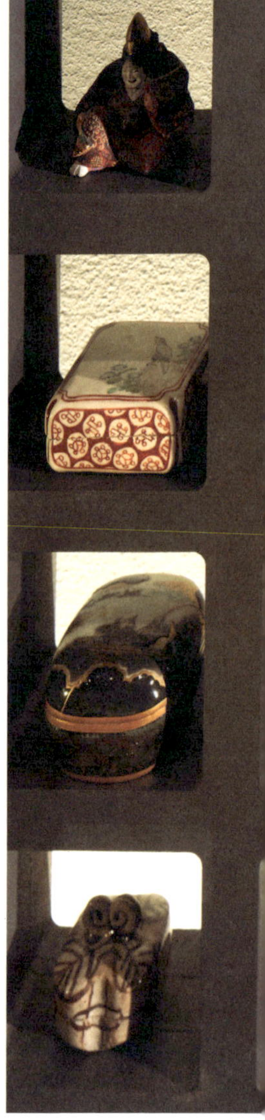

Fig. 1.19
Clemenceau's office desk with incense boxes.

Courtesy of Musée Clemenceau, Paris, 2017

Fig. 1.18
Group of Clemenceau's incense containers in the collection of the Montreal Museum of Fine Arts.

Asian Art Gallery; Stephan Crétier and Stéphany Maillery Wing for the Arts of One World, Montreal Museum of Fine Arts
Photo: MMFA, 2025

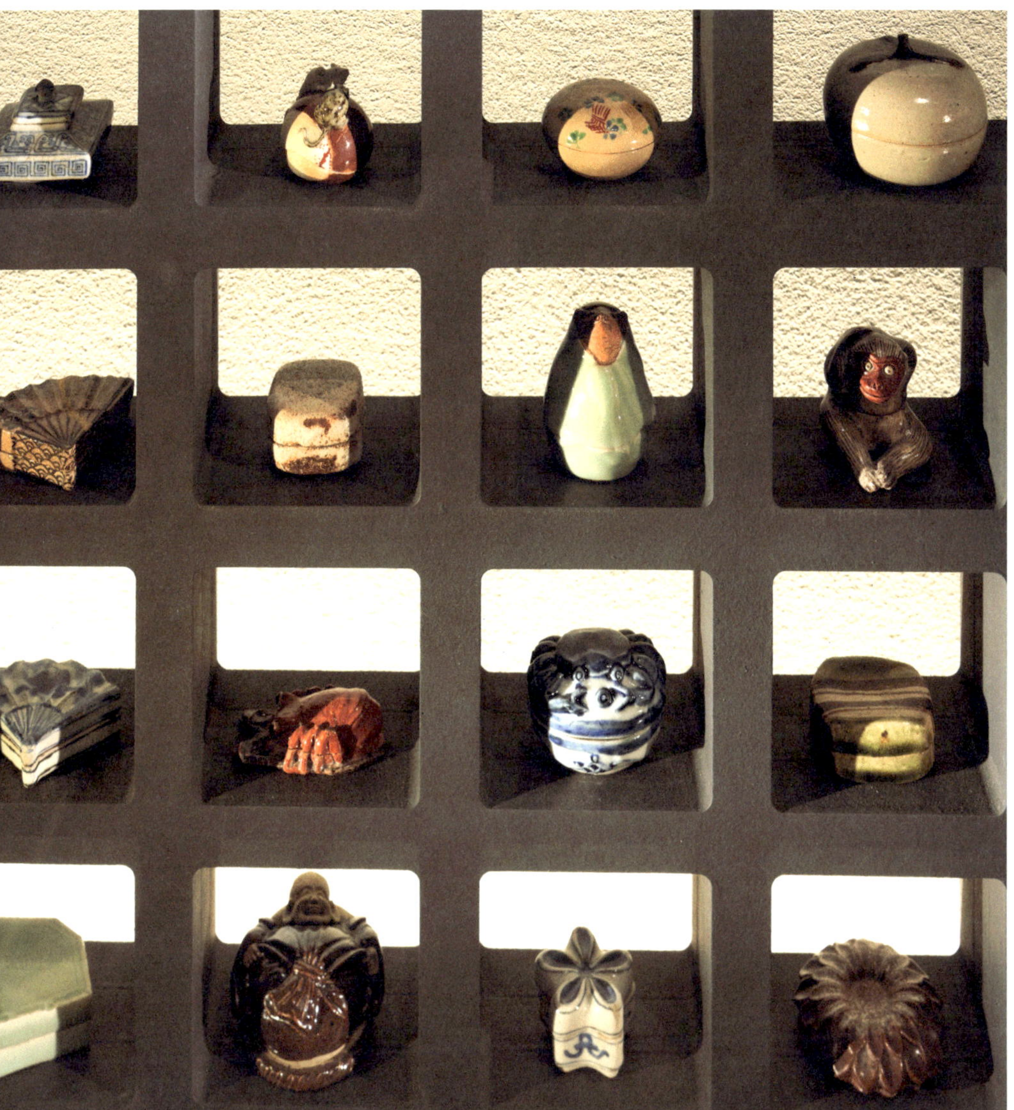

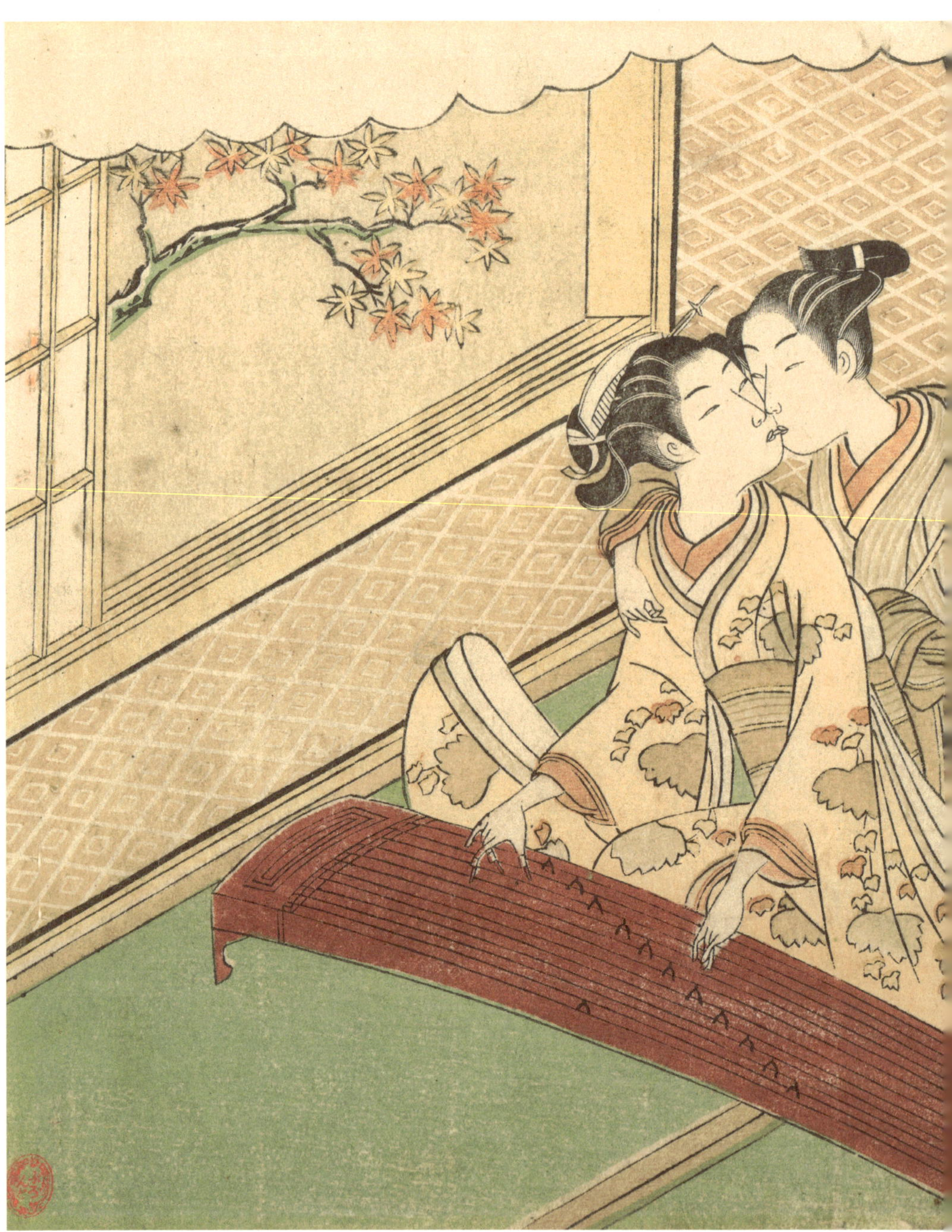

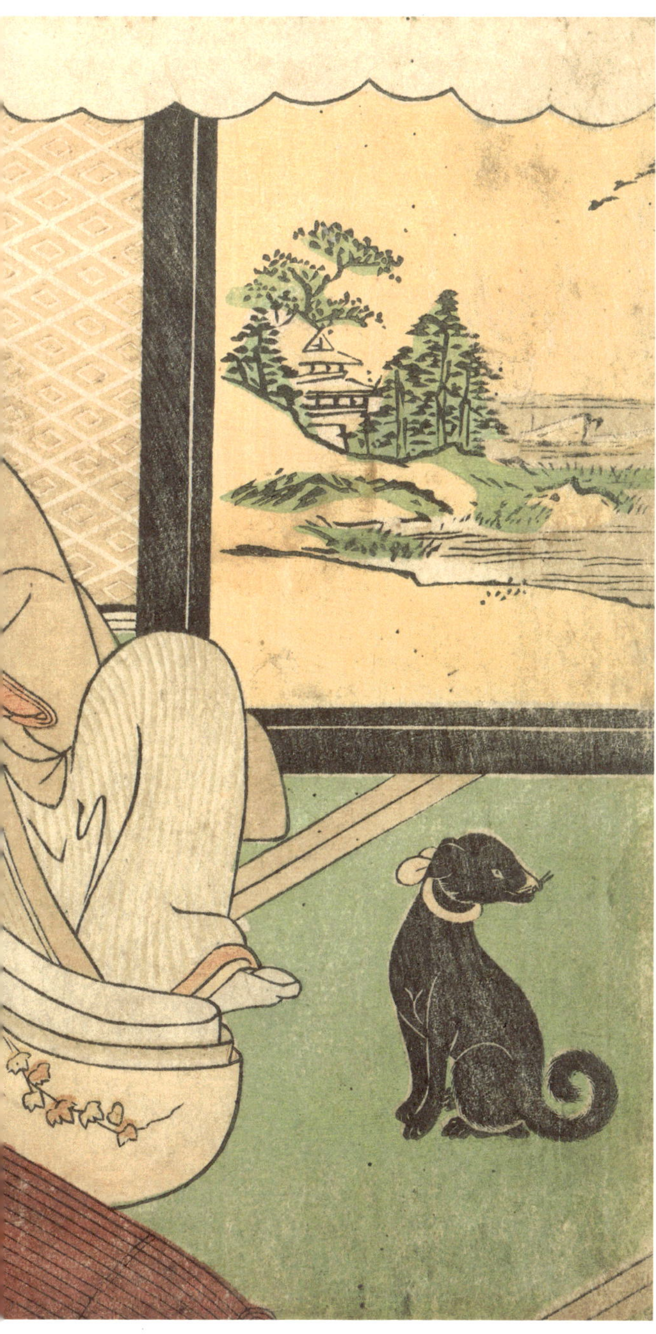

Fig. 1.20
Suzuki Harunobu (1725–70)
Two Lovers: A Wakashu and a Young Woman Kiss
Edo period, 1768–70
Woodblock print on paper
18.5 × 25.7 cm
ROM 926.18.114

Sir Edmund Walker Collection

While few scholarly studies have been conducted on the subject of shokkan in Japanese art, many descriptions of tactile encounters with Japanese art can be found in Western literary works. Edmund de Waal, for example, includes tactile descriptions of Japanese objects in his 2010 novel, *The Hare with Amber Eyes*: "When you held a Japanese *objet*, it revealed itself. Touch tells you what you need to know: it tells you about yourself … Japanese art was a brave new world: it introduced new textures, new ways of feeling things … *Japonisme* and touch were a seductive combination … What they collect are objects to discover in your hands, 'so light, so soft to the touch.'"[11] David Howes's essay in this volume also touches on Maureen Gibbon's description of how the French painter Édouard Manet (1832–83) encountered a netsuke through the sense of touch.[12] While these literary descriptions of the experiences of historical Western collectors are the product of modern imaginations, they nonetheless attest to the evocative, tactile nature of the appreciation of Japanese art during the japonisme time.

In addition to small 3-D objects, Japanese woodblock prints could evoke the sense of touch. *Shunga*, literally "spring pictures," which were Edo-period erotic prints depicting explicit sexual activities, were also one of the most popular items for Western collectors (Fig. 1.20). While shunga were subject to official suppression in the Edo period, they were nonetheless accepted and enjoyed by all social classes and genders as a form of humorously entertaining visual art and were commonly part of bridal trousseaux, given as auspicious gifts at New Year's, or used as talismans for samurai in the battlefield.

After Japan opened up to global trade in the mid-19th century, shunga were exported in large quantities to the West. The French art critic Edmond de Goncourt (1822–96) was the first person to introduce the shunga of Katsushika Hokusai and Kitagawa Utamaro, writing in the 1890s that their artistic level was comparable to that of European masters.[13] While the comparative openness to sexuality in Japan must have been a trigger for Westerners' interest in shunga,[14] the sensual nature of these prints evoking the sense of touch must have also been a crucial element of their popularity.

Why might the tactility of Japanese art have been a factor in its popularity at the time, apart from sheer exoticism? A broader socio-cultural shift occurring in the West might help explain it: tactility was being degraded at the time from "the origin of all senses" in favour of vision, which was increasingly thought of as the "civilized" sense during the advent of modernity in the late 18th to the 19th centuries. Touch, along with taste and smell, came to be seen as "a crude and uncivilized mode of perception," associated with irrationality and primitivism.[15] This way of thinking was in contrast to the view before the 18th century, when touch was considered to possess the power to "access interior truth of which sight was unaware."[16] Constance Classen argues that the degradation of the sense of touch resulted from cultural changes in the West during the transition from medieval times to modernity, including the decline of the medieval "tactile" cosmology, the development of a culture of comfort, the "discovery of the nervous system," and the industrialization of touch.[17] Given such cultural circumstances, the popularity of Japanese art in the West in the mid- to late 19th century might have symbolized the revival of, or nostalgia for, the sense of touch in Western cultures.

It is notable that the objects collected during the craze for things Japanese in the mid-19th and early 20th centuries have since formed the essential parts of Japanese collections in many Western museums, including ROM. Reinterpreting Japanese objects held by the museum via touch is thus also an attempt to explore the multiple layers making up Western perspectives toward collected Japanese objects.

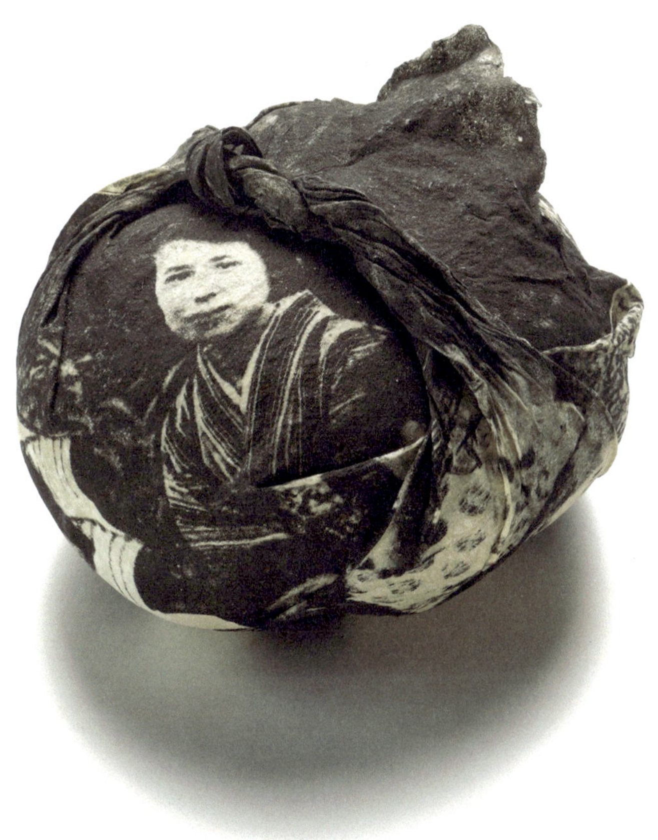

Fig. 1.21
Emma Nishimura (b. 1982)
Bundle from *An Archive of Rememory*
2016–18
Mixed media
8.7 × 9.3 × 6.0 cm
ROM 2019.108.14

(pp. 44–45)
Emma Nishimura (b. 1982)
Group of 23 bundles from *An Archive of Rememory*
2016–18
Mixed media
Dimensions vary
ROM 2019.108.1-.23

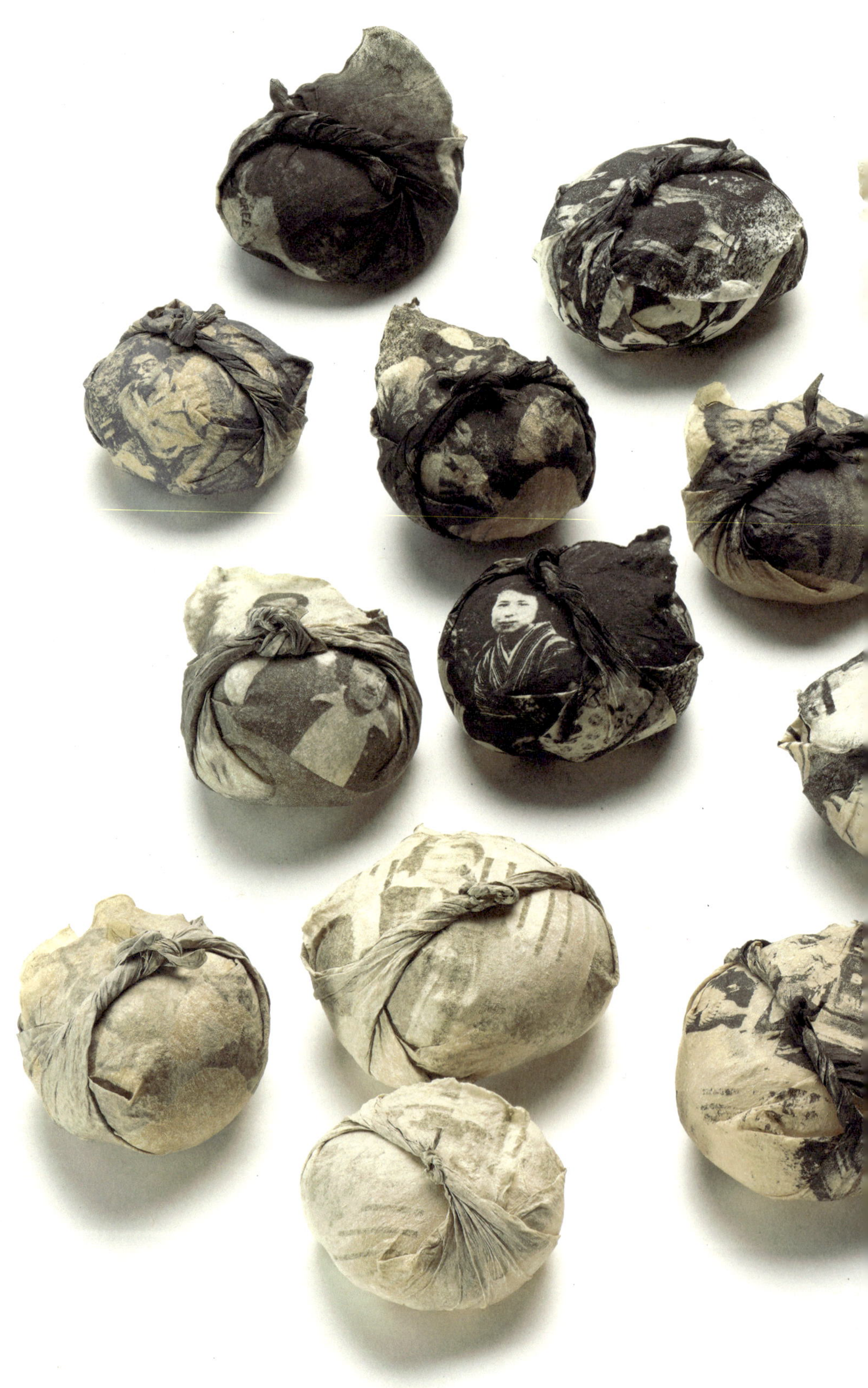

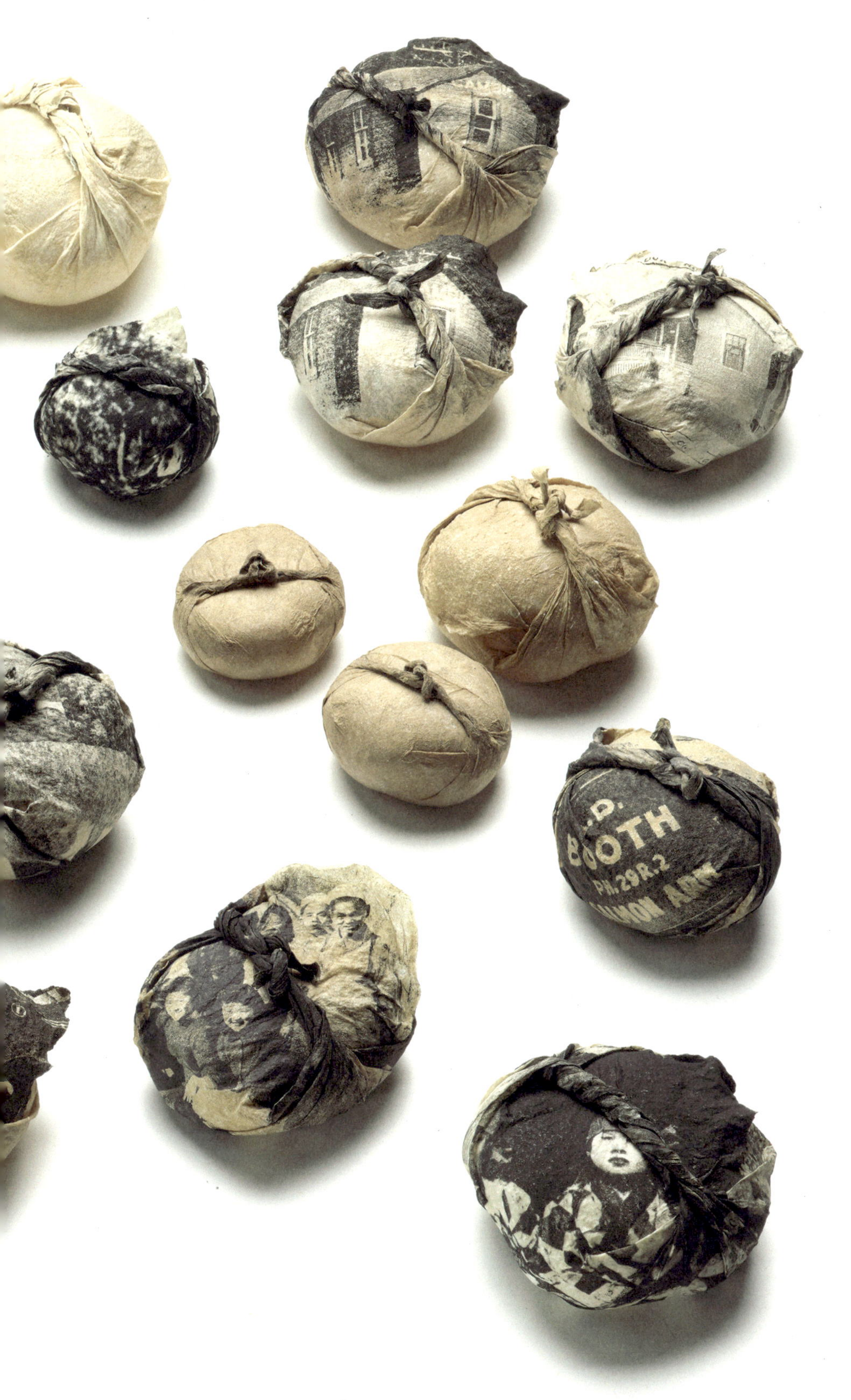
BOOTH
PH.29R.2

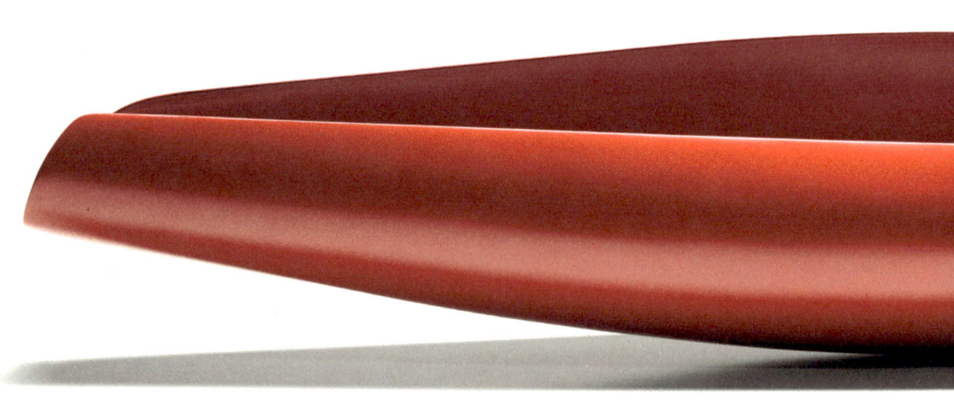

The keyword "tactility" may also be used as a valid way to (re)interpret contemporary Japanese artworks even when the artists do not explicitly intend it. Japanese Canadian artist Emma Nishimura's *An Archive of Rememory* is an ongoing project consisting of hundreds of small bundled forms, known as *furoshiki* in Japanese (Fig. 1.21). Furoshiki, a versatile fabric-wrapping technique, has long been used in Japan to wrap and carry items and gifts. Nishimura's bundles—wrapped instead with paper with printed photographs and containing seemingly stone-like objects—invite the viewer to imagine the artist's intimate acts of wrapping and tying, as well as the weight of the thing inside. The fact is that the bundles are empty, and the photos are of her family in the Japanese internment camp during WWII. The bundles now symbolize the trace of the weighty memory, with the paper furoshiki as its fragile shell. This work exemplifies an intricate entanglement of tactility, materiality, memory, and illusion.

The smooth, flowing texture of the lacquer piece by Nobuyuki Tanaka gives the viewer a strong illusion of touching its surface (Fig. 1.22). His series *Tactile Memory*, as its title indicates, invites one to explore the interconnection of facade and interior—the inner state of mind—through tactile memory. Likewise, Yayoi Kusama's soft sculptures embodying her obsession with phallic forms strongly evoke sensual touch the moment one lays eyes on them (Fig. 1.23). Photographs can also evoke the sense of touch: Michiko Kon's "simultaneously seductively beautiful and shockingly disturbing" photographs have strong tactile elements conjured by biological motifs like salmon roe and chicken feet (Fig. 1.24).

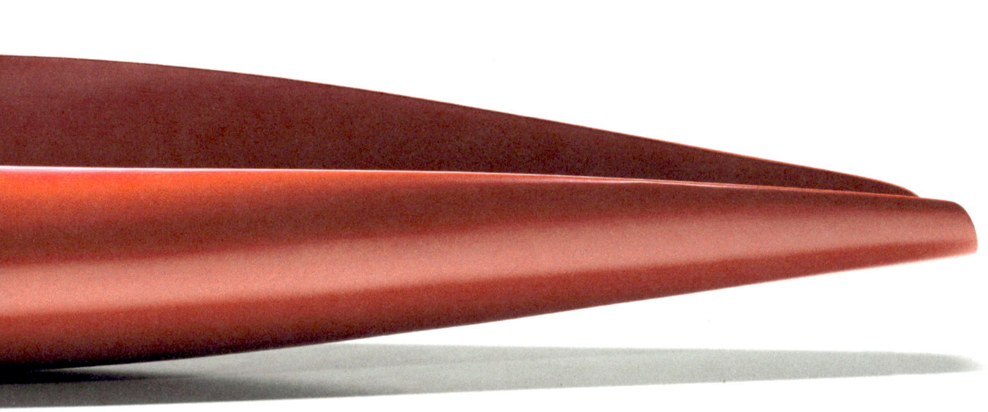

Besides artists, museums in Japan and around the world are also exploring the possibilities for multi-sensory experiences in museum spaces. The National Museum of Ethnology in Osaka is a leading institution in the field, led by Professor Kōjirō Hirose. In his essay in this volume, he describes his life work of establishing the "Universal Museum" that everyone can enjoy using multiple senses (pages 110–27). As Hirose emphasizes, the Universal Museum is not about accessibility and inclusion, concepts that address disability from the perspective of the able-bodied, but rather about creating a "culture of tactility"[18] in which everyone can broaden and deepen their understanding of the world and capacity to appreciate beauty through touch.

Fig. 1.22
Nobuyuki Tanaka (b. 1959)
Tactile Memory: Floral Impression (2011-II)
Heisei period, 2011
Lacquer, hemp cloth
32.2 × 23.9 cm
MIA 2015.35.1
Copyright: © Nobuyuki Tanaka
Photo: Minneapolis Institute of Art

Gift of the Clark Center for Japanese Art & Culture

Fig. 1.23 (pp. 48–49)
Yayoi Kusama (b. 1929)
Violet Obsession
Heisei period, 1994
Sewn and stuffed fabric over rowboat and oars
109.8 × 381.9 × 180 cm
MoMA 819.1996
Copyright: © Yayoi Kusama

Gift of Mr. and Mrs. Joseph Duke
Digital Image © The Museum of Modern Art/Licensed by SCALA / Art Resource, NY

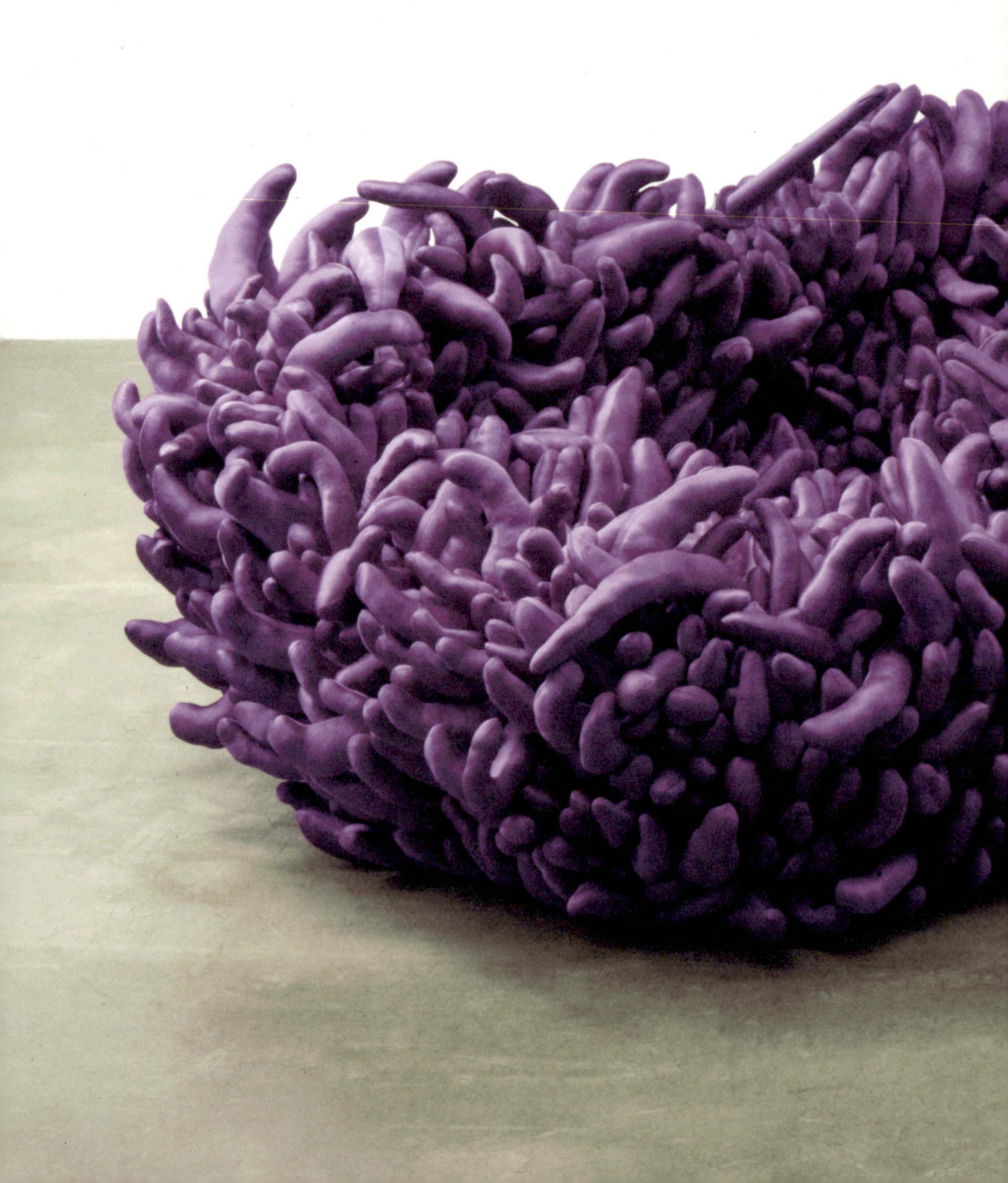

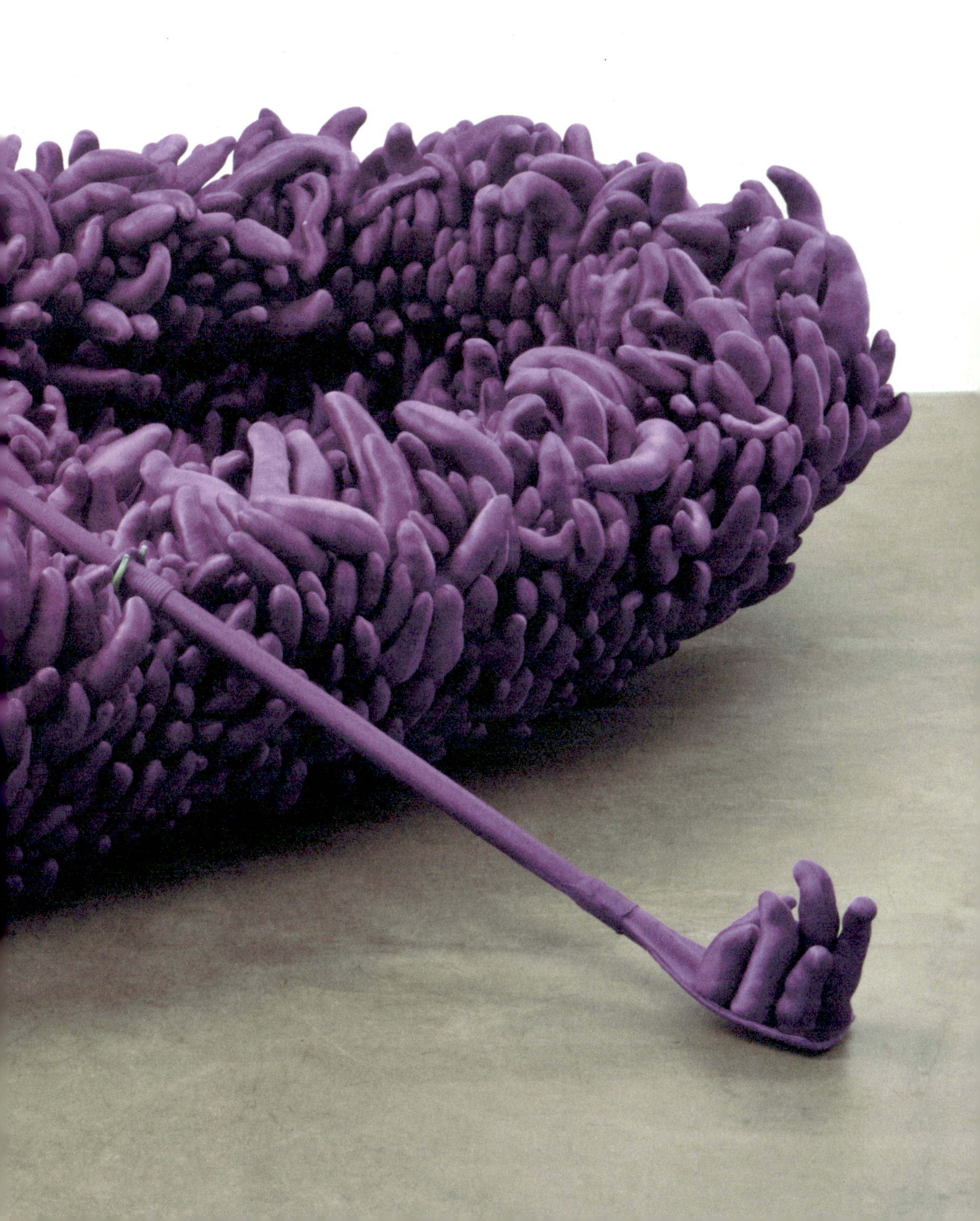

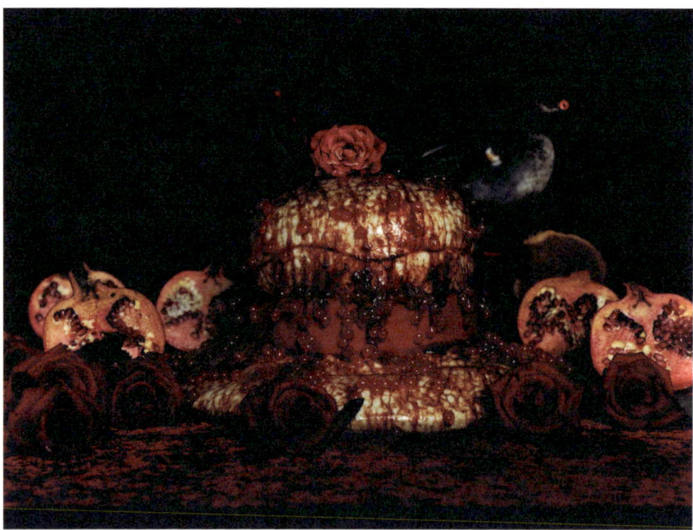

Fig. 1.24
Michiko Kon (b. 1955)
Red Hat
Heisei period, 1994
Dye coupler print
Image: 43.2 × 55.7 cm
NGC 42499
Copyright: Michiko Kon

This book and the accompanying exhibition explore Japanese art through the sense of touch, but touch is ubiquitous; every culture experiences tactile beauty. Thinking about touch is also highly relevant to today's social conditions. The global experience of the COVID-19 pandemic has made us suddenly conscious of the warmth of another's body, of touching the surfaces around us—acts that had been taken for granted. Similar to the Black Death in the 14th century, the pandemic has had a huge impact on our lives and how we communicate.[19] While on the one hand, it has made us cherish in-person communication even more, on the other, it has made digitally mediated, contactless communication ubiquitous, a form of communication that emphasizes vision, hearing, and language above all else. While virtual communication may make us feel connected, our sense of "skin perception" knows something is missing—Masashi Nakatani and his co-authors call the situation "a separation of mind and body," a condition to which many people have found it hard to adapt.[20]

Unlike other senses, our sense of touch cannot be "shut down."[21] In times like these, it is meaningful to foreground this easy-to-forget sense of tactility as an alternative way to engage with art—"from inside" and "from in between," to borrow Classen's phrasing.[22] We all experience it, even as taking it for granted is easy. Tactile beauty is all around us, just waiting to be discovered.

1 The exhibition will be held at the Royal Ontario Museum from April to September 2026.
2 Masashi Nakatani et al., *Shokuraku Nyūmon* [Introduction to the joys of touch] (Tokyo: Asahi Shuppansha, 2016), 31.
3 Charles Spence, "Making Sense of Touch: A Multisensory Approach to the Perception of Objects," in *The Power of Touch: Handling Objects in Museum and Heritage Contexts*, ed. Elizabeth Pye (New York: Routledge, 2007), 46.
4 David Howes, "The Skinscape: Reflections on the Dermalogical Turn," *Body & Society* 24, no. 1–2 (2018): 226.
5 Jonathan Hay, *Sensuous Surfaces: The Decorative Object in Early Modern China* (Honolulu: University of Hawai'i Press, 2010), 78–80.
6 Muneyoshi Yanagi, *Teshigoto no Nihon* [Japan, a country of handwork] (Tokyo: Seibun-sha, 1948), 5. My translation.
7 Shigemi Inaga, *Sesshoku Zokei-ron: Fure-au Tamashii, Tsumugareru Katachi* [In search of haptic plasticity: Souls touching each other, forms interwoven] (Nagoya: Nagoya University Press, 2016), 272.
8 Morgan Pitelka, *Handmade Culture: Raku Potters, Patrons, and Tea Practitioners in Japan* (Honolulu: University of Hawai'i Press, 2005), 27.
9 Nakatani et al., *Shokuraku Nyūmon*, 226.
10 A statement made by Hannah Thompson at a webinar, "The Sensational Museum: Theory and Practice," (from the virtual lecture series "Multisensory Museology," Centre for Sensory Studies, Concordia University, September 19, 2024).
11 Edmund de Waal, *The Hare with Amber Eyes: A Family's Century of Art and Loss* (London: Farrar, Straus and Giroux, 2010), 44–54.
12 Maureen Gibbon, *The Lost Notebook of Édouard Manet* (New York: W.W. Norton, 2021), 89, quoted in Howes, see page 68.
13 Monta Hayakawa, "Use of Shunga and Ukiyo-e in the Tokugawa Period," in *The Tokugawa World*, ed. Gary P. Leupp and De-min Tao (New York: Routledge, 2022), 647.
14 For example, the diary of Francis Hall (1822–1902), an American merchant who came to Yokohama in 1859, well illustrates his surprising reaction to the fact that "a seemingly proper and model wife in a good home" was "entirely unashamed in viewing erotic art with men." Hayakawa, "Use of Shunga," 665.
15 Constance Classen, *The Deepest Sense: A Cultural History of Touch* (Champaign: University of Illinois Press, 2012), xii, xiv.
16 Classen, *Deepest Sense*, 141.
17 Classen, *Deepest Sense*, xiii.
18 Nakatani et al, *Shokuraku Nyūmon,* 222.
19 Classen, *Deepest Sense*, 150.
20 Nakatani et al., *Shokuraku Nyūmon*, 14.
21 Nakatani et al., *Shokuraku Nyūmon*, 16.
22 Classen, *Deepest Sense*, xvii.

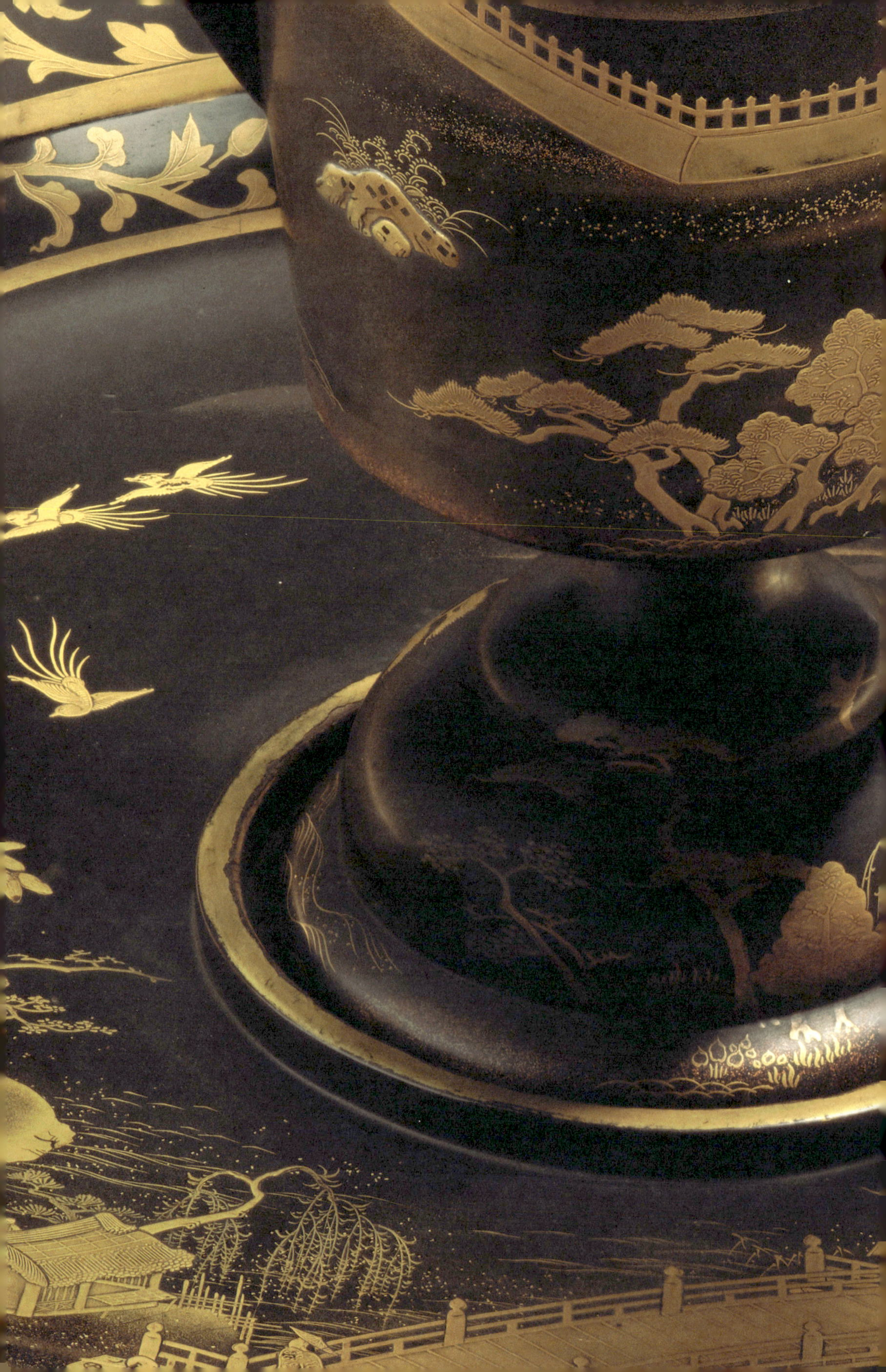

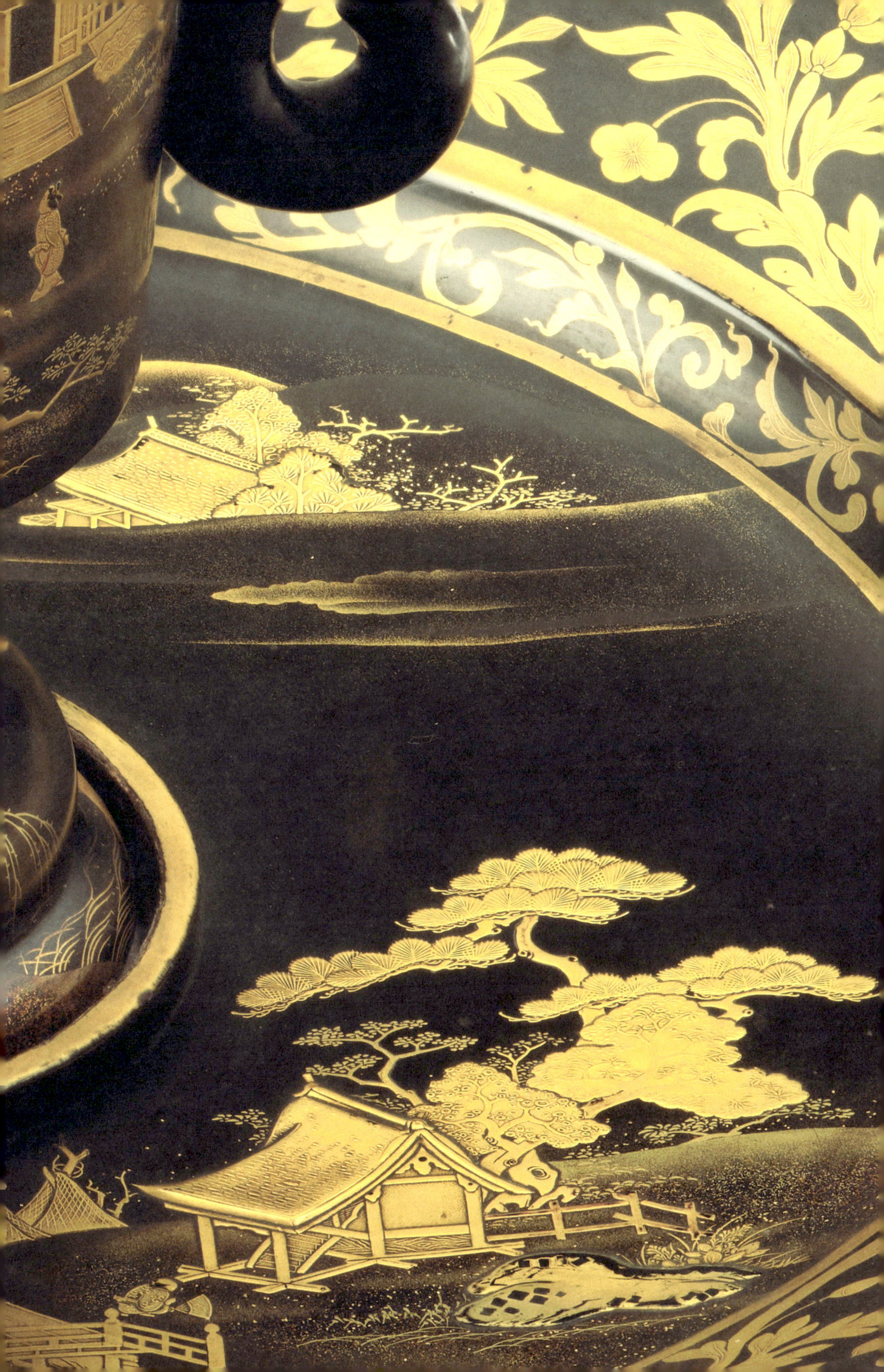

CHAPTER TWO

Seeing-Touch, Touching-Sight: Navigating the Chasm between Western and Japanese Habits of Perception-Expression

DAVID HOWES

I NOTICED A CURIOUS REACTION in myself when I encountered my first netsuke. I wanted to reach out and hold one in my hand, of course; I also could not help but smile. What accounts for the extraordinary appeal of these little figurines, for the spell they cast on us? My attempt to fathom this response in what follows will range over many topics, from sensory atomism in Western psychology (after Locke) to the debt which the avant-garde in Western art owes to traditional Japanese aesthetics. I hope that this odyssey can pleasure the reader's senses as much as composing the ensuing *étude sensorielle* did mine. I am deeply grateful to Akiko Takesue for curating *Shokkan: Material Encounters in Japanese Art*. The exhibition is so magnificent in itself and stimulated so many sensuous recollections of my own six-day trip to Japan, back in 2011, as well as a range of cross-cultural reflections in the spirit of Lafcadio Hearn and François Laplantine, not to mention Sadakichi Hartmann.

In *An Essay concerning Human Understanding*, the philosopher John Locke (1632–1704) recounts the anecdote of "a studious blind man who ... bragged one day, that he now understood what scarlet was—upon which his friend, [demanded] to know what scarlet was? The blind man answered, it was like the sound of a trumpet." Precisely! the reader might think at first blush. But not Locke, who proceeds to ridicule the blind man's suggestion: "For, to hope to produce an *idea* of light or colour by a sound, however formed, is to expect that

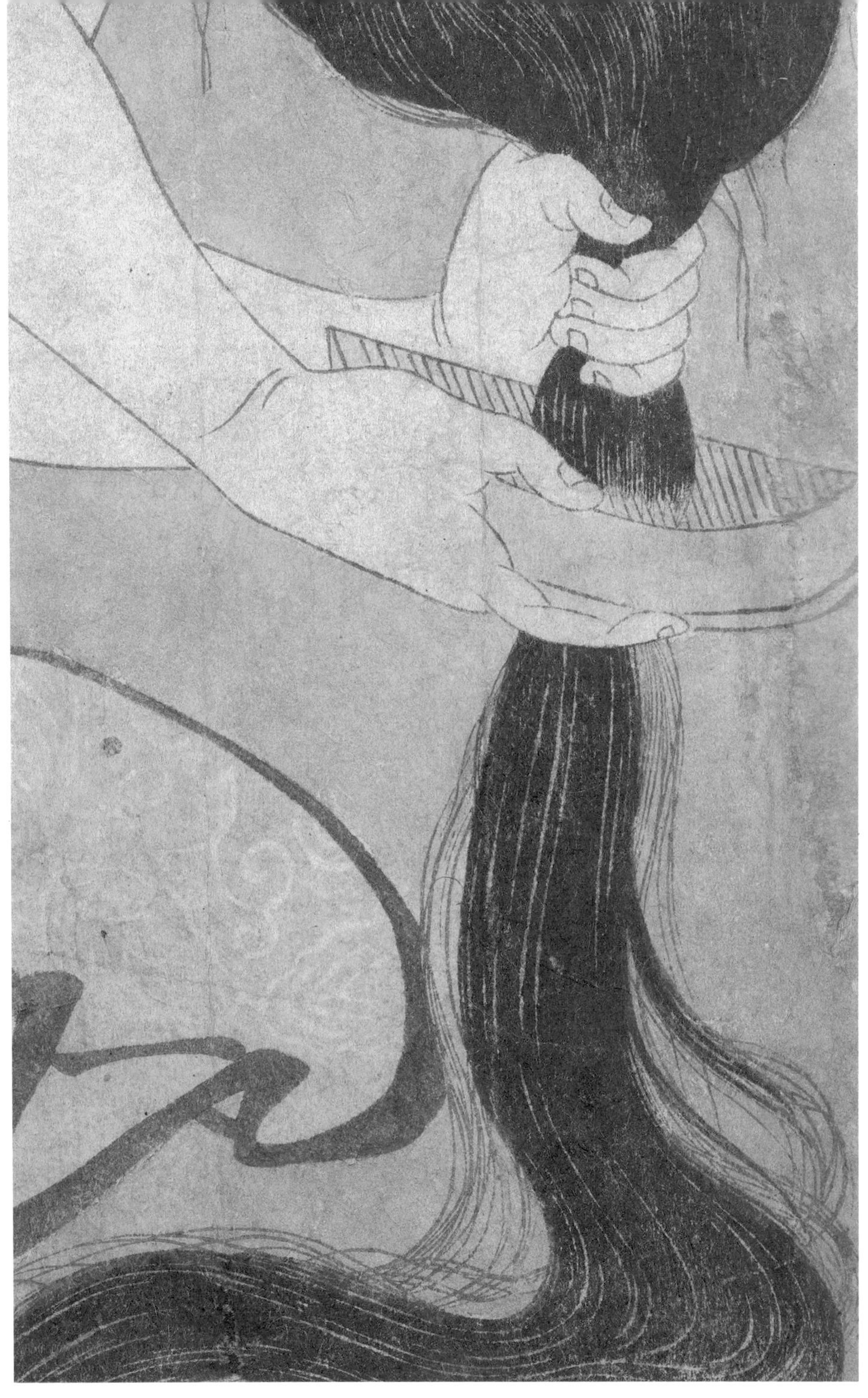

Detail, *Yamauba Combing Her Hair with Kintarō*

sounds should be visible or colours audible; and to make the ears do the office of all the other senses. Which is all one as to say, that we might taste, smell, and see by the ears."[1] This is utter nonsense, as far as Locke is concerned.

Locke's dismissal of the blind man's analogy expresses the empiricist philosophy of sensory atomism peculiar to the Western sensorium in its basest (and most lasting) form. Now, consider this haiku poem of Matsuo Bashō (1644–94):

As the bell tone fades
Blossom scents take up the ringing
Evening shade

According to Steve Odin, this poem describes "an intensely synaesthetic experience of nature," and it produces "a total aesthetic effect": "The reverberating sound of a fading bell tone merges with the fragrant perfume of flower blossom, which, in turn, blends with the shadowy darkness of evening shade."[2] Contrary to Locke's sensory atomism, the focus of Bashō's poem is on the intersensory.

Between Locke's empiricist philosophy and Bashō's sensibility lies a gaping aporia. How can we navigate this chasm? Let us take our lead from another poem, a *waka* poem said to have been spoken by Sen no Sōtan (1578–1658), who was a grand master in the Urasenke tradition of *chanoyu*, or "tea ceremony," founded by his grandfather, Sen no Rikyū (1522–91):

If asked
The nature of chanoyu,
Say it's the sound
Of windblown pines
In a painting[3]

The painting we are invited to listen to—or see with our ears—would have been a sumi-e ink painting.[4]

Chanoyu presents a wonderful way into the Japanese sensorium (Fig. 2.1 and 2.2). Odin characterizes chanoyu as "a synthesis of various arts and crafts," including the landscaped garden in which the tea hut is set; the humble architecture of the hut; and, within its confines, the hanging scrolls, the flower arrangements, the incense burner, the utensils, the choreographed movements, the coarse texture of the unusually shaped ceramic tea bowls, and the warmth of the tea: "Chanoyu functions to stimulate and harmonize the diverse sense modes through a refined orchestration of subtle tastes, scents, sights, and sounds as well as tactile and thermal sensations. In his book on chanoyu, Hamamato Soshun writes:

'The six sense organs signify the modes of perception—eyes, ears, nose, tongue, body (touch), and consciousness—that we see constantly in daily life. True practice of Tea brings all senses to function simultaneously and in accord, and leads to the realm of immovable tranquility.'"[5]

In 2011, I went on a trip to Japan for six days, which was somewhat longer than Sadakichi Hartmann's famous 16-minute foray from New York to Kyoto on a waft of smells and sounds[6] but nowhere near long enough. I gave a series of lectures on the anthropology of the senses at Keio University, at the invitation of fellow anthropologist Keizō Miyasaka. My itinerary was packed with sensory delights, thanks to Professor Miyasaka's connoisseurship and extensive contacts, such as having tea (like President Obama before me) in the traditional Japanese home adjacent to the Great Buddha of Kamakura at Kōtoku-in Temple, at the invitation of one of his colleagues, who was also the temple priest.

During our walks about Tokyo, Professor Miyasaka would bring numerous little details to my attention, like the fact that no two high-rise towers may abut their whole height: a space must remain, according to the building code in Tokyo, even though it be no more than a few centimetres. This observation arose in connection with our discussion of the Japanese notion of *ma*. Ma means "gap" or "interval." The concept of the interval is both spatial and temporal. It is the space between the figures in a painting or the instant between two notes in a piece of music. This area, left empty, is no less important than the areas that are filled in, for without this in-between, nothing could exist, at least nothing that stands out. As Tomie Hahn observes in *Sensational Knowledge*, "*Ma* is a particularly Japanese aesthetic where aspects of 'negative' space and time are not believed to be empty but are considered to be expansive and full of energy."[7]

Our discussion of the significance of negative space led to a further discussion of Japanese proxemics. The average interpersonal distance (or personal space) in Japan is reported to be 360 cm, compared with 240 cm in Western Europe and 120 cm in Latin America. This measurement makes the Japanese seem even more reserved than the British, who are (or were) notorious for their formality. Other factors contribute to Japan's reputation as a "no-contact culture," to use the terminology of Ashley Montagu in *Touching: The Human Significance of the Skin*,[8] such as the practice of bowing instead of kissing on the cheek when greeting someone;

Fig. 2.1
Nonomura Ninsei
(act. late 17th century)
Rounded Square Tea Bowl with Flowing Glaze
Edo period, late 17th century
Glazed stoneware
8.1 × 13.2 cm
ROM 944.16.24

Given in memory of my grandfather, the late Sir William Van Horne

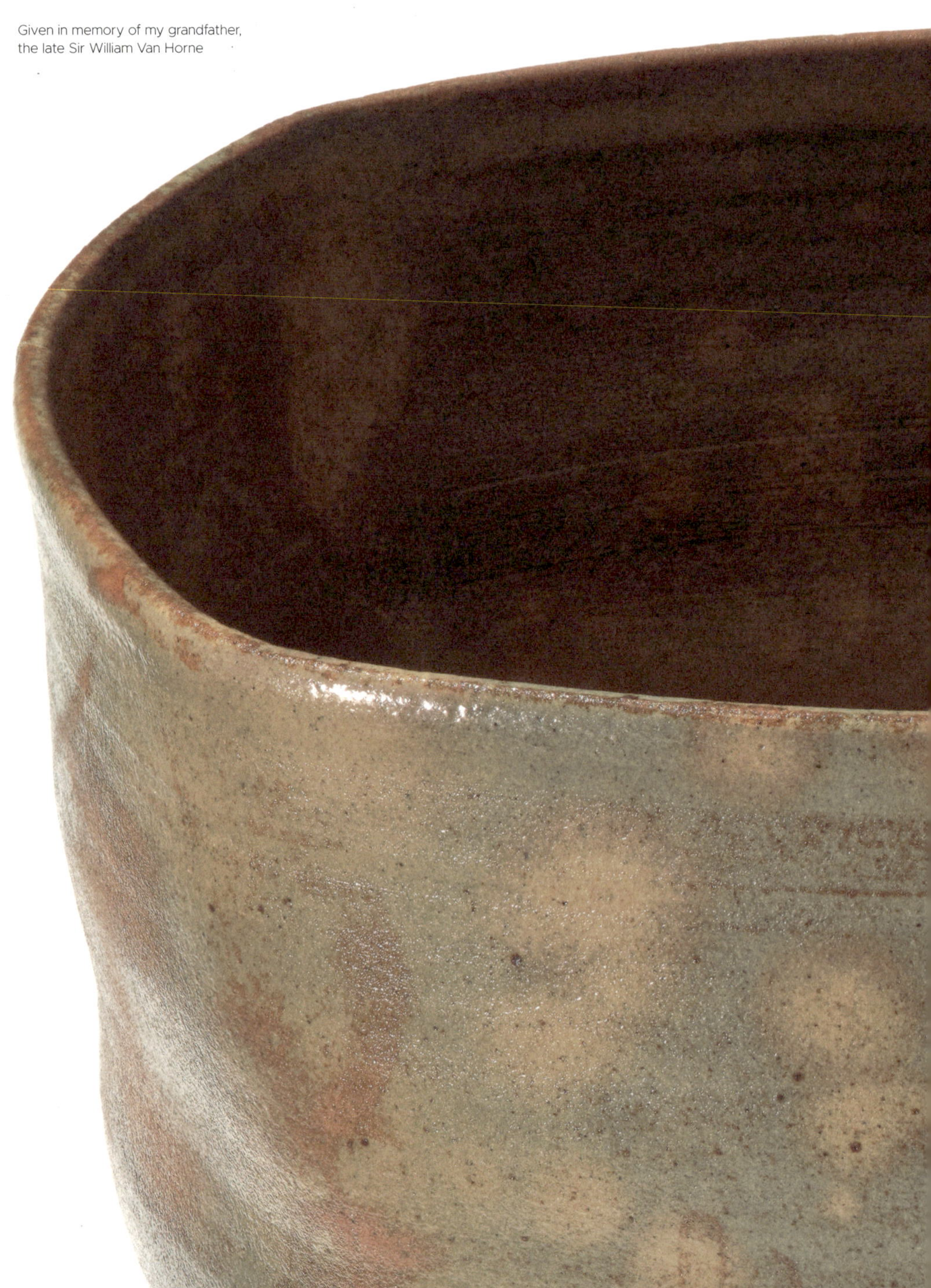

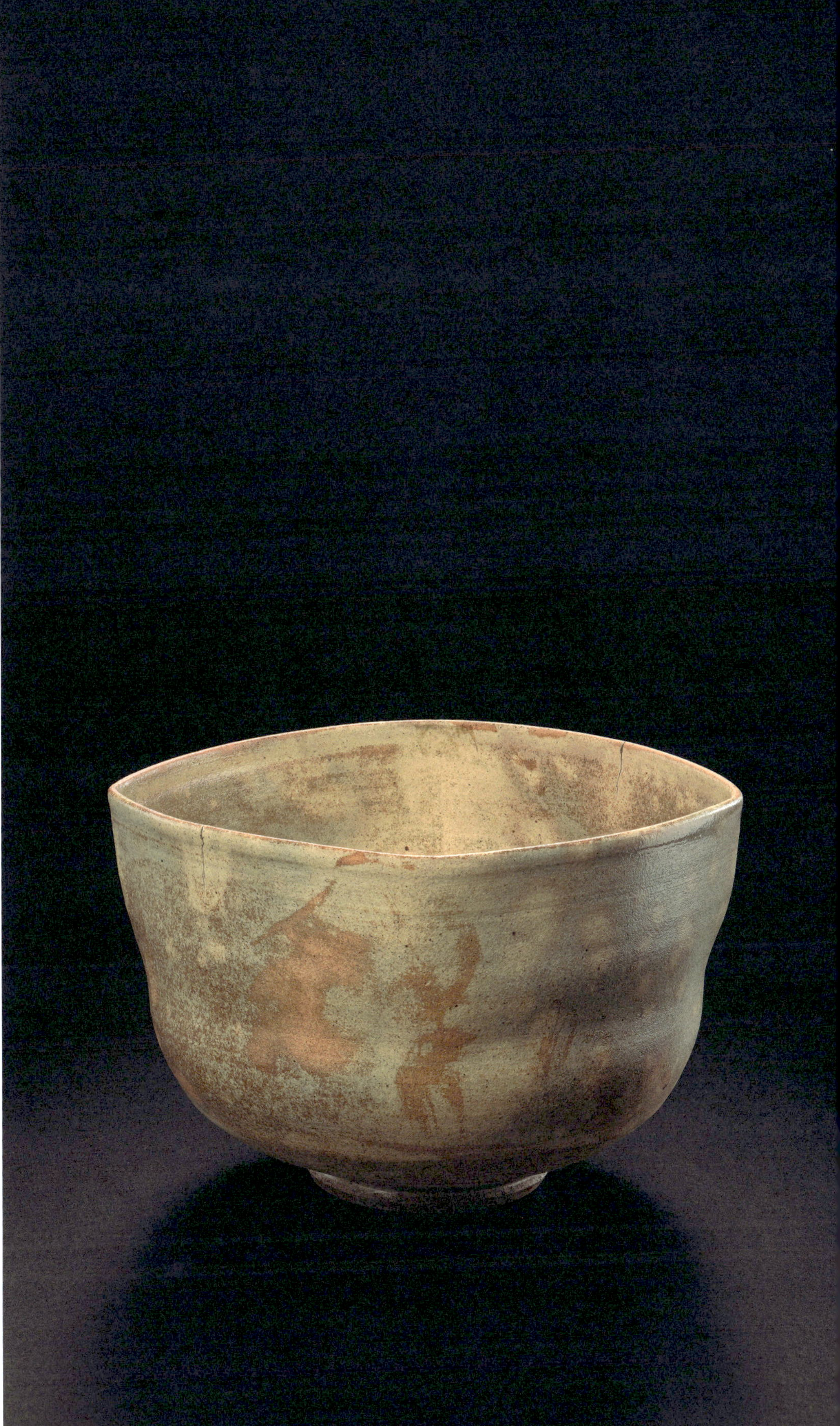

Fig. 2.2
Ōmine Jissei (b. 1933)
Tea Bowl
Heisei period, late 20th–
early 21st century
Earthenware
9 × 10 cm
ROM 2015.63.12

Gift of Deanna Horton

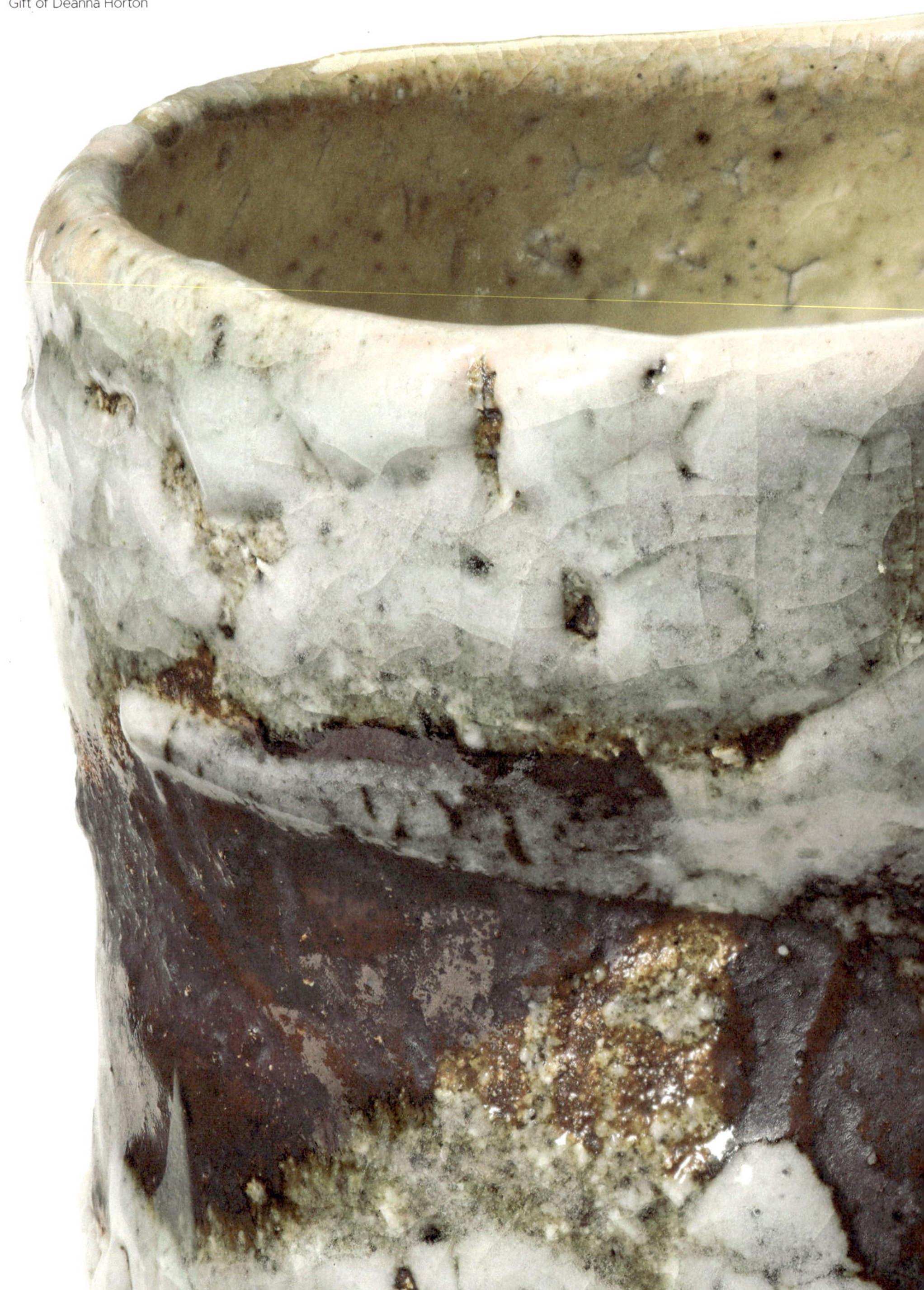

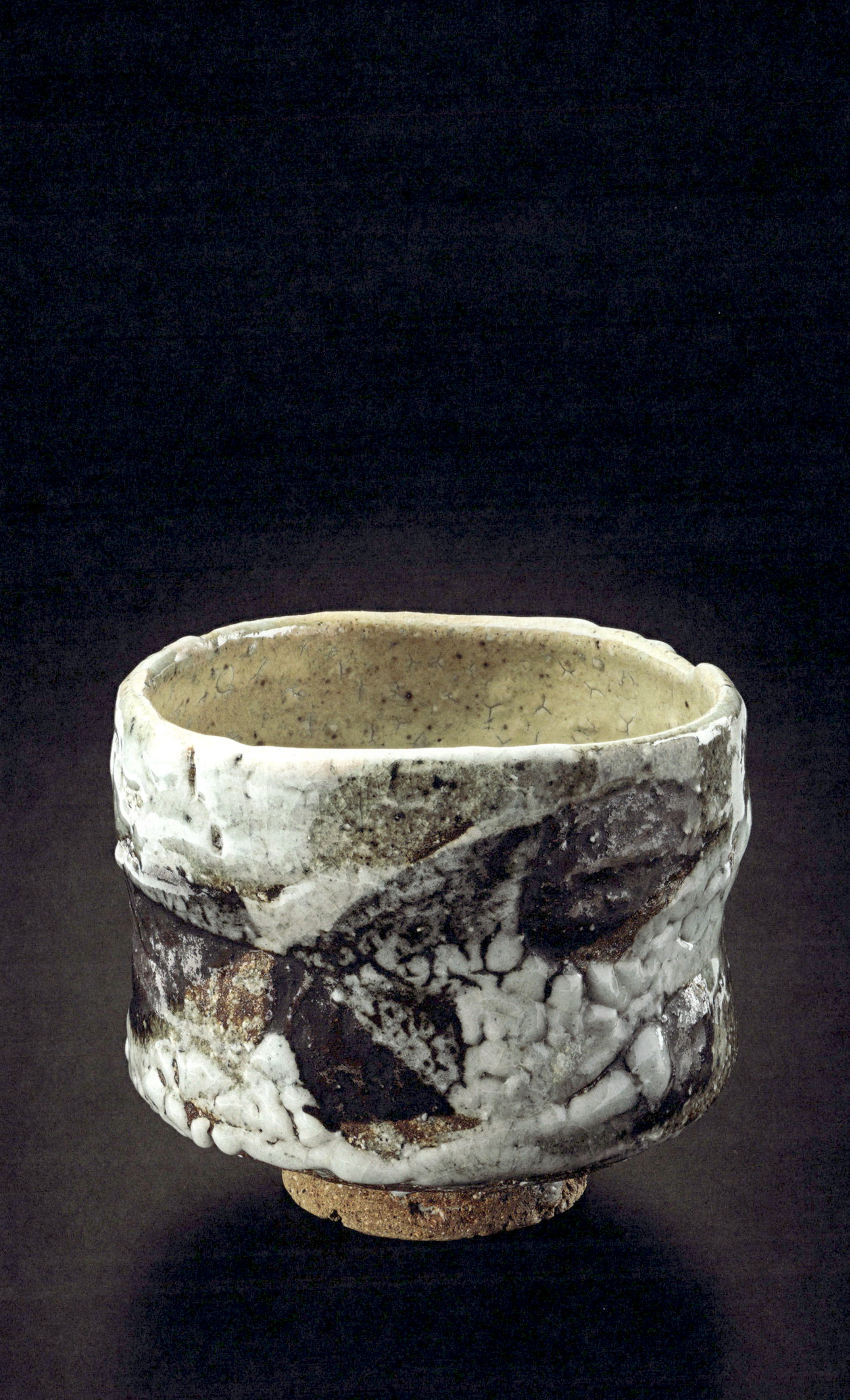

the tradition of masking, both in the theatre and in everyday life (for hygienic reasons); and the importance attached to "face" (or "keeping face").

The perimeters of personal space are indeed more extensive in Japan than in the U.S. or the U.K., and social interaction does tend toward greater formality. However, the characterization of Japan as a no-contact culture is false, for it ignores the fact that two kinds of contact zone are present in Japan, one public, the other private. As Professor Miyasaka noted, in the home, there is a great deal of emphasis on physical proximity and reliance on non-verbal communication, particularly in comparison with Americans, who, according to Montagu again,[9] resort more to verbal communication.

This pattern is manifested in the popularity of co-sleeping arrangements in Japan, whereby children sleep together with their parents or grandparents until they start attending elementary school and sometimes even until they reach puberty. This is in contrast to the American child, who is assigned their own bed (starting with a crib) and own room from very early on (Fig. 2.3). Significantly, a vogue for private children's rooms in Japan began in the 1980s, but this arrangement has since declined because of the perceived social benefits of co-sleeping. As one of Inge Daniels's middle-class female informants explained, "Until a few years ago it was considered good to have a children's room just like people in Europe. But recently, cases in which families cannot create smooth internal relationships have increased. That is why the view that it is good to be [i.e., sleep] together as a family is regaining popularity."[10]

It is interesting to contemplate how Japanese culture appears to outflank American culture when it comes to personal space and contact. The Japanese are both more reserved and more intimate than the average American. Traditional Japanese aesthetics also confound Western tastes—for example, in the way that art and craft are not distinct from one another (the two pursuits are equally refined)—as does Japanese etiquette. When I would go to pay for a meal at a restaurant, for instance, the cashier would receive and return my credit card with two hands. Out of respect, I tried to emulate this gesture, but due to the pre-eminence of my right hand,[11] I repeatedly fumbled the exchange.

Fig. 2.3
Kitagawa Utamaro (c. 1754–1806)
Yamauba Combing Her Hair with Kintarō
Edo period, c. 1800
Woodblock print on paper
Image: 37.4 × 25.1 cm
ROM 926.18.396

Sir Edmund Walker Collection

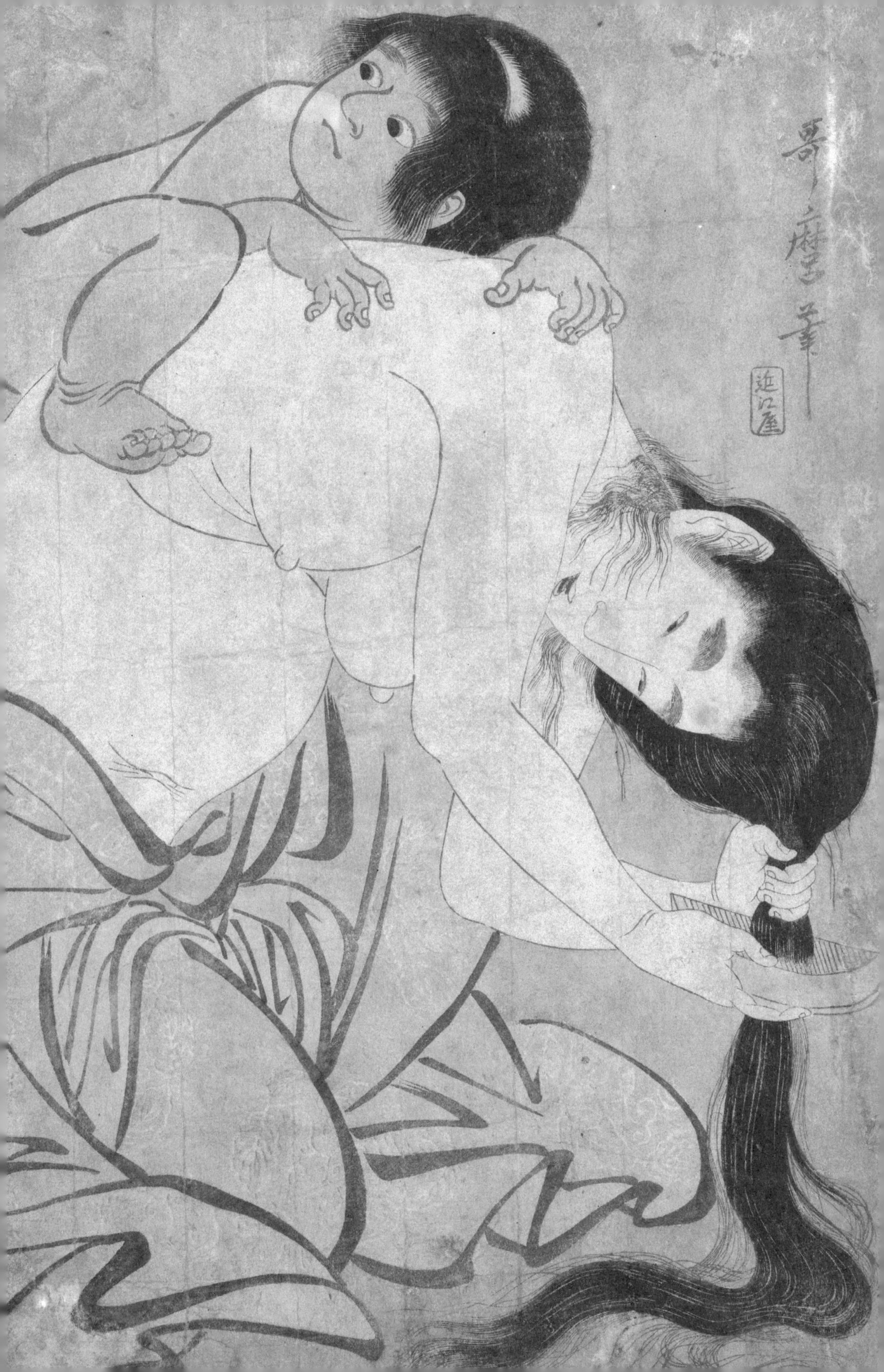
哥麿筆
近江屋

It may seem as though our attempt to navigate the gulf between Japan and the West has so far only exposed more barriers to understanding and social interaction, more reefs than bridges. But the Western imagination is not wholly insensible to the entreaties of Japanese culture. For example, while Bashō's poem would have made no sense to Locke, to a symbolist, such as the poet Charles Baudelaire (1821–67), with his doctrine that "scents and sounds and colours correspond,"[12] it would have made perfect sense. Significantly, after the late Meiji period (1868–1912), the poetry of Baudelaire and other French symbolists was warmly received in Japan due to its perceived correspondence to the poetry of Bashō. This reception, in turn, inspired a florescence or renaissance of sensualism in Japanese literature, as exemplified by the symbolist poetry of Kanbara Yumei and Miki Rofū; the neo-sensualist novels of Kawabata Yasunari (winner of the Nobel Prize for Literature in 1968); and the literary theory of Kitahara Hakushū and Yokomitsu Riichi.[13]

The reception of traditional Japanese aesthetics in Europe was equally enthusiastic and energizing. For example, *japonisme* had a profound influence on the painterly style of the expatriate American artist James McNeill Whistler (1834–1903), who was an ardent collector of Japanese prints and crafts and had a long-standing correspondence with the adventurer Lafcadio Hearn (1850–1904).[14] Whistler began by incorporating depictions of Japanese objects (kimonos, fans, or parasols) into his paintings (Fig. 2.4) and gradually internalized and came to express an eminently Japanese way of sensing—for example, in his treatment of the expanse (ma) of the Thames and the way he gave his paintings musical titles, such as *Nocturne: Blue and Silver* and *Symphony in White*.[15] The avant-garde Russian filmmaker Sergei Eisenstein (1898–1948) fell under the spell of haiku poetry and kabuki theatre, as can be discerned, according to Odin, in Eisenstein's invention of such techniques as montage (overtonal montage and multi-sensory ensemble), which he saw as "the basic element of traditional Japanese culture" and transposed into his style of "synaesthetic cinema."[16] Eisenstein even coined a new (sixth) sense, "the film sense," to denote the intersensory potential of the medium of film.[17]

Parenthetically, other "alien," or cross-cultural, influences on the development of Western avant-garde art include African arts. For example, the chief inspiration for Pablo Picasso's break with linear perspectivalism and invention of the multiperspectivalism of his cubist period would appear to have been his exposure to African masks and other statuary, with their "distorted" features, during the afternoons he whiled away at the Musée du Trocadéro.[18] The conclusion is inescapable: the roots or wellsprings of modernism were not exclusively European in origin; rather, they sometimes originated from exposure to diverse non-Western aesthetic traditions.

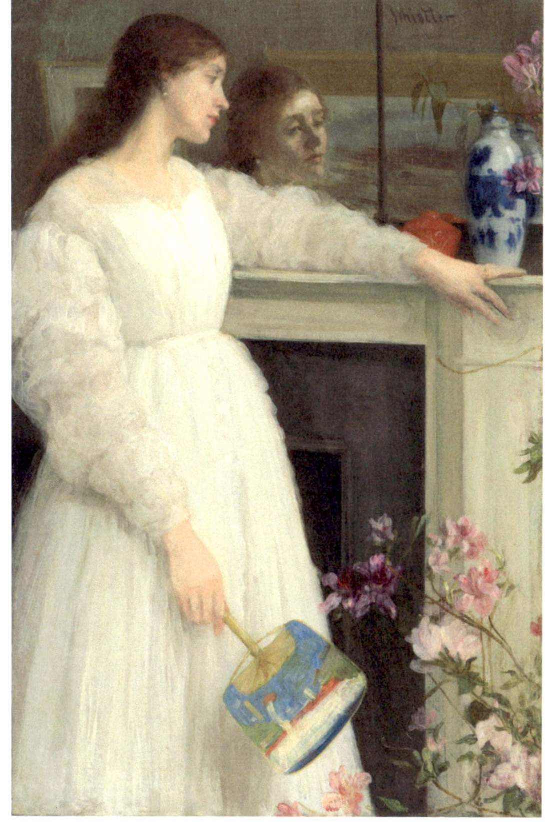

Fig. 2.4
James McNeill Whistler (1834–1903)
Symphony in White No. 2 (*The Little White Girl*)
1864
Oil paint on canvas
Support: 765 × 511 mm
Tate N03418

Tate, presented by Arthur Studd Bequest, 1919. Photo: Tate

Netsuke constitute another such cultural and sensory transplant. The vogue for collecting netsuke blossomed in the West during the 19th century, when collections in ROM and other prominent museums, such as the Met,[19] as well as private collections, came into existence (Fig. 2.5 and 2.6). Why was this? Was it because advances in mass production stimulated a counter-longing for the handcrafted and exotic? Evidently, netsuke rubbed the Western imagination the right way: they called out to be handled, to be possessed. But there is more. Rather than mere objects to be collected, netsuke embody (or are alive with) an alternative way of sensing, which is given in the notion of *shokkan*, a psychological experience of a haptic sensation, composed of inputs from vision, hearing, memory, and languages. Vision and touch are poles apart in the Western sensorium,[20] whereas in the term shokkan and in the experience of netsuke, they are conjoined: netsuke are grounded in and radiate the intersensory.

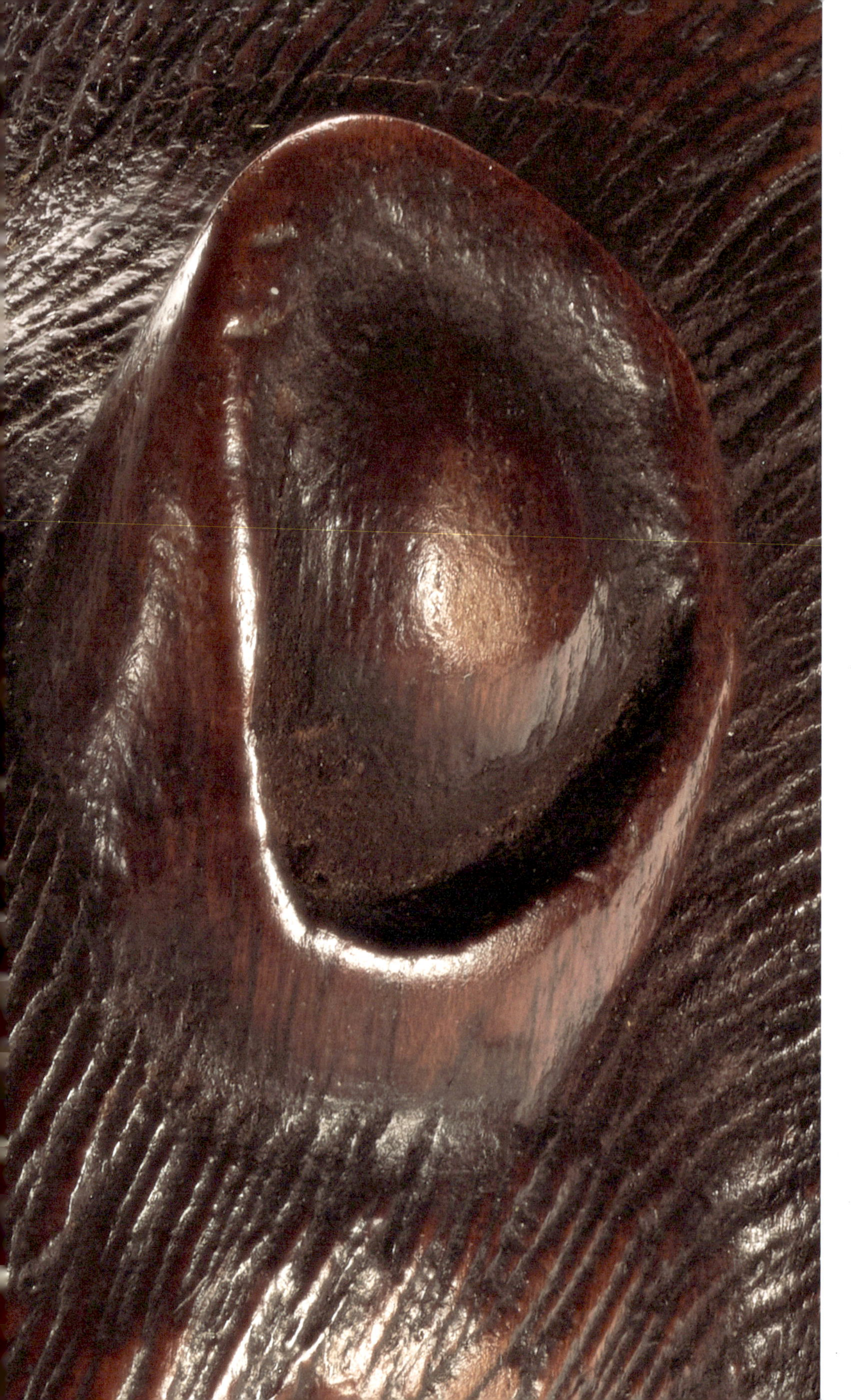

Fig. 2.5
Kokei (act. late 18th century)
Netsuke of Mouse
Edo period, late 18th century
Carved wood
3 × 2.5 cm
ROM 988.102.1

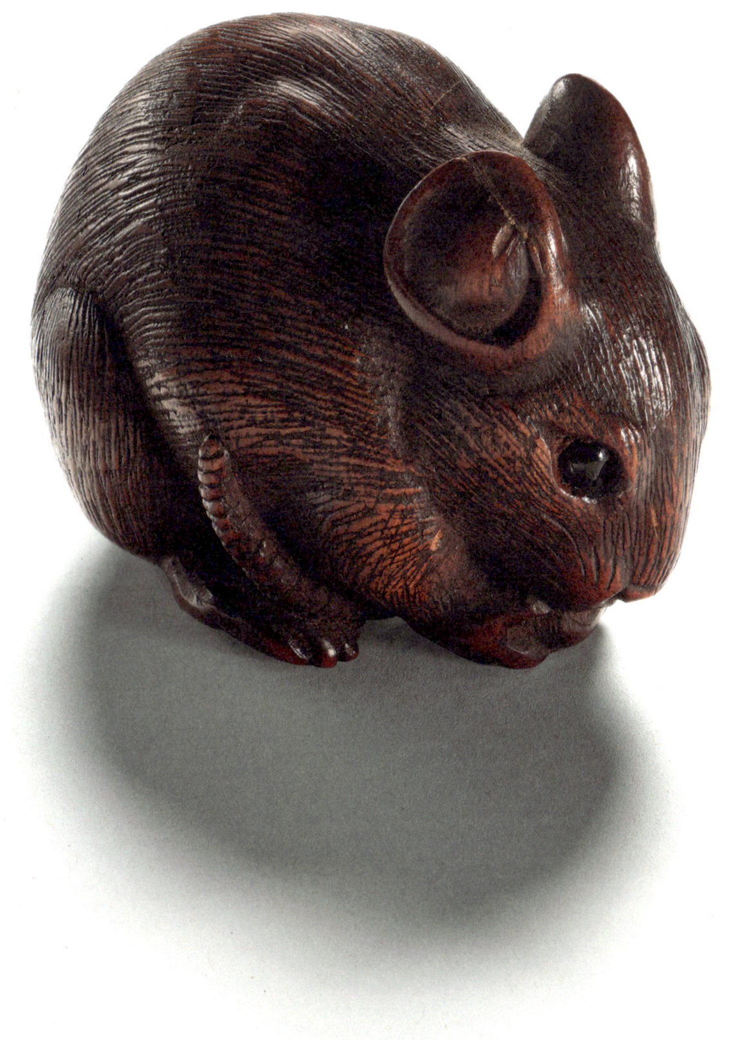

This nexus is nicely captured by the novelist Maureen Gibbon in a passage in *The Lost Notebook of Édouard Manet*. While in a curio shop in Paris, the French artist picks up a netsuke, which is described as follows: "A woman bathes in a tub. One foot in the water, the other foot up on the rim of the tub, where she bends to soap it. A small frog also perches on the rim of the tub. He sits behind the woman and looks up. At her *chose*."[21] Manet is so engrossed by the netsuke in his hand that he does not notice the approach of an associate, who asks to see it. Manet reluctantly relinquishes the netsuke. After a while, when the netsuke is finally returned to him, he wonders:

> What is it about the smallness of such things? Do they remind us of trinkets we had as children? Is it that you see them as much with your fingertips as you do with your eyes? Yet small paintings also have a charm that larger works cannot.
>
> I think some of it is that you have to get close to see. You come in as if for a kiss, so there is that nearness. The intimacy is built in—first by the artist, who had to work so close to make the piece, and then by the viewer, who must finish the embrace.[22]

Precisely! Gibbon evokes the intersensoriality of netsuke very well in this passage. In other parts of her novel, she manifests a flair for drawing out the extra-visual sensory dimensions of Manet's paintings as well.[23]

I prepared myself—that is, I primed my senses—for my 2011 trip to Japan by reading ethnographies, such as the work of the French anthropologist François Laplantine, author of *Le social et le sensible* and *Tokyo, ville flottante*.

In a chapter of the former book, called "The Sensible, the Social, Category and Energy," Laplantine traces the history of the opposition between categorical thinking and modal thinking in Western philosophy, arguing that the latter, latent way of thinking (which is also a way of sensing) is vital while the former kills.[24] According to Laplantine, categorical thought, which Western culture inherited from the Greeks, attributes properties to those things it isolates from the flux of existence and cleaves to the logic of the excluded middle. As such, it is inimical to life and living (*la vie et*

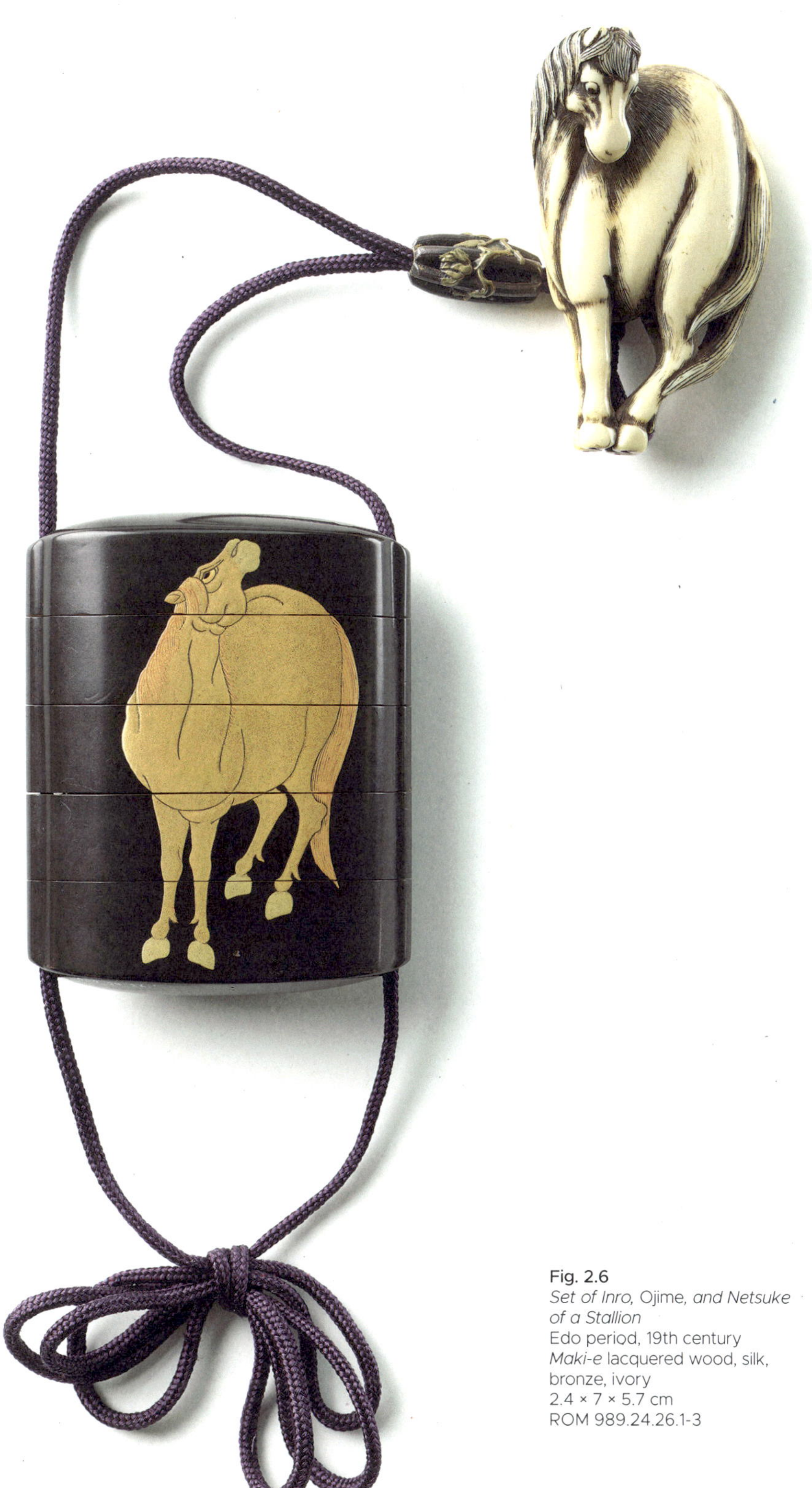

Fig. 2.6
Set of Inro, Ojime, *and Netsuke of a Stallion*
Edo period, 19th century
Maki-e lacquered wood, silk, bronze, ivory
2.4 × 7 × 5.7 cm
ROM 989.24.26.1-3

le vivant), which are processes of continuous transformation. Life itself is rhythmical, and to model or categorize it—which is to say, to fix it—is false, for the model overrides the temporal and processual in the name of the essential.

Laplantine's second book, *Tokyo, ville flottante*, was conceived during his two-month sojourn as a visiting professor in Tokyo in 2008–9.[25] It is part sensory ethnography and part film studies. His attentiveness to contemporary Japanese film[26] and penchant for modal thinking appear to have primed him to pick up on the many nuances, and also the enduring polarities, of Japanese culture. According to Laplantine, the Japanese privilege form (not idea), percept (not concept), concrete (not abstract), and transformation (not essence). The culture oscillates between high tech and tradition, the pragmatic and the frivolous, extravagance and asceticism, extreme flexibility and standing on ceremony, a strong sense of duty and a craving for distraction (for example, by karaoke and pachinko parlours), self-effacement and national pride. Japanese society is a highly disciplined—even "hypercivilized"—society with an overwhelming emphasis on security, serenity, harmony, and integration; but it is also pervaded by a profound consciousness of "impermanence" (the seasonal cycle, seismic activity, and the fact that Tokyo itself is built on a marsh). In what other society, we might ask, do we find aesthetic appreciation of a few unpretentious objects, as in the paraphernalia of chanoyu—or, as described here, in netsuke—and expertise in seasonal representation, as in the art of flower arranging, so bound up with social distinction? Social distinction is normally about permanence, not fugacity.[27]

Netsuke give expression to an analogous conjuncture, or kind of *coincidentia oppositorum*. Netsuke are not for collecting and not a form of cultural capital; they are for caressing with the eyes and hands successively in unison. Their charm is a function of their "intersensoriality,"[28] or shokkan.

---

1 John Locke, *An Essay concerning Human Understanding* (Oxford: Clarendon Press, 1975), chap. 4, para. 11.

2 Steve Odin, "Blossom Scents Take Up the Ringing: Synaesthesia in Japanese and Western Aesthetics," *Soundings: An Interdisciplinary Journal* 69, no. 3 (1986): 261.

3 Quoted in Odin, "Blossom Scents," 261.

4 The incense ceremony (*kōdō*), which involves "listen[ing] to the incense" (*kō wo kiku*), is also grounded in such an appeal to the intersensory. See David Howes, *Sensorium: Contextualizing the Senses and Cognition in History and across Cultures* (Cambridge: Cambridge University Press, 2024), 23–24.

5 Odin, "Blossom Scents," 258. Six sense organs? In Buddhism, the mind (or "consciousness") is classified as a sixth sense. It is positioned on a par with the other five, unlike in the West, where the mind lords it over

the body and senses. See Howes, *Sensorium*, 7. For a more sequential and nuanced interpretation of the orchestration of the senses in chanoyu, see Dorrine Kondo, "The Tea Ceremony: A Symbolic Analysis," in *Empire of the Senses*, ed. David Howes (Abingdon, U.K.: Routledge, 2005), 192–211.

6 The New York-based art critic Sakadichi Hartmann's 1902 scent concert (which sought to transport the audience from New York City to Kyoto on wafts of scent and sound) was a bust but has recently been revisited and restaged. See "A Trip to Japan in Sixteen Minutes, Revisited," posted 2014, by Hammer Museum, YouTube, 2 min., 18 sec., https://www.youtube.com/watch?v=6TX6xYSrGig.

7 Tomie Hahn, *Sensational Knowledge: Embodying Culture through Japanese Dance* (Middletown, CT: Wesleyan University Press, 2007), 76.

8 Ashley Montagu, *Touching: The Human Significance of the Skin* (New York: Harper and Row, 1978).

9 Montagu, *Touching*, 280. See further William Caudill and Helen Weinstein, "Maternal Care and Infant Behavior in Japan and America," *Psychiatry* 32, no. 1 (1969): 12–43. Compare Fusako Innami, *Touching the Unreachable: Writing, Skinship, Modern Japan* (Ann Arbor: University of Michigan Press, 2021).

10 Inge Daniels, *The Japanese House* (Abingdon, U.K.: Routledge, 2010), 38.

11 Robert Hertz, "The Pre-Eminence of the Right Hand," *Right and Left: Essays on Dual Symbolic Classification*, ed. Rodney Needham (Chicago: University of Chicago Press, 1973), 3–31.

12 Constance Classen, *The Color of Angels: Cosmology, Gender and the Aesthetic Imagination* (New York: Routledge, 1998), chap. 5.

13 Odin, "Blossom Scents," 262–63. For another striking example of such West-East sensory exchange, see Fusako Innami, "Falling Dance: Hijikata's Recomposition of the Body via Bacon," *Senses and Society* 16, no. 1 (2021): 1–15.

14 See Stefano Evangelista, "Symphonies in Haze and Blue: Lafcadio Hearn and the Colors of Japan," in *The Colours of the Past in Victorian England*, ed. Charlotte Ribeyrol (Oxford: Peter Lang, 2016), 71–94.

15 Howes, *Sensorium*, 49–61.

16 Odin, "Blossom Scents," 274–76.

17 David Howes, *The Sixth Sense Reader* (Abingdon, U.K.: Routledge, 2009), 357–58.

18 Howes, *Sensorium*, 51–52.

19 Barbra Teri Okada, *Netsuke: Masterpieces from the Metropolitan Museum of Art* (New York: Harry N. Abrams, 1982).

20 Classen, *Color of Angels*. See further Constance Classen, *The Deepest Sense: A Cultural History of Touch* (Champaign: University of Illinois Press, 2012).

21 Maureen Gibbon, *The Lost Notebook of Édouard Manet* (New York: W.W. Norton, 2021), 89.

22 Gibbon, *Lost Notebook*, 89–90.

23 On the intersensory dimensions of avant-garde art, see David Howes, "The New Intersensory Music and Art History," *Senses and Society* 20, no. 1 (2025): 143–50.

24 François Laplantine, *Le social et le sensible : Introduction à une anthropologie modale* (Paris: Tétraèdre, 2005). English translation: *The Life of the Senses: Introduction to a Modal Anthropology* (Abingdon, U.K.: Routledge, 2015).

25 François Laplantine, *Tokyo, ville flottante : Scène urbaine, mises en scène* (Paris: Éditions Stock, 2010).

26 According to Laplantine, cinema is inherently temporal (compared with painting, for example, which is spatial), and it traffics in images rather than ideas and emotions rather than reason. Cinema, which is the very embodiment of continuous transformation, can therefore serve as a model (in a positive sense) for integrating life into thought.

27 See further Daniels, *Japanese House*, 108–12.

28 David Howes, *The Sensory Studies Manifesto: Tracking the Sensorial Revolution in the Arts and Human Sciences* (Toronto: University of Toronto Press, 2022), 11, 69–70, 98–99.

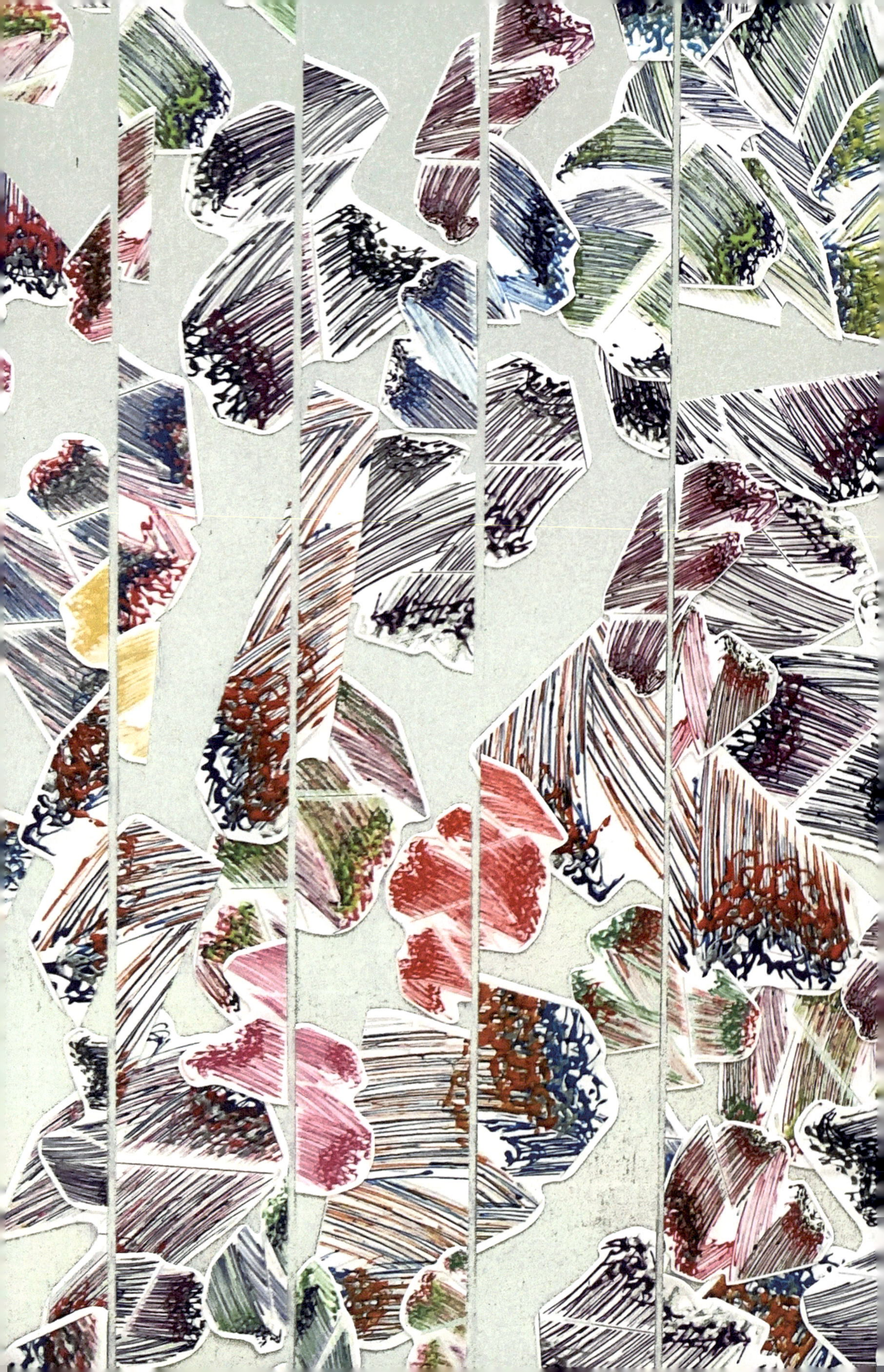

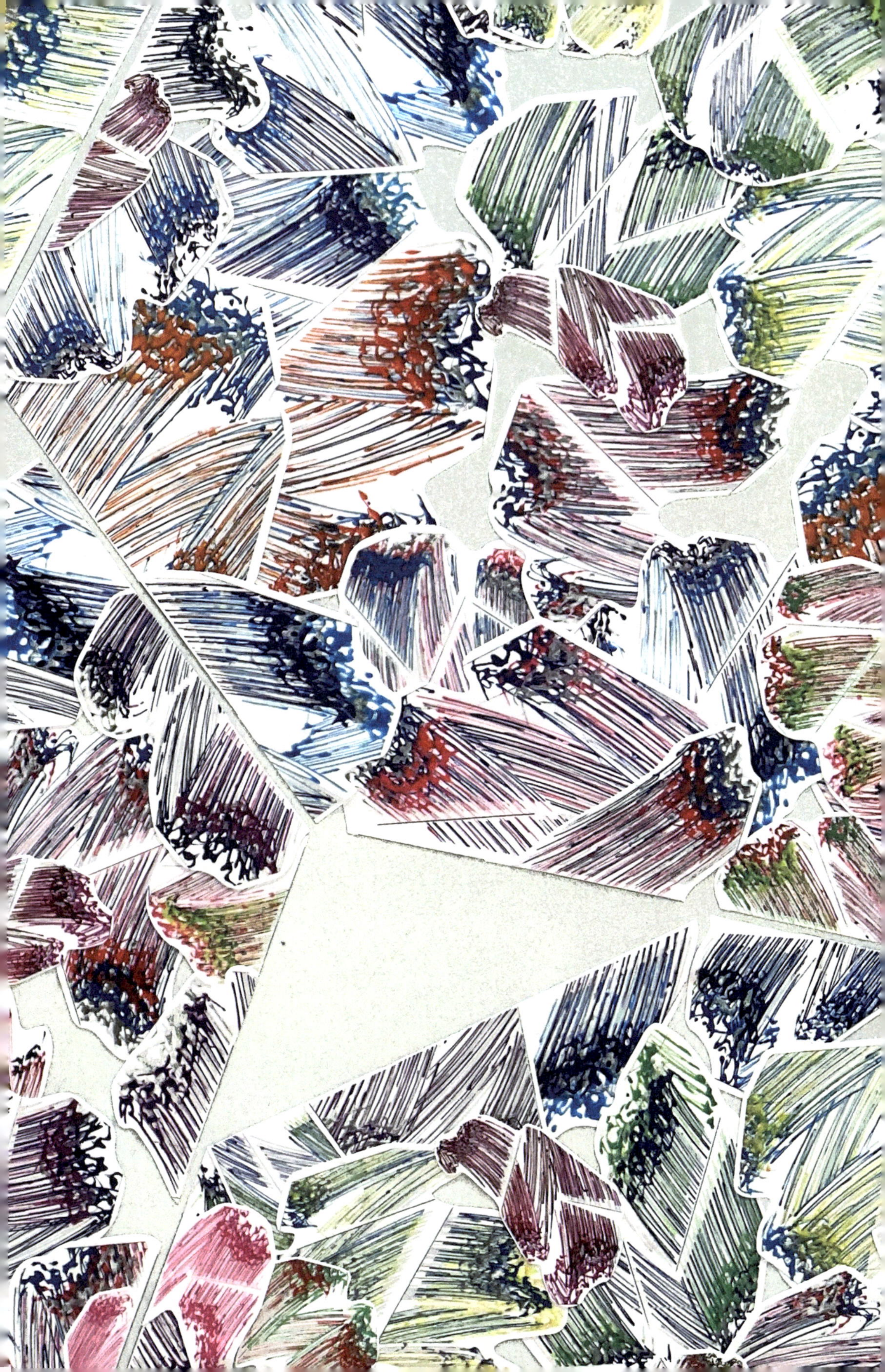

CHAPTER THREE

In the Gaps between Folding Screens: On *Abstract/Expression/Byōbu*

KŌSUKE IKEDA
TRANSLATED BY BRIAN BERGSTROM

EVERY TABLE AT EVERY RESTAURANT AND CAFÉ had sprouted unsightly clear plastic dividers; every cash register at every supermarket and convenience store was suddenly draped in a clear plastic sheet. Every face passing in the street was covered in a rectangular mask, while every face conversing online was isolated in its own frame. Had there ever been a time when our living environment was so filled with dividers? The years since 2020, this passage through the pandemic and beyond, have felt like a time when the entire world has become increasingly cut up by partitions of all sorts.

The Shock of *Screens within Screens*

During this time when the world was partitioned in so many ways, I happened upon some images of pieces on display in museums in the U.S. Among these, one piece in particular caught my eye: *Screens within Screens*, held by the Metropolitan Museum of Art. Part of a show that ran from 2021 to 2022 called *Japan: History of Style*, the piece consists of a pair of six-fold screens dating from somewhere between the late 17th century and the early 18th (Fig. 3.1). The moment I laid eyes on it, I became enamoured by its strangeness—it is a pair of folding screens (*byōbu*) covered in images of overlapping folding screens.

Plenty of examples come to mind of other folding screens decorated with images of objects arranged in overlapping rows or scattered across the space.

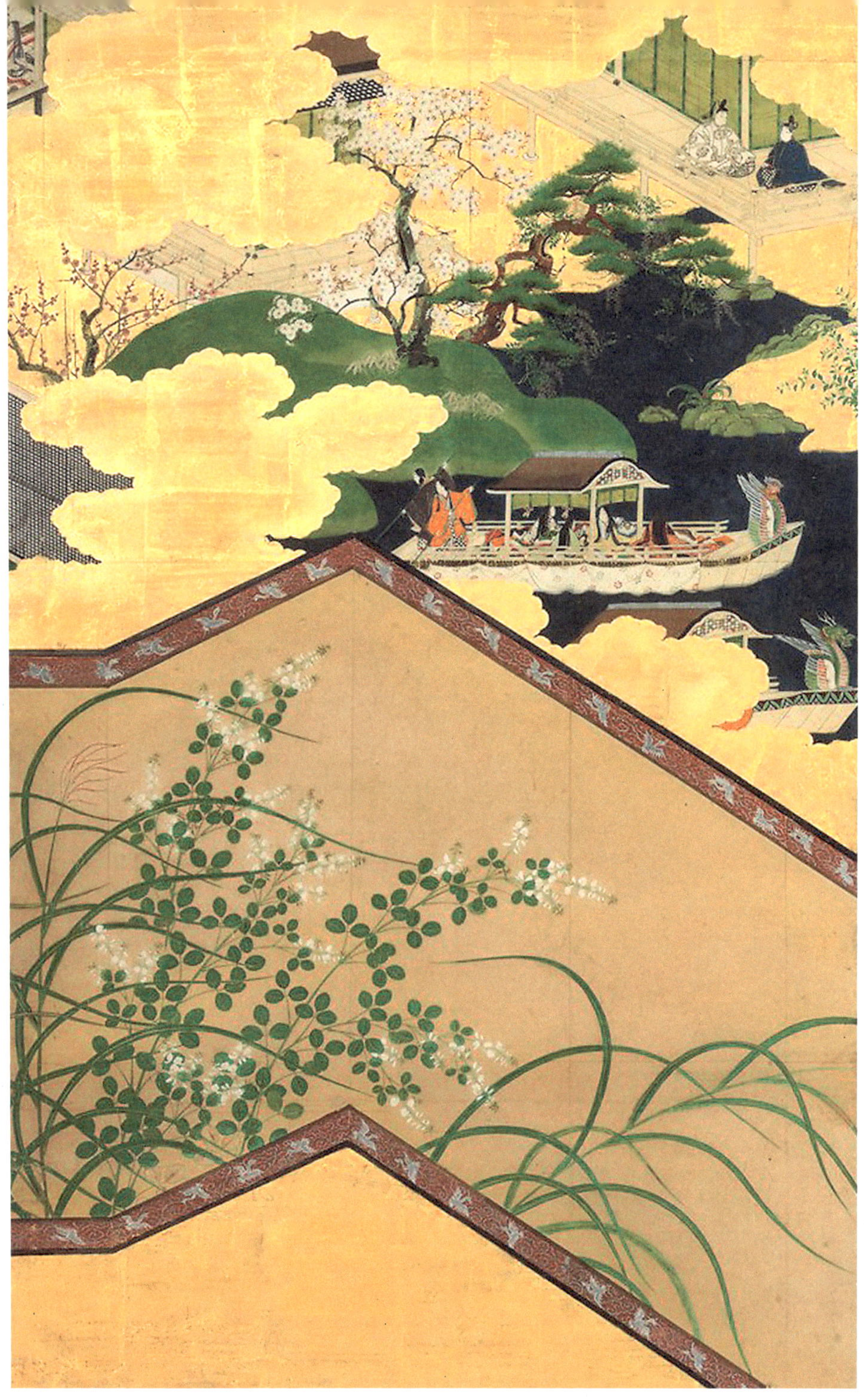

Detail, *Screens within Screens*

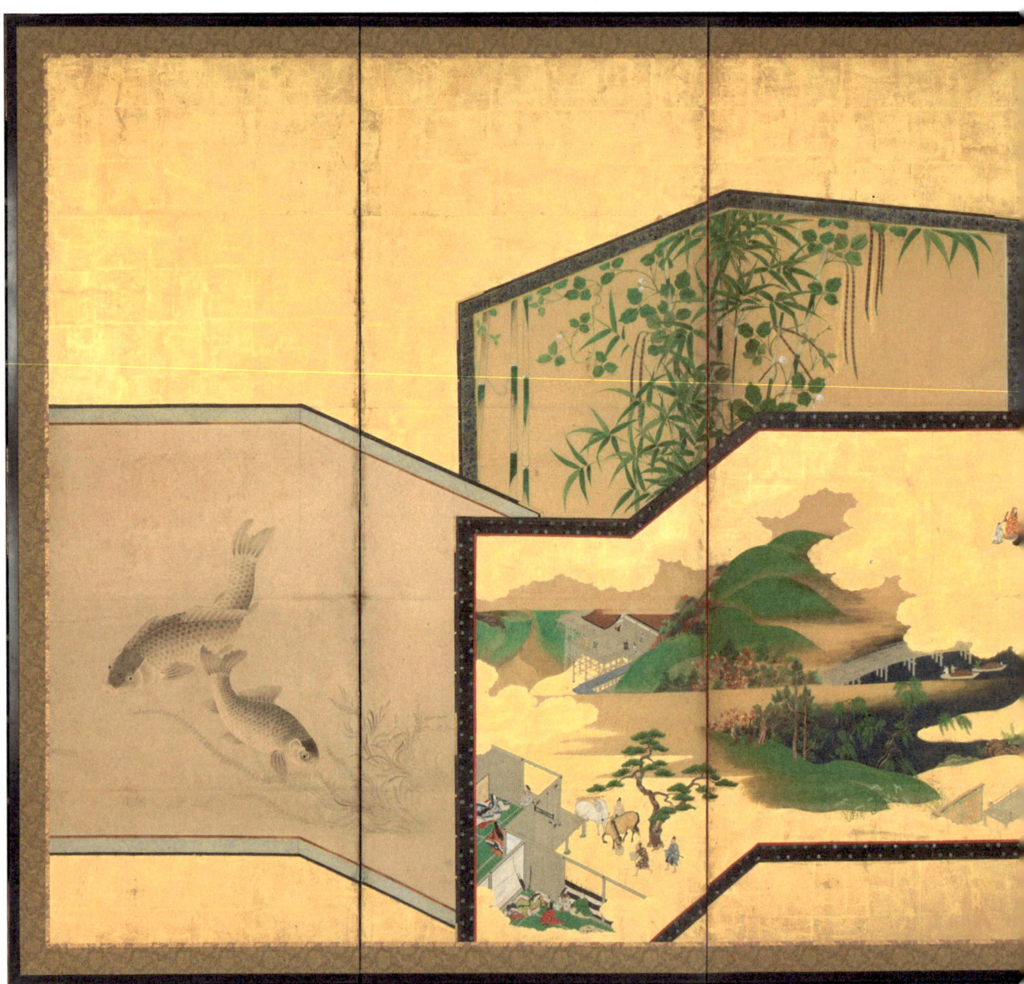

Fig. 3.1
Screens within Screens,
left screen
Edo period, late 17th–
early 18th century
Pair of six-panel folding screens;
ink, colour, and gold on gilt paper
170 × 376 cm each
Metropolitan Museum of Art
2010.402.1-.2

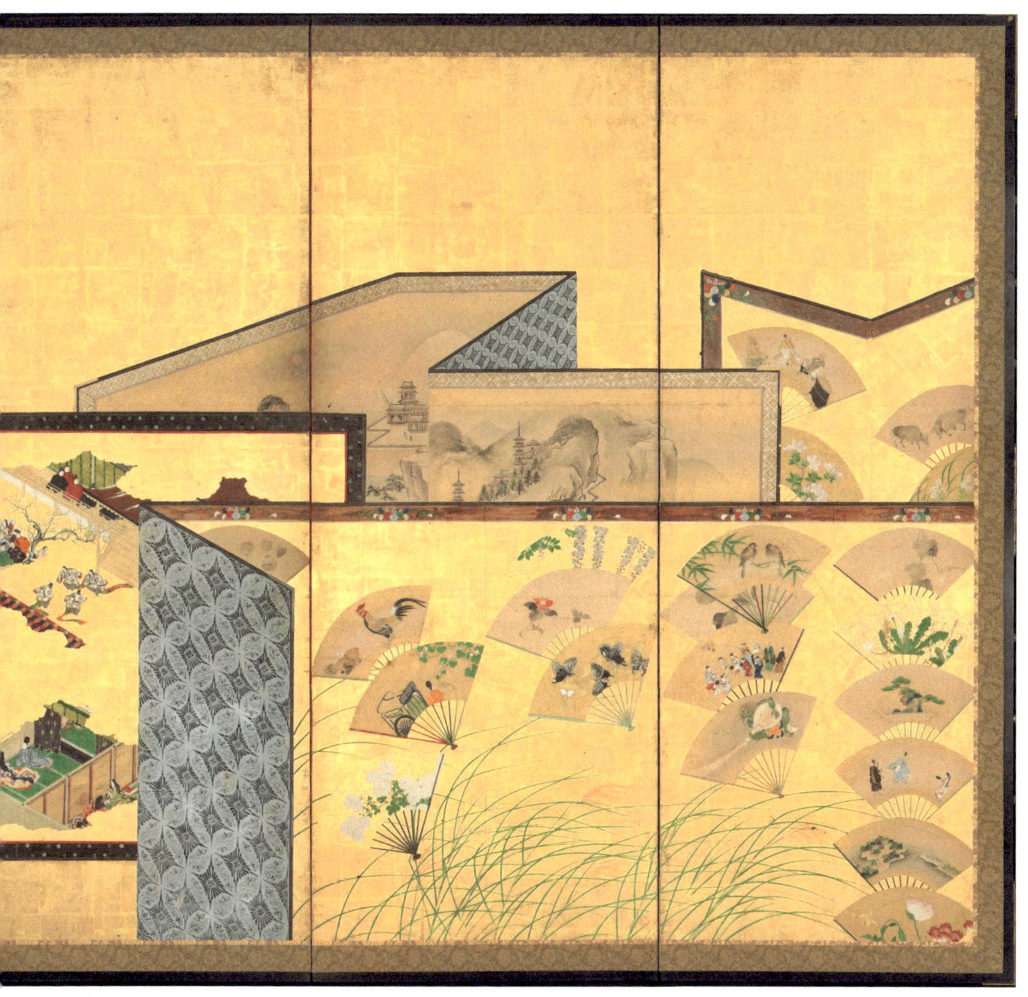

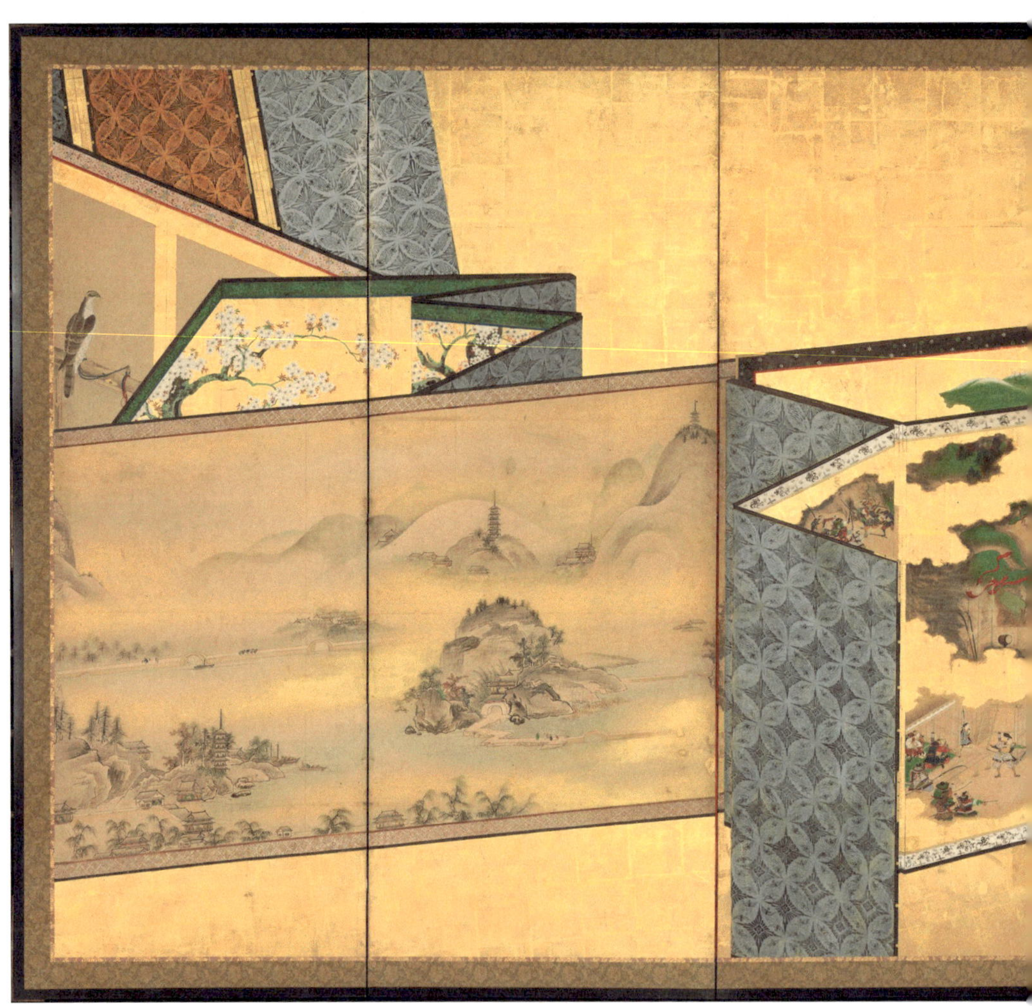

Screens within Screens,
right screen

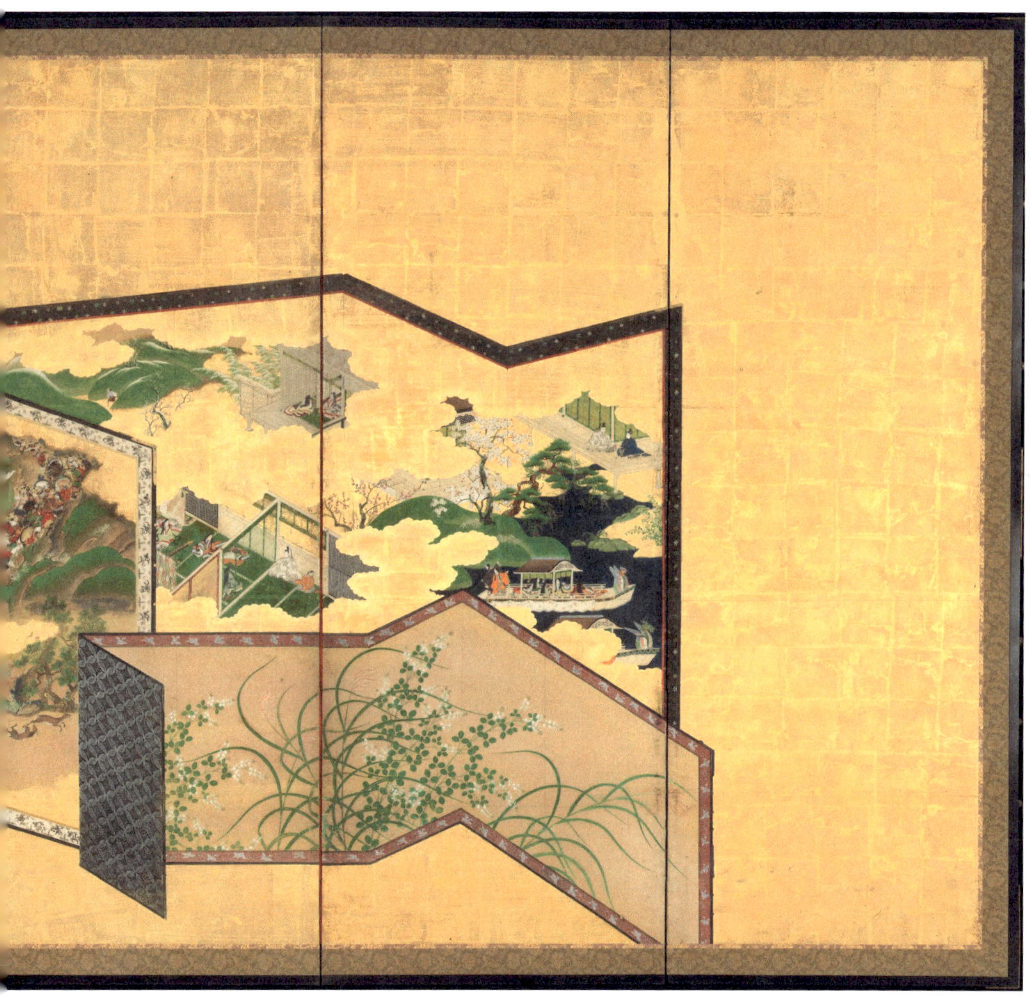

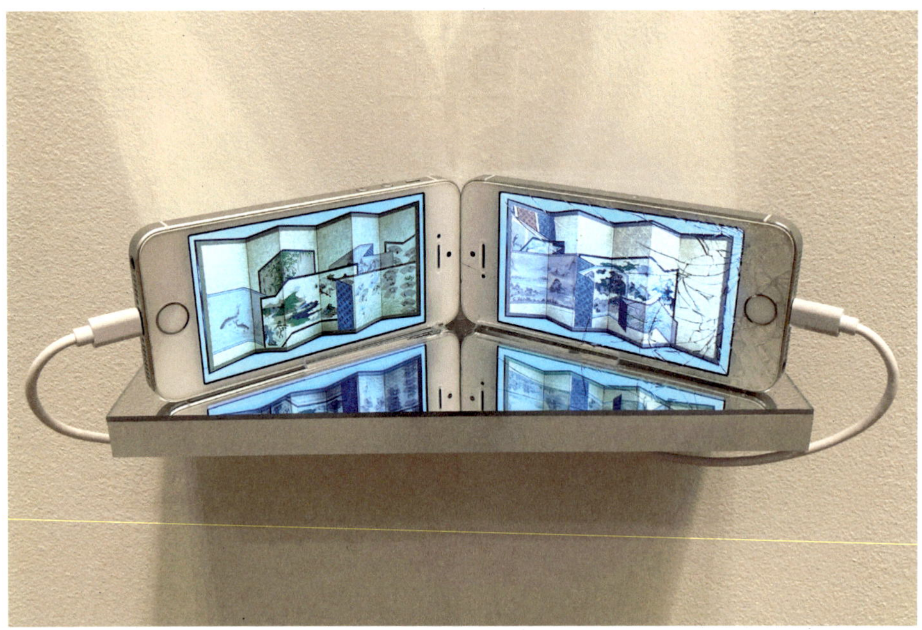

Classic examples include the *Tagasode (Whose Sleeves?)* screens, which feature images of kimonos of all kinds draped over rods, and the *Screen with Scattered Fans* screens, which are covered in images of various fans, each with its own patterns and pictures drawn on it. In screens like these, the fans and kimonos bear their own designs and images, which means that even though they are presented in a more or less orderly manner on the screen, the overall effect disrupts the unity of the screen's visual space.

The history of Chinese painting also shows a clear lineage of screens and room dividers being decorated with images of screens and room dividers, as well as of paintings featuring images of paintings within them—in short, a history of "meta-painting." As Chinese art historian Wu Hung has discussed in depth in his book *The Double Screen*, the Chinese painting tradition includes many works featuring layered images of screens and dividers that themselves have images painted on them.

Fig. 3.2
Kōsuke Ikeda (b. 1980)
Screened Screens
Reiwa period, 2021
Smartphones
5.6 × 24.6 cm

Collection of Artist

Even as I point out these precedents, however, I still find myself struck by the uniqueness of *Screens within Screens*. These are screens decorated with images of screens, and that is it—they have nothing else on them. Most of these screens-within-screens feature traditional landscape paintings, images of plants and animals, or scenes from everyday life, but one of them, located on the right-hand side of the left screen, is covered in images of fans, each decorated with various other images and designs. A screen within a screen, itself covered in fans that each bear their own image—it was this dizzyingly nested composition spreading across the folded surface of the screen that gave me a sort of quiet shock.

I printed out the image and then folded the paper to imitate the way the screens folded, which only added to the multi-layered, multi-planar nature of it; the physical folding of the screens to make them stand up turned the images into something like a labyrinth. The 2022 installation I discuss below includes a piece displaying *Screens within Screens* as images on smartphones propped up at an angle like two folding screens (Fig. 3.2).

On *Abstract/Expression/Byōbu*

The quiet shock of *Screens within Screens*, combined with the increasingly partitioned nature of everyday life, led me to create the installation *Pandemic and (Folding) Screens* for a pandemic-themed group show. I set up walls at angles like chains of folded screens throughout my installation space, each one displaying artwork on its surface (Fig. 3.3). It may seem a bit convoluted, but my screen included in the *Shokkan: Material Encounters in Japanese Art* exhibition, *Abstract/Expression/Byōbu*, first appeared within this folded screen-shaped installation—that is, as a screen within a space defined by other screens (Fig. 3.4).

A folding screen, or byōbu, is a partition made of multiple surfaces that, when folded, stands on its own. You must open a folding screen to stand it up, but if you open it too much, it falls over. This aspect of folding screens might be interpreted as a painfully ironic version of society, which is in a constant process of opening up to globalization, a continuous expansion that has become the overriding concern of our era. The global exchange of people and goods and the unstoppable spread of a virus into every part of the world are two sides of the same coin. During the crisis we were experiencing, perhaps it was time to think seriously about exactly *to what degree* we should open ourselves up—this was my concern as I put together the show in 2021, while still in the midst of the pandemic.

Abstract/Expression/Byōbu includes stickers printed with several patterns formed from brushstrokes. These brushstroke-stickers are derived from "original images"—that is, various paintings I had created previously (Fig. 3.5). Brushstrokes are more than simply a visual element of the image conjured by a painting; they are also

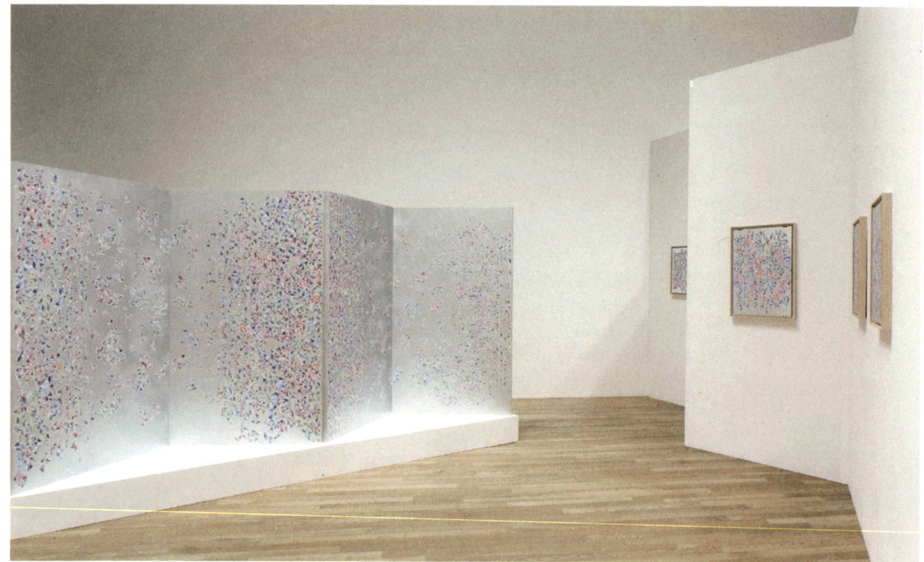

direct, tactile traces attesting to the physical basis of that image. The brushstroke-stickers end up alternately closely packed and loosely scattered as they are stuck to the screen, creating undulating flows of density and sparseness.

A brushstroke in a painting is the trace of a one-time bodily movement. By making them into stickers, I end up replicating them again and again. This deactivates the brushstroke's tactility and directness, but at the same time, it enables the creation of a new type of tactility as the stickers are stuck to the screen.

These stickers become the element connecting the brushstroke-as-image to the surface of the folding screen. The stickers are stuck to the screen the same way children place stickers onto bookshelves and refrigerators. In this way, the painterly act of applying brush to canvas becomes the everyday act of sticking a sticker onto a surface—something that everyone (at least in Japan) has had experience with while growing up. A byōbu is something meant to be placed in a living space, and thus, it suits this transformation more than would a painting, which presents images as illusions severed completely from the space around them.

Fig. 3.3
Kōsuke Ikeda (b. 1980)
Pandemic and (Folding) Screens
Reiwa period, 2021
Installation, mixed media
Dimensions variable

Collection of Artist
Photo: Gin Hasegawa

Unlike the wall-mounted tableau, which is standard in Western traditions of painting, the folding screen stands on its own, dividing a space into rooms with exteriors and interiors. A tableau is by nature untouchable, a form of art that privileges the visual experience, while the Eastern tradition of images painted on screens and dividers places these images within physical spaces, creating bodily relations between them and anyone in the same room with them (in this sense, it seems natural that partitions of all sorts popped up so frequently during the pandemic). In other words, a folding screen possesses the quality of being an object placed in the spaces where people conduct their lives. Layering brushstroke-stickers onto folding screens accentuates this physical aspect of the screen as something sharing the same floor space as a part of everyday life.

The brushstrokes appearing on the screen are part of a long-time motif in my work, a foundational, critical concern with abstract painting as exemplified by action painting; the Gutai Art Association; and calligraphy, which emphasizes physical movement and the one-time-only essence of brushwork. In a different work, I cut into brushstrokes, the direct traces of the artist's physicality, as a way to deal with the continuity and discontinuity of that physicality, and in this sense, I was addressing the same issues as I do with my current interest in partitions, which cut into space.

As stated above, the four-fold screen of *Abstract/Expression/Byōbu* was placed within a labyrinthine space defined by layers of walls set at angles in the manner of a folding screen, along with the original paintings from which the stickers were made and the other works on the walls; the entire space thus became a single installation work. In other words, the screens and paintings were nested within the spatial arrangement of their installation; at the risk of repeating myself, this means that the work appearing in the *Shokkan* show, *Abstract/Expression/Byōbu*, was originally created as a work-within-a-work or rather a folding-screen-within-a-folding-screen-space.

Alongside *Views of Kyoto and Its Environs*

The piece *Views of Kyoto and Its Environs*, held by ROM, is a pair of six-fold screens showing Nijō Castle on the left screen and Hōkō-ji Temple on the right-hand side of the right screen—a common arrangement and subject matter for a genre of folding screens first appearing in the early Edo period (1603–1868) (see pp. 10–14). Famous sites in Kyoto are glimpsed through gaps between golden clouds, offering detailed views of people living their everyday lives.

On the left screen, one can see a dense group of people forming a procession at the gate of Nijō Castle, while at the bottom of the right screen, one can see the typical summertime sight of the Gion Festival; both scenes offer spectacles

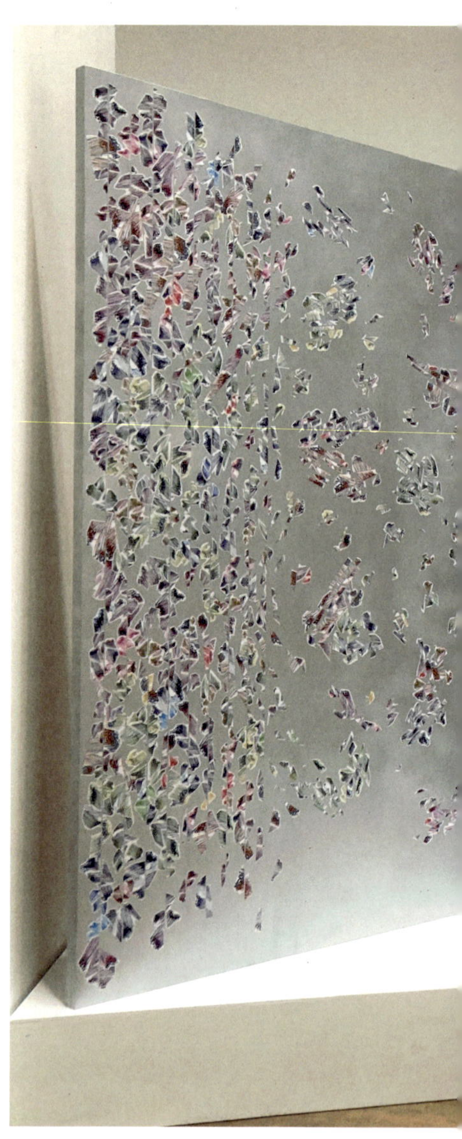

Fig. 3.4
Kōsuke Ikeda (b. 1980)
Abstract/Expression/Byōbu
Reiwa period, 2021
Four-panel folding screens;
stickers, acrylic, wooden panel
162 × 384 cm

Collection of Artist

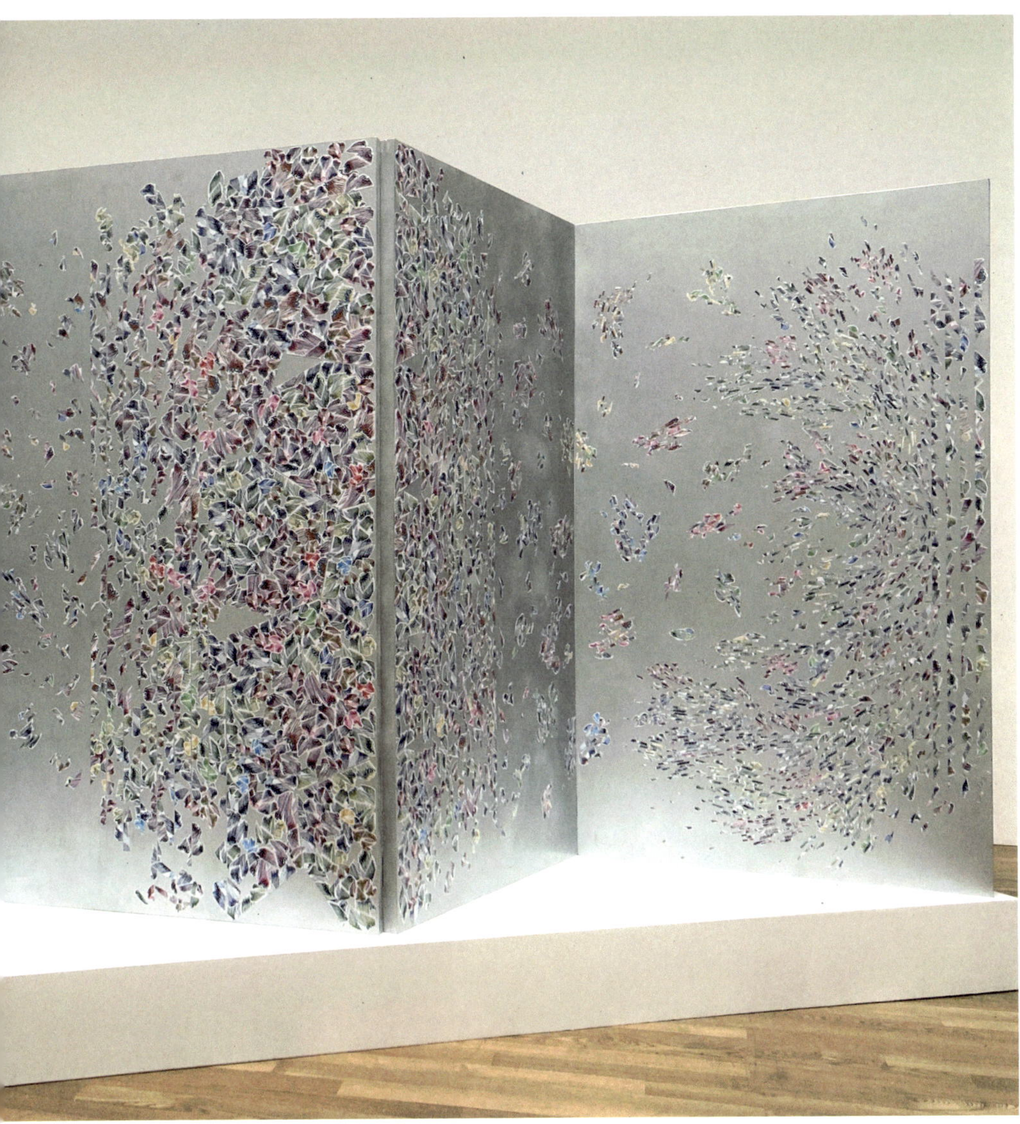

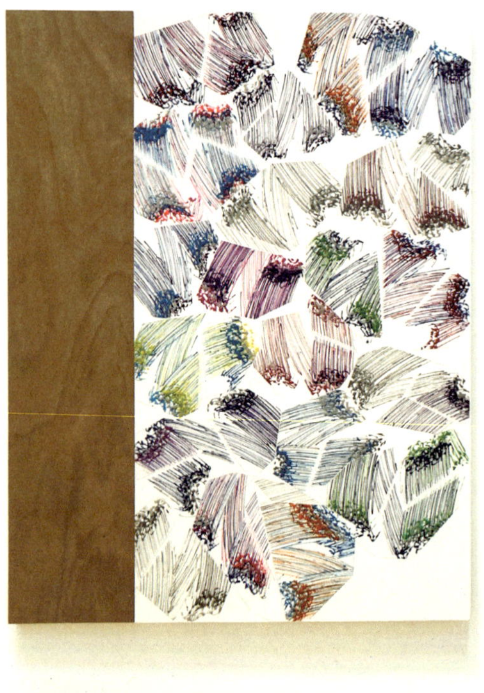

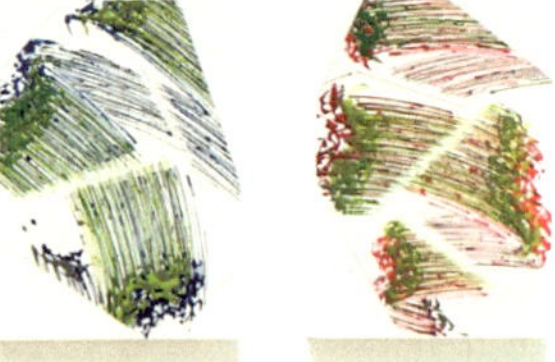

Fig. 3.5
Kōsuke Ikeda (b. 1980)
Abstract/Expression/Stroke
Reiwa period, 2020
Acrylic on wooden panel
Left: 91 × 116.7 cm
Right: 24.2 × 33.3 cm each

Collection of Artist

of people gathering into crowds. On the other hand, the upper sections of both screens feature views of the mountains surrounding Kyoto, scenes in which people are only sparsely glimpsed.

These famous sites are presented in the form of street scenes and groups of people that alternate rhythmically between dense crowds and sparsely scattered individuals, all connected by billowing golden clouds. While it at first appears to offer a bird's eye view of the city and its surroundings, *Views of Kyoto and Its Environs* presents images of well-known spots in Kyoto more in the manner of a guidebook or tourist map, making it impossible to take in the entire landscape at once. The golden clouds connecting the various scenes to each other are what particularly caught my attention, as they seem to me to function quite like the frames around manga panels.

A forerunner to my *Abstract/Expression/Byōbu* piece is one I made using a motif of brushstrokes taking the form of a manga, called *Abstract/Expression/Manga* (Fig. 3.6). Brushstrokes move from panel to panel, until in the last panel, they end up isolated from each other completely. A panel in a manga is a frame that cuts an image off from its surroundings, isolating it, but at the same time, it connects these images to one another; in this sense, it possesses a double valence, connoting both continuity and discontinuity. To me, the manga panel is something that both cuts up space and, as a partition, brings these isolated spaces together.

In this sense, I had already been using the brushstroke and the manga panel as a way to interrogate the issue of physicality being cut up and then reconstructed, so when the pandemic led to an increased division of space into sections, this naturally led me to become interested in partitions. Now, as I see my own folding screen-based work, inspired in part by my encounter with *Screens within Screens*, become liberated from the labyrinthine space of my installations and displayed alongside a piece like *Views of Kyoto and Its Environs*, which hails from the same Edo period that produced *Screens within Screens*, it feels strangely fated, a stroke of good fortune.

What sorts of continuities and discontinuities will emerge from placing my work in the same space as the historical *Views of Kyoto and Its Environs* in the context of the *Shokkan* exhibition? It is my hope that, even as they are both screens, the contrasts between the two pieces—past versus present, representation versus abstraction—will, in the gaps between them, allow for a new space-time to be constructed from their conjunction.

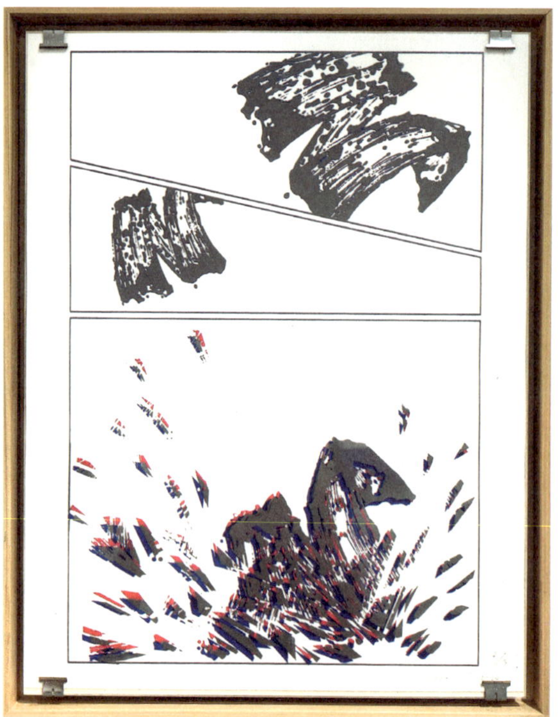

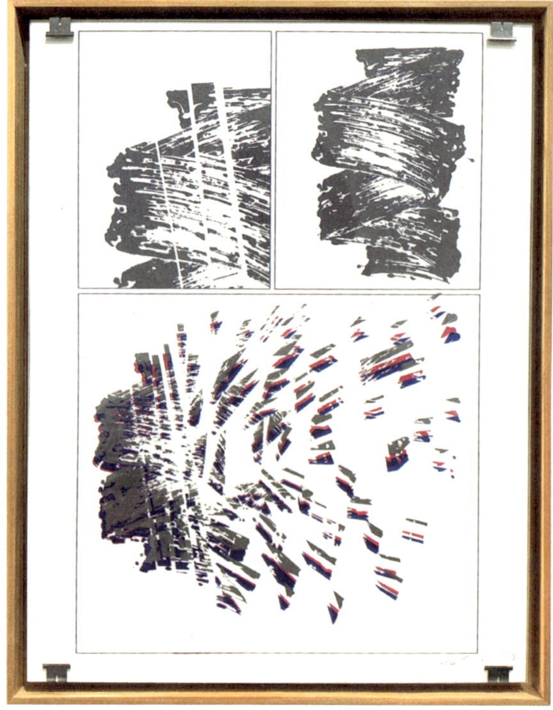

Fig. 3.6
Kōsuke Ikeda (b. 1980)
Abstract/Expression/Manga
Reiwa period, 2020
Ink on paper
36 × 28 cm

Collection of Artist

---

1 The Metropolitan Museum of Art's website includes explanatory notes on both *Tagasode (Whose Sleeves?)* and *Screen with Scattered Fans*. See "Screens within Screens," The Met, accessed September 4, 2025, https://www.metmuseum.org/art/collection/search/76113.

2 Wu Hung, *The Double Screen: Medium and Representation in Chinese Painting* (London: Reaktion Books, 1996).

3 Various artists, *New Ways to Grow: Artists Envision a Post-COVID World*, the University Art Museum at Tokyo University of the Arts, 2021.

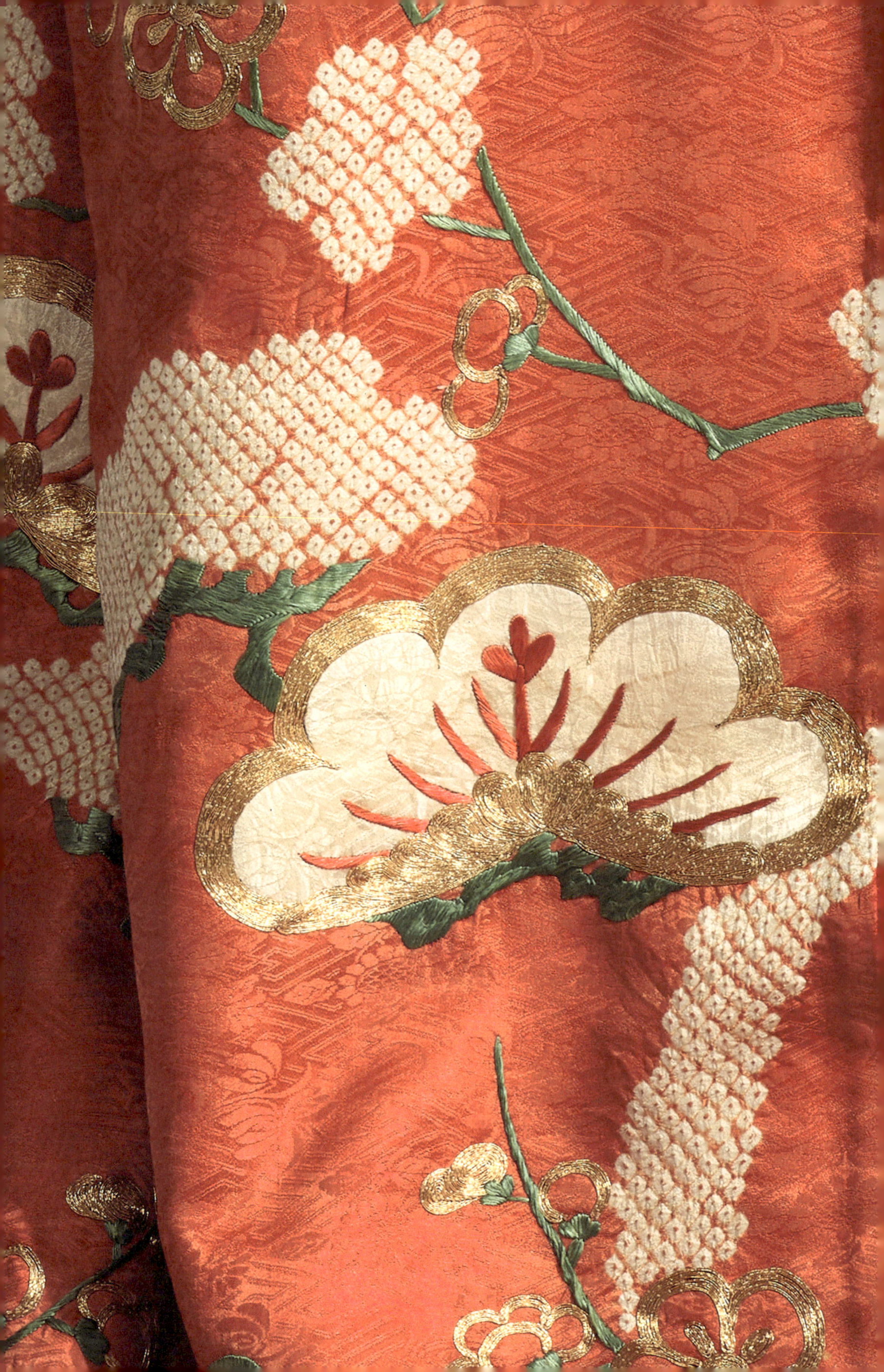

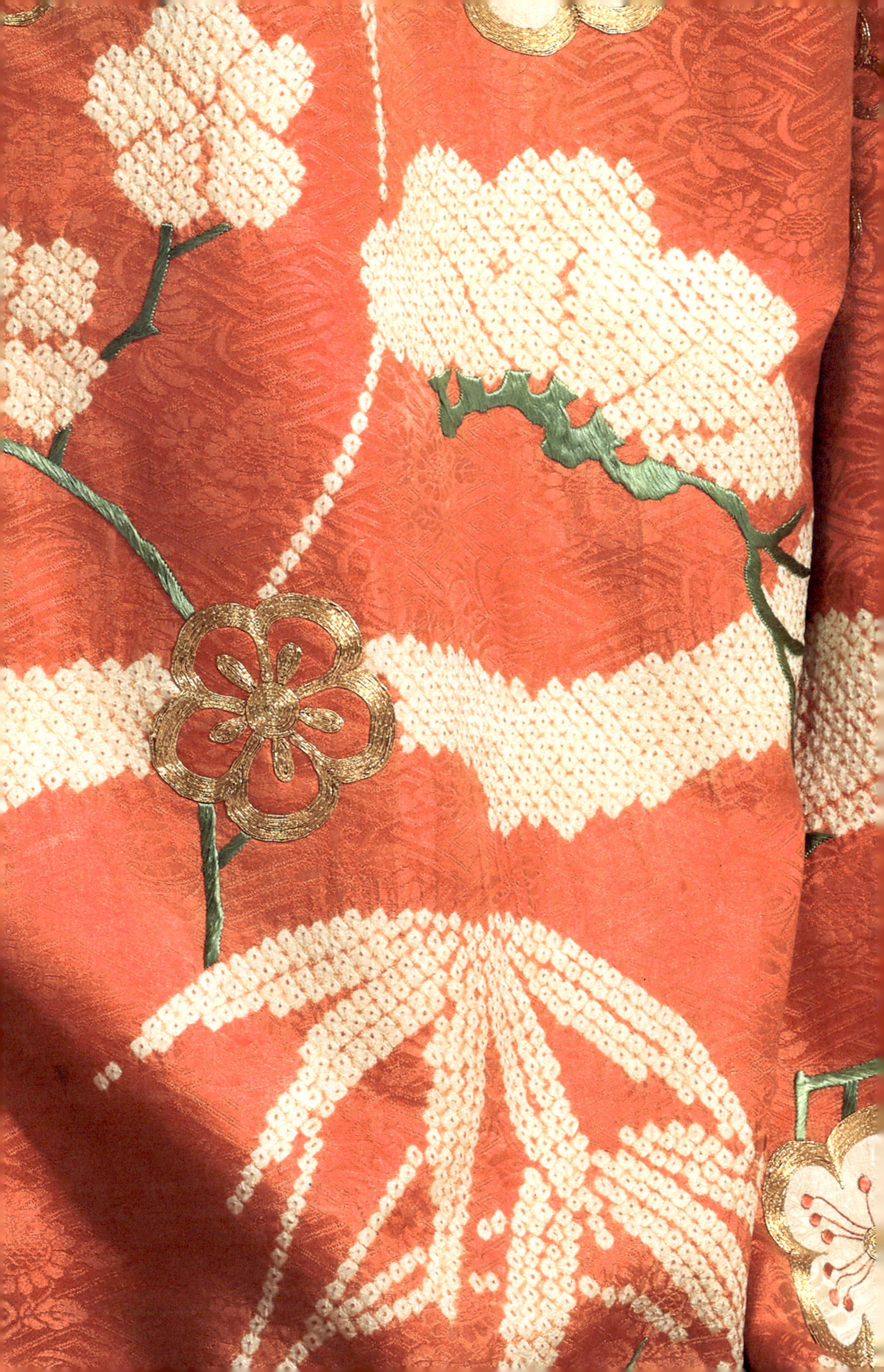

CHAPTER FOUR

Appreciating Tactility in Japanese Tea Ceramics

NATSU OYOBE

IN NOVEMBER 2024, I had a rare experience while attending a *chanoyu*, commonly translated as "Japanese tea ceremony," in Nara, Japan. The setting was at a *sōan* ("thatched hut") style tea house, which was developed in the 16th century. Through a narrow door, I entered the tea house, which was very dark because the only light was coming through a few windows with a paper screen. In this dark and intimate space, my five senses seemed to be heightened, while I watched the host solemnly preparing *koicha*, a thickly made tea. When the tea was ready, a tea bowl was handed to me from a person next to me; I gently held it with both hands and sipped warm tea. Later, during the dedicated viewing and handling session, I was able to touch three tea bowls used in the tea gathering: a Raku tea bowl by Hon'ami Kōetsu (1558–1637), a Karatsu tea bowl, and a Korean tea bowl. I felt the thick structure of the Kōetsu bowl, the grainy surface of the Karatsu bowl, and the sturdy body and foot of the Korean bowl. I mostly remember their tactile sensation in my hands, while I have only vague recollections of the outer appearances of these tea bowls. This experience made me contemplate the sense of tactility in the historical evolution of the practice of chanoyu and its tea wares. Indeed, the emergence of tea bowls with these textures was deeply affected by the evolution of chanoyu during Japan's Momoyama period (1583–1615).

From *Kaisho* to Sōan: Invention of Tactile Wares

Tea drinking in Japan came from China in the ninth century and was enjoyed by the courtiers of the Heian period (794–1185). The tea, at that time, was steeped

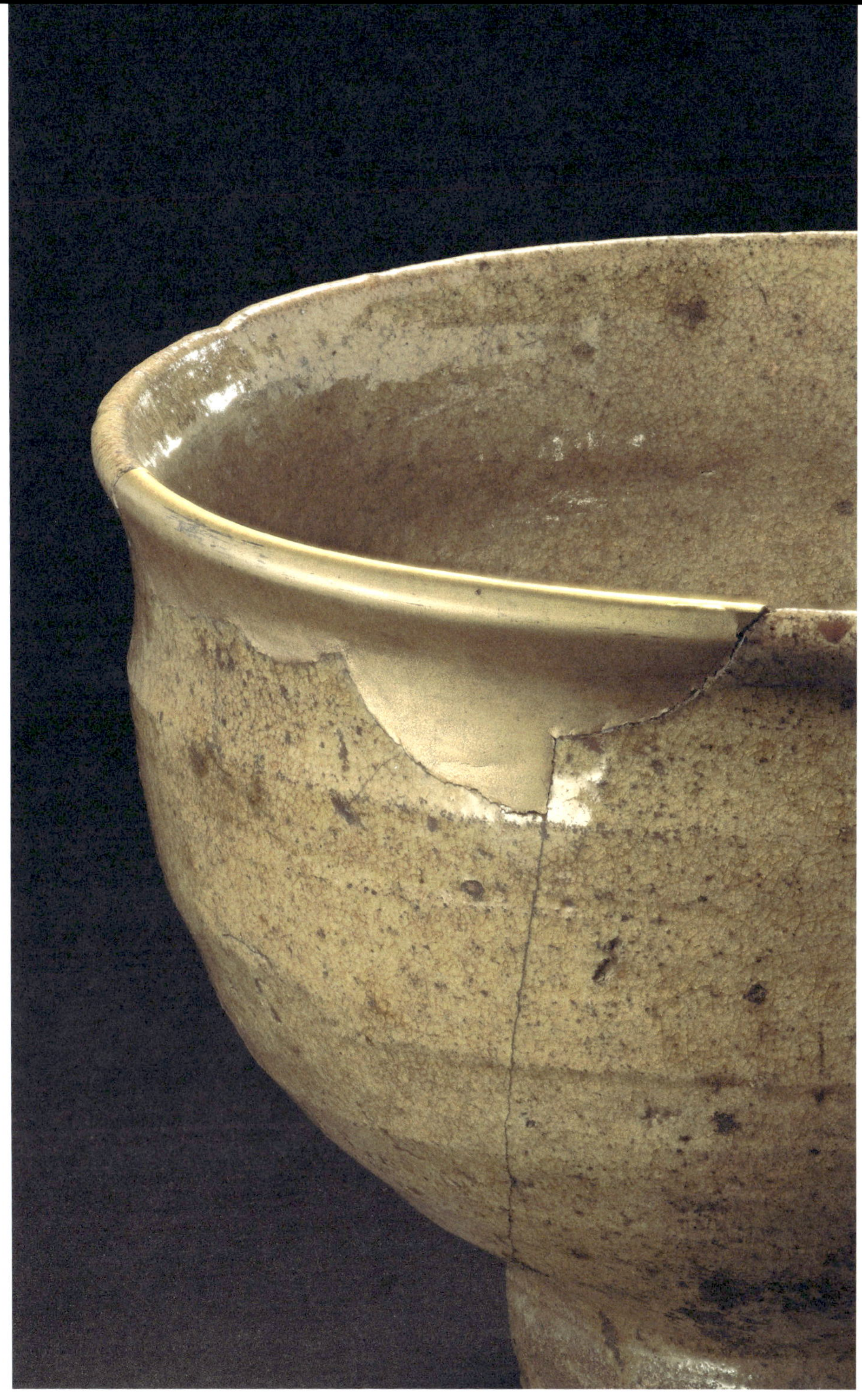

Detail, *Karatsu Ware Tea Bowl of Komogai-nari Shape*

from tea leaves in the form of a brick. Toward the end of the 12th century, a new practice of whisking tea powders was brought to Japan by Buddhist monks who had studied in Zen monasteries in China, along with tea plants, which were soon to be cultivated in Japan. As the tea practice spread beyond temples and among military elites and aristocrats in Kyoto and Kamakura, a large number of tea wares and decorative objects for the tea room, such as tea bowls, lacquer bowl stands, tea containers, flower vases, and paintings, were imported from China (Fig. 4.1). Symbols of power and wealth, these Chinese objects were valued for their visual appearance: a perfectly symmetrical form, mesmerizing glaze colour, and intricate patterns. The tea was prepared by servants in a separate room and brought to kaisho, or a "large meeting room," where guests were entertained by the host.[1]

In the late 15th century, a new trend emerged called *wabi-cha* ("tea of rusticity and simplicity") among merchants and intellectuals of the Kansai region. Dictated by wabi-cha aesthetics of simplicity, austerity, a withered quality, and tranquility, the new tea room (sōan) was drastically small, around the size of three or four tatami mats (one tatami mat is about 190 × 96 cm) and located away from the main house (Fig. 4.2). Hot tea was made by the host within the room, which was equipped with a heating unit. Sen no Rikyū (1522–91, Fig. 4.3), who established the style and rules of wabi-cha, pushed the aesthetics even further. He shrunk the guest entrance into a small square wooden door called *nijiri-guchi* ("a crawl-in entrance"; see the small door on the side of the circular window in Fig. 4.2) of about only 65 cm in width and height. The maximum number of guests was three or four, and sometimes, only one guest was invited. The room was dark, with a few paper-screened windows.

This kind of small setting creates intimacy and invites close communications between the host and the guests, as well as between each guest. It was natural for Rikyū to develop chanoyu as a space of care and hospitality. Many tea gathering procedures he invented were guided by this core principle, and one of them was serving tea in a new type of tea bowl that he developed with Raku Chōjirō (d. 1589), a ceramic tile maker in Kyoto. The tea bowl was a hand-formed black cylinder-shaped one, which would be later called "the Raku tea bowl" (Fig. 4.4).

Rikyū understood that the tactile sensation would lead to great satisfaction and fulfill a human desire. Before the invention of the Raku tea bowls, he and other wabi-cha practitioners had already decreased the use of visually arresting Chinese tea bowls, staples of the kaisho tea gathering of the previous era, and more frequently used Korean tea bowls, which were made of unrefined clay and clear glaze. The feet of these tea bowls were proportionally large and roughly made, and their visual quality aligned with the simple and withered aesthetic of wabi-cha. The new black Raku tea bowl followed the same aesthetic, but the cylindrical

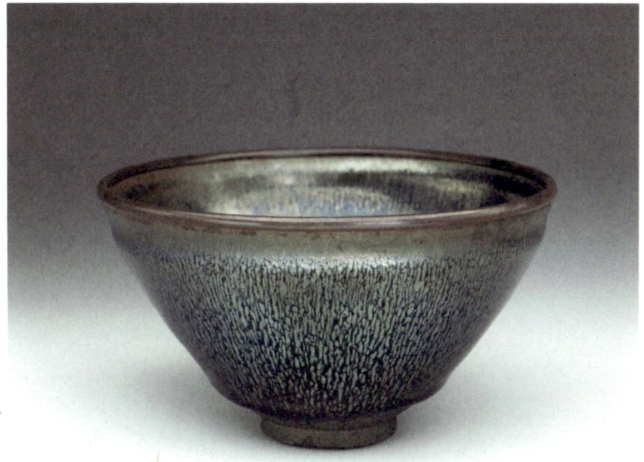

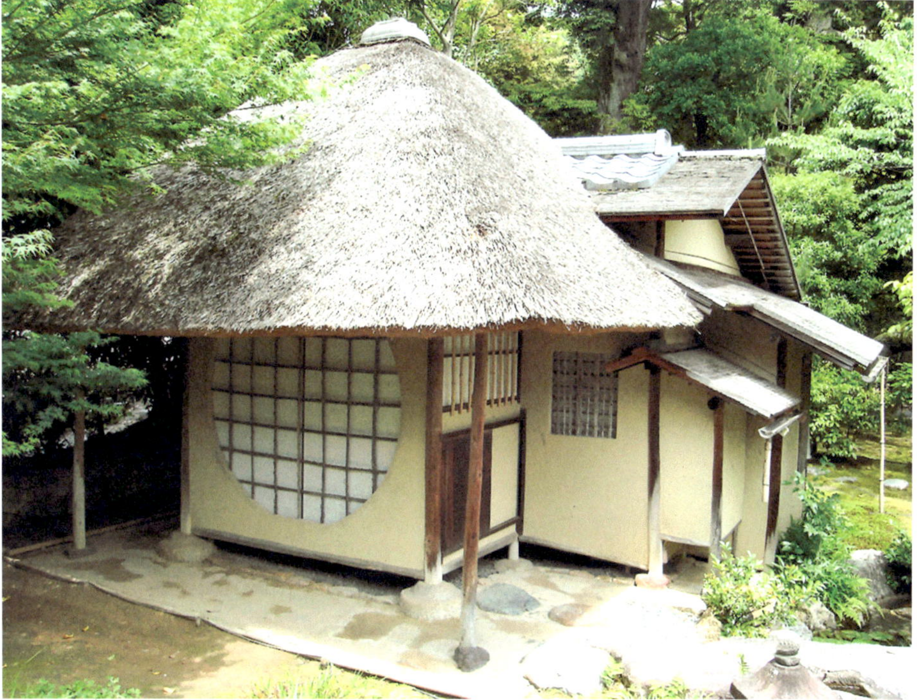

Fig. 4.1
Jian (Tenmoku) Ware Tea Bowl with Metal Rim
China, Southern Song dynasty (1127–1279), 12th–13th century
Stoneware with black iron glaze
7.1 × 12.4 cm

Collection of National Museum of Asian Art, Washington, DC

Fig. 4.2
Ihō-an, Kodai-ji in Kyoto, Japan, originally constructed in the Momoyama period, early 17th century.

Photo: PlusMinus, 2005

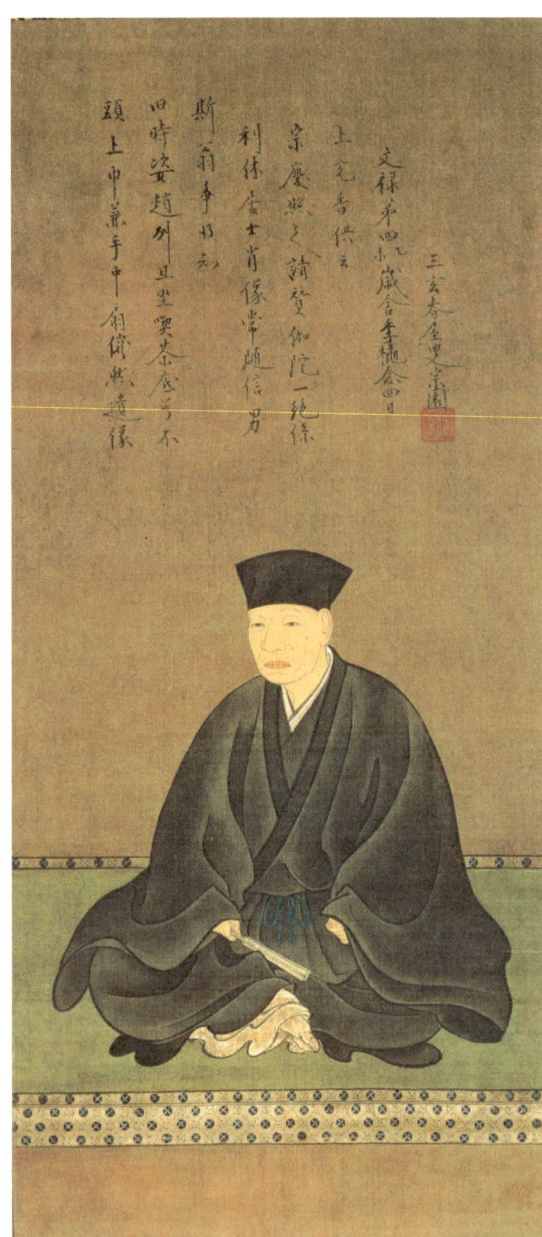

Fig. 4.3
Hasegawa Tōhaku (1539–1610), inscription by Shunoku Sōen (1529–1611)
Portrait of Sen no Rikyū
Momoyama period, 1595
Ink and colour on silk
80.6 × 36.5 cm

Photo: Taken of painting in collection of Omotesenke Fushin'an Foundation, 2006

Fig. 4.4 (opposite)
Black Raku Ware Tea Bowl
(part of a tea box)
Meiji period, late 19th to early 20th century
Earthenware
8.7 × 10 cm
ROM 920.26.1.2

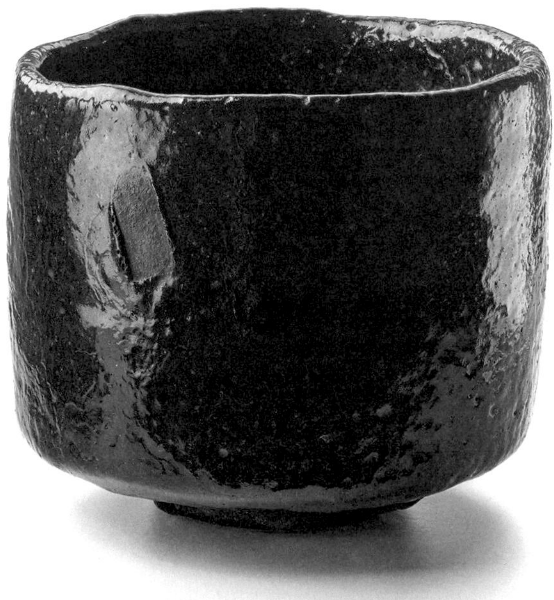

shape was revolutionary.[2] Compared with the flare shape of Korean tea bowls (called "*Ido*-type"), the cylinder shape could retain the heat better. Moreover, while the Korean tea bowl was wheel thrown, comparably thinly built, and fired at a higher temperature, the Raku tea bowl was hand formed, thickly built, and fired at a lower temperature. These properties allowed the Raku tea bowl to fit on the hands gently and emit the warmth of the tea gradually onto the human skin. When the guest was drinking tea, the thick rim would softly touch their lips. Rikyū invented the Raku tea bowl to serve hot tea in the most ideal condition for the guest's tactile enjoyment.

In addition to the Raku tea bowl, many tactile wares were invented, incorporated, and popularized during Rikyū's and his direct disciples' times. ROM's collection features some of these wares: a tea bowl of Karatsu ware (Fig. 4.5), which was invented by Korean potters who immigrated during and after the Imjin War (1592–98), and a serving bowl of Shino ware (Fig. 4.6), known for its thick milky glaze invented in Mino (present-day Gifu prefecture).

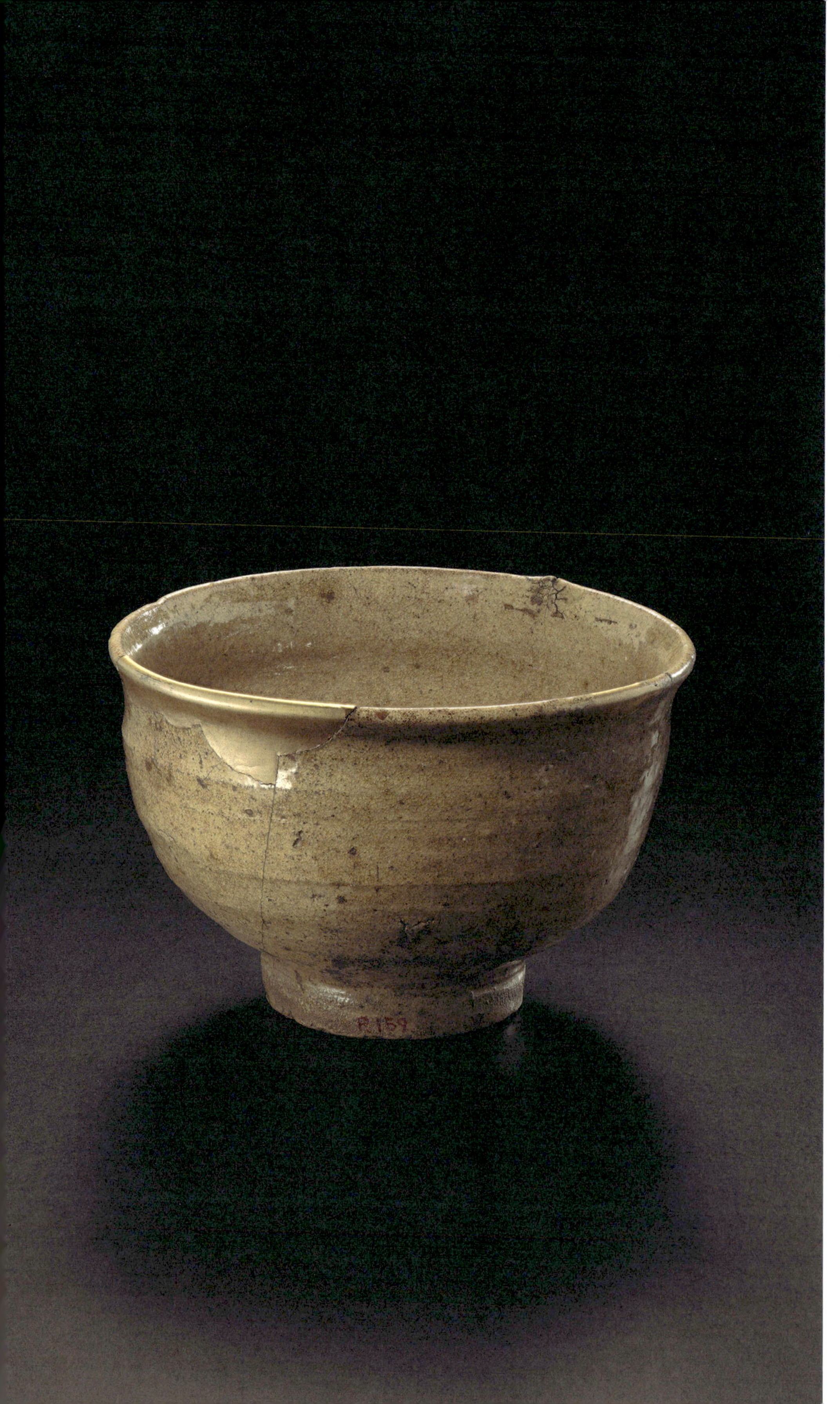
P.159

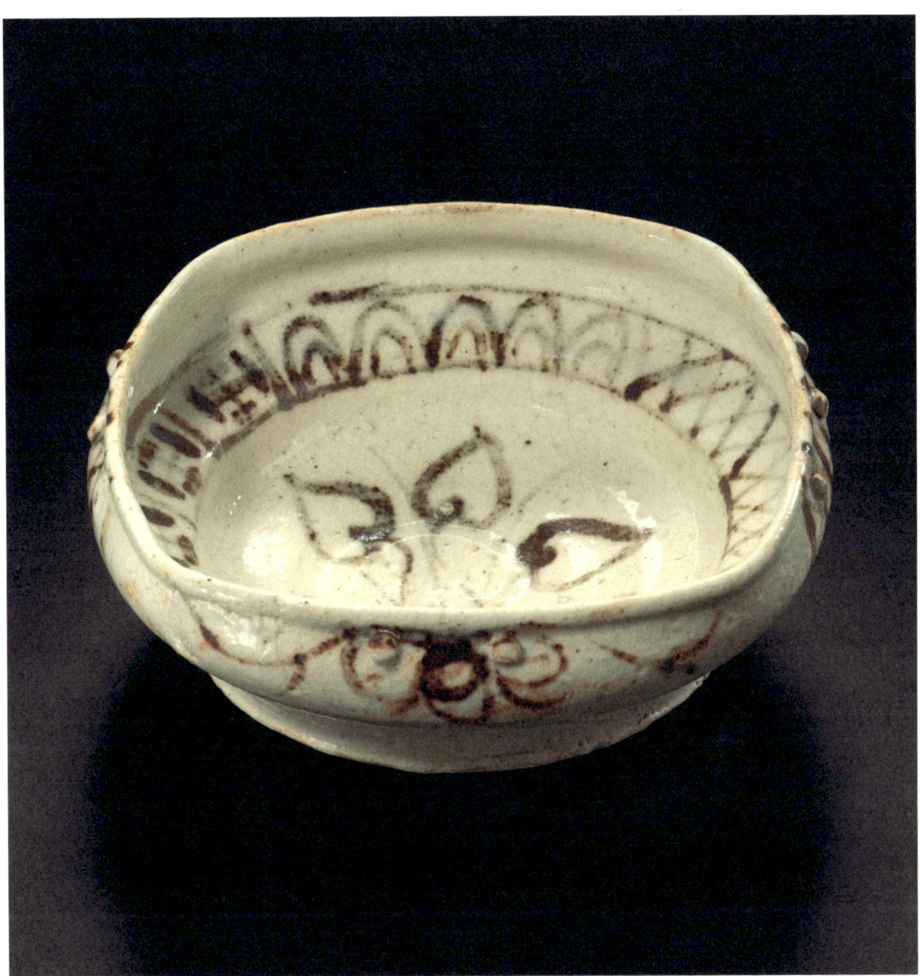

Fig. 4.5
Karatsu Ware Tea Bowl of Komogai-nari Shape
Edo period, early 17th century
Glazed stoneware
8.3 × 12.6 cm
ROM 909.22.46

Gift of Sir William C. Van Horne

Fig. 4.6
Mino Ware, e-Shino–Type Serving Bowl
Momoyama period, late 16th century
Glazed stoneware
6.3 × 16.2 cm
ROM 964.84.2

Shigaraki Tea Ware

One of these cherished tactile wares, Shigaraki ware, is made in a style called *yakishime* ("hardened by firing"), which refers to non-glazed or naturally ash-glazed stonewares. To make the hard body, they are fired for up to seven days in a kiln. The history of Shigaraki ware started in the late 13th century, when farmer-potters made jars, pots, and pestles for their farming community, using clays and woods sourced locally. As tea cultivation spread in Uji (the south side of Kyoto and the west side of Shigaraki) in the late 15th century, Shigaraki ware jars were used to preserve the freshness and flavours of expensive tea leaves.[3] Around the same time, wabi-cha practitioners in urban centres not too far from Shigaraki started using Shigaraki ware farming and cooking vessels as *mizusashi* ("water jars") and *kensui* ("wastewater containers"). A letter written by merchant-monk tea master Murata Jukō (1422–1502) in Nara, located on the southwest side of Shigaraki, complained that many tea practitioners, despite their lack of knowledge of wabi aesthetics, were using Shigaraki and Bizen wares (another wood-fired, non-glazed ware from current-day Okayama prefecture).[4] His comment shows how much wares like Shigaraki were in fashion at that time.

By the early 16th century, kilns in Shigaraki were producing wares specifically for chanoyu. According to the diaries of tea practitioners, water jars and wastewater containers were the most frequently used Shigaraki ware. In the late 16th century, more varieties of tea wares appeared, including vases, tea bowls, tea caddies, incense containers, and plates and bowls for *kaiseki* (meals served at tea gatherings). Unlike water jars and wastewater containers, many of these smaller vessels were intimately handled by invited guests. Tea bowls and kaiseki plates and bowls were of course touched with hands and lips. The guests also had dedicated time to handle and observe bowls and plates afterwards.

Specific terminologies were created to describe both visual and tactile features of Shigaraki ware. *Ishihaze* ("stone burst") refers to protrusions of feldspar (a mineral with a glassy lustre) and silica stones that are not easily melted. Unrefined Shigaraki clay contains many of these stones, and when fired at high temperatures, the clay shrinks and they protrude from the surface, looking like exploded stones.

Fig. 4.7
Shigaraki Ware Storage Jar
Momoyama period,
late 16th century
Stoneware with natural ash glaze
34 × 27 cm
ROM 2019.70.1

Gift of Eberhard and Jane Zeidler

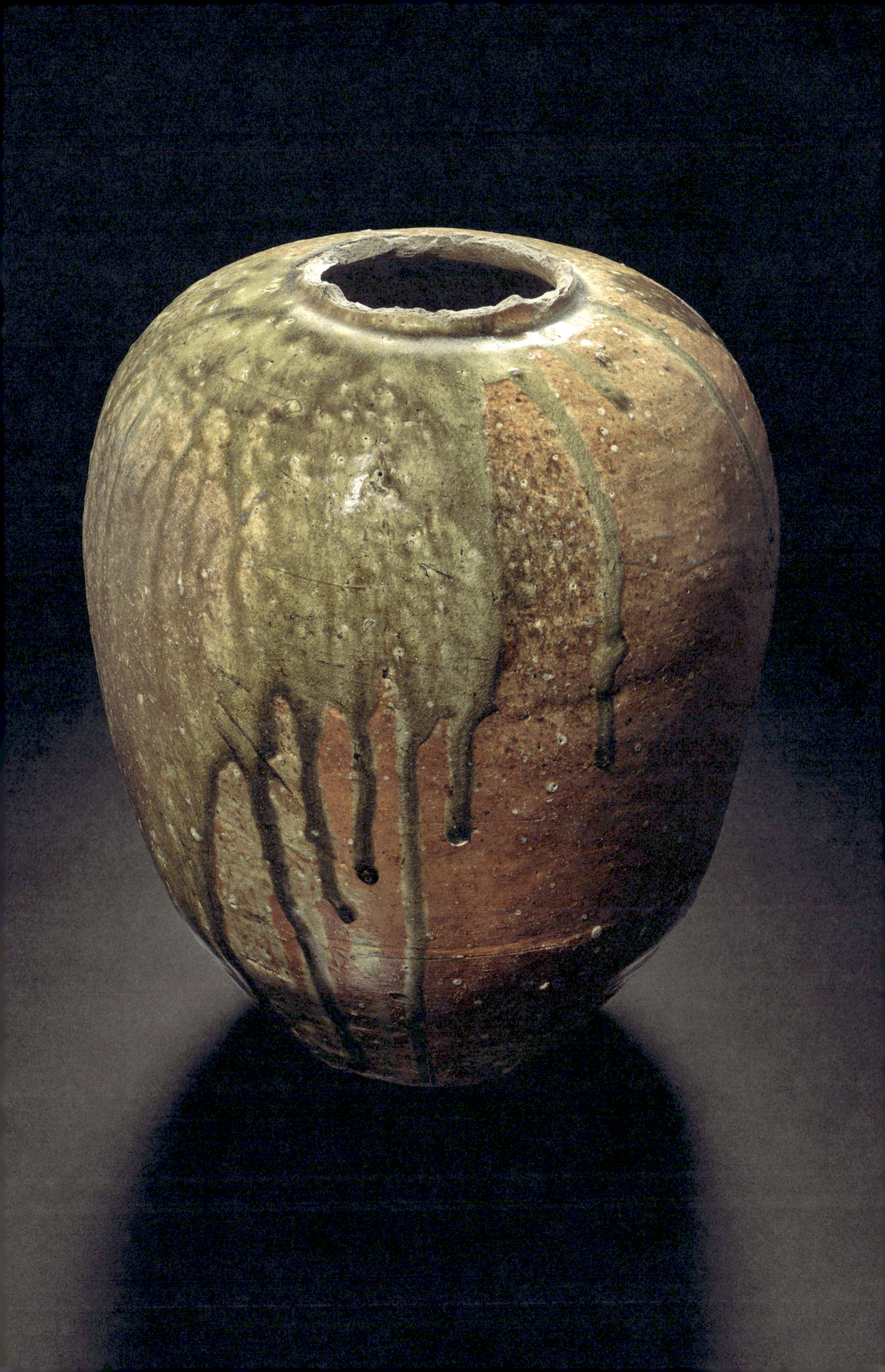

Also, the feldspar would melt at temperatures between 1,250 and 1,300 degrees Celsius and turn into glassy white grains. These bumpy spots are called *kani-no-me* ("crab eyes") or *arare* ("hail"). Moreover, the smooth ash-glazed area, called *hai-kaburi* ("ash-covered"), and the rough unglazed surface would create pleasing tactile contrast.[5] Imagine sliding your hands on the 16th-century jar in ROM's collection (Fig. 4.7): feeling the different sensations between the cool streaks of ash glaze and the undulated unglazed sections would be an enjoyable experience. Although the objects at a tea gathering were much smaller scale, the guests would admire these same features of Shigaraki ware.

Mixing Textures: Tea Gathering Sequence and *Shukō*

Tactile sensation also became an important element in a tea ware arrangement of chanoyu. Keeping in mind care and hospitality, Rikyū changed the norm and focused on tea itself in the gathering. Before Rikyū's time, chanoyu was part of a day-long entertainment: in addition to having elaborate meals with sake and drinking tea, guests engaged in activities such as poetry making, dancing, singing, and, if it was summer, even bathing.[6] Rikyū's new tea-centred sequence was as follows: after meals and sake, the guests had koicha ("thick tea") and *usucha* ("thin tea") prepared by the host, and that was all. This more simplified and refined chanoyu was dictated by shukō, or "a thematic program," that involved arrangements of the tea room, tea wares, tea making performance, and conversation according to a chosen theme. The host put their creativity into the sole purpose of pleasing the guests through shukō, which, at its best, would have had many joyful discoveries and surprises. As chanoyu developed further after the 17th century, shukō became a site of creative outputs.[7]

How the selection and arrangement of tea wares became the centre of attention within shukō can be seen in their frequent mentions in the tea diaries of the time. Along with the visual appearance and pedigrees, the tactility of the tea wares was an important element. Rikyū and his contemporary tea practitioners used different types of tea bowls for koicha and usucha in a tea gathering.[8] Often when a smooth Chinese tea bowl was used for koicha, a sturdy Korean tea bowl was given for usucha. Or a Korean tea bowl was used for koicha and a thick Raku tea bowl appeared for usucha. Offering tea with tea bowls of different textures could please the guests by enabling them to experience a variety of tactile sensations.

Although it is not a ceramic ware, the inclusion of a tea scoop, which was usually viewed at the end of the chanoyu sequence, is noteworthy. A tea scoop, usually made of bamboo, is an important tea utensil despite its humble nature. A tea scoop can be handmade by tea masters and practitioners, because unlike ceramics or

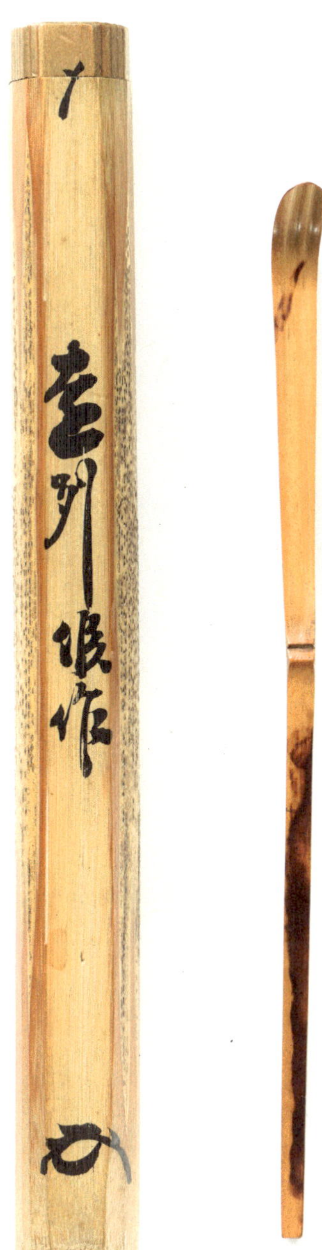

Fig. 4.8
Attributed to Kobori Enshū (1579–1647)
Tea Scoop
Edo period, first half of 17th century
Bamboo
18.6 × 0.9 cm
ROM 990.156.6

The Yamagami Sōju (Akio, 1873–1957) Collection; gift of Mrs. Yamagami and the Umezawa family. Certified by the Canadian Cultural Property Export Review Board under the terms of the Cultural Property Export and Import Act. Attesté par la Commission canadienne d'examen des exportations de biens culturels en vertu de la Loi sur l'exportation et l'importation de biens culturels.

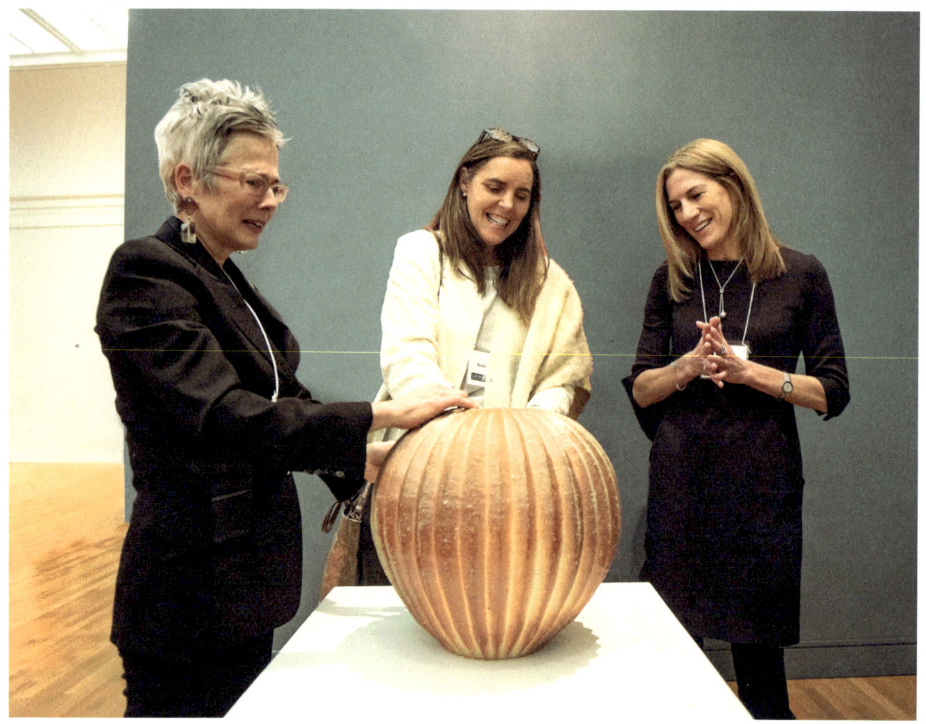

Fig. 4.9
Takahashi Yoshiko (b. 1988)
Shigaraki Jar
Reiwa period, 2021
Stoneware with natural ash glaze
3.7 × 37.3 × 37.3 cm

Collection of the University of Michigan Museum of Art
Gift of the artist, 2025/1.112
In the exhibition *Clay as Soft Power: Shigaraki Ware in Postwar America and Japan*, University of Michigan Museum of Art
Photo: Leisa Thompson, 2021

lacquerware, a tea scoop does not require special materials, tools, or skills. ROM's collection features a tea scoop made by tea master Kobori Enshū (1579–1647, Fig. 4.8). Enshū served tea to the third Tokugawa Shogun, Iemitsu, and Enshū's sophisticated, elegant taste and affection for classical poetry of the Heian period (794–1185) set the trend of the early Edo period. A tea scoop made by past tea masters like Enshū could be the highlight of the entire shukō for the guests, as they could touch and feel Enshū's traces. In koicha, the viewing sequence of the tea scoop comes between the tea caddy and the silk pouch for the caddy. Again, textural differences, from ceramics to bamboo and then to a smooth silk cloth, can be an enjoyable experience for the guests.

Future of Sensory Experiences for Museums

Attending a tea gathering is analogous to visiting an art museum, where the guests have an elevated experience of appreciating various kinds of artistic objects, including painting, calligraphy, ceramics, lacquerware, bamboo crafts, metalware, and textiles. The selection and arrangement of these objects on a specific theme is like curation and installation choreographed by the host. However, a fundamental difference is apparent: the collection and settings of a tea gathering are in the hands of a private individual, while a museum is a public institution and its collection and facilities are meant for the public good. A collecting museum's important mission is to preserve the collection for education and research purposes for the present and the future. Because of the importance of chanoyu history in Japanese culture, many museums in Japan and overseas collect and display tea wares, but due to the public nature of the collection, they are not allowed to be touched. Considering the great importance of tactile sensations in chanoyu, can this situation be changed?

In recent years, several museums have begun trying to respond to this desire to provide tactile experience in the appreciation of tea ceramics. At the University of Michigan Museum of Art, for example, I included a touchable jar by a contemporary artist as part of the exhibition *Clay as Soft Power: Shigaraki Ware in Postwar America and Japan* (November 2022–May 2023; Fig. 4.9). The jar, commissioned specifically for touching and feeling the uneven surface of wood-fired, unglazed Shigaraki ware, is a work by Takahashi Yoshiko. In conversation with the artist, we chose a larger work, rather than a smaller object like a tea bowl, so that the artwork would be stable while being touched. In another instance, at the 2017 opening of the Japanese gallery of the Detroit Institute of Arts in Michigan, visitors were encouraged to hold a 3-D printed tea bowl modelled after a black ceramic Raku tea bowl while sitting around a table monitor showing a tea gathering video. The tea bowl was light compared with an actual Raku bowl,

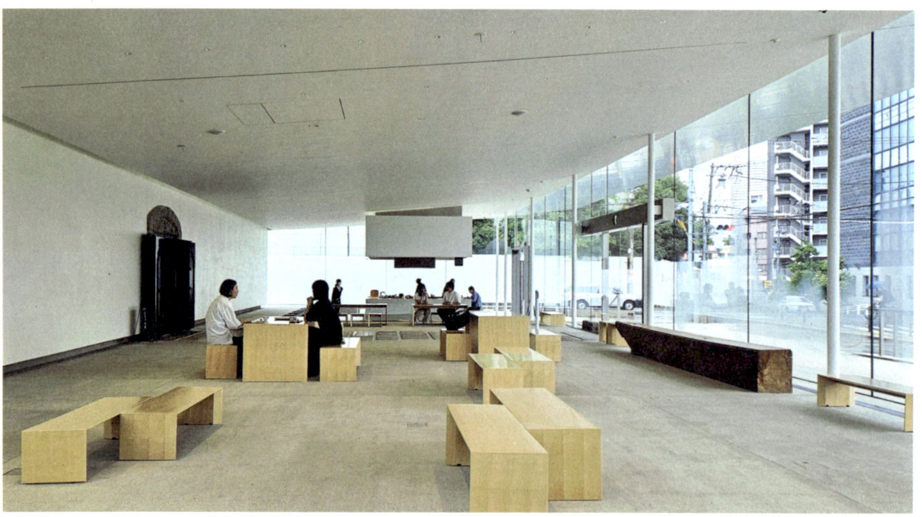

but the bumpy and warm feeling of hand-formed Raku was there.[9] Finally, the Fujita Museum in Osaka provides the most comprehensive experience of touch, smell, taste, and even sound. For a nominal fee, visitors can drink tea (they can choose matcha or steeped green tea) and eat rice cakes at the entrance café (Fig. 4.10). The tea bowls, made by contemporary artists in Momoyama period styles, invite visitors to enjoy tactile sensations. Unlike many museum cafés, the Fujita Museum's is located in an open space between the building entrance and the gallery, without any partitions. Visitors can hear the sound of tea whisking. If they wish, they can sit in a tatami-matted tea room in the same space. From my short time there, I observed that most visitors chose to have tea in that space. Although visitors cannot touch the museum's splended tea ware collection, they can experience the sensation through contemporary tea bowls. I am hoping that many other museums will explore more creative ways to bring the sense of touch to the introduction of Japanese chanoyu.

Fig. 4.10
Amishima-chaya café at the entrance of the Fujita Museum.

Photo: Akiko Takesue, 2023

1 For the early history of tea in Japan, see Yasuhiko Murai, "The Development of Chanoyu: Before Rikyū" in *Tea in Japan: Essays on the History of Chanoyu*, ed. Paul Varley and Isao Kumakura (Honolulu: University of Hawai'i Press, 1989), 3–32.

2 Extant examples exist of Chinese blue-and-white and red-and-green overglaze tea bowls of cylindrical shape between the late 15th and 16th century, which were converted from incense burners to tea bowls. A Chinese blue-and-white cylindrical tea bowl named *Kimiidera* (Kimiidera Temple) was said to have been owned by Sen no Rikyū. See Tokugawa Art Museum and Gotoh Museum, eds., *Chanoyu Meiwan: Aratanaru Edo no Biishiki* [Masterpiece tea bowls of chanoyu: New aesthetics of the Edo period] (Nagoya and Tokyo: Tokugawa Art Museum and Gotoh Museum, 2005), 12–13. Rikyū might have instructed Chōjirō to model his bowls after these types of Chinese tea bowls. Tea historian Yoshiaki Yabe points out that behind Rikyū's choice of a minor, cylindrical shape was his strict commitment to realize a tea bowl of wabi aesthetic. Yoshiaki Yabe, *Miwaku no Momoyama chanoyu: Rikyū, Hideyoshi, Oribe no kakushin* [Enchanting chanoyu of the Momoyama period: Innovations by Rikyū, Hideyoshi, Oribe] (Kyoto: Miyaobi Shuppansha, 2019), 130.

3 Louise Allison Cort, *Shigaraki: Potters' Valley* (Tokyo: Kodansha International, 1979; Bangkok: Orchid Press, 2001), 104.

4 Murata Jukō, *Kokoro no fumi* [Letter of the heart], cited in Murai, "Development of Chanoyu," 21.

5 For more of these terminologies and descriptions, see Shigaraki Ceramic Cultural Park, *Shigaraki yaki: Naokata no Chatō, Shunsai no Tsubo* [Shigaraki ware: Tea wares of Naokata and jars of Shunsai] (Shigaraki: Shigaraki Ceramic Cultural Park, 2010), 139–41.

6 Isao Kumakura and Martha J. McClintock, *Japanese Tea Culture: The Heart and Form of Chanoyu* (Tokyo: Japan Publishing Industry Foundation for Culture, 2023), 42–54, 120, https://doi.org/10.2307/jj.2840648.

7 Kumakura and McClintock, *Japanese Tea Culture*, 137–45. Also see Hiroichi Tsutsui, *Rikyū no chakai* [Tea gatherings of Rikyū] (Tokyo: Kadokawa, 2015), 10.

8 Until the mid-16th century, no clear distinction existed between koicha and usucha. If the guest wanted thicker tea, more tea powder was simply added. The distinction was first recorded at a tea gathering hosted by Satsumaya Sōsetsu in 1542, around the same time that Rikyū's tea gathering was first recorded. Hiroichi Tsutsui points out that the distinction between koicha and usucha coincided with the time when tea leaves began to be categorized and named according to the quality. Tsutsui, *Rikyū no chakai*, 21–23. Also see Akio Tanihata, "Chakaiki to koicha usucha no chawan [Tea diaries and tea bowls for koicha and usucha]," in *Chadō Shūkin*, vol. 11 (Tokyo: Shōgakkan, 1983), 175–79; and tea diaries in Isao Kumakura, ed., *Chanoyu no koten 3: Yondai chakaiki* [Classics of chanoyu 3: Four great tea diaries] (Tokyo: Sekaibunkasha, 1984), 52, 54, 66, 96.

9 During the 2020 pandemic, the tea bowl was unfortunately removed from this interactive display.

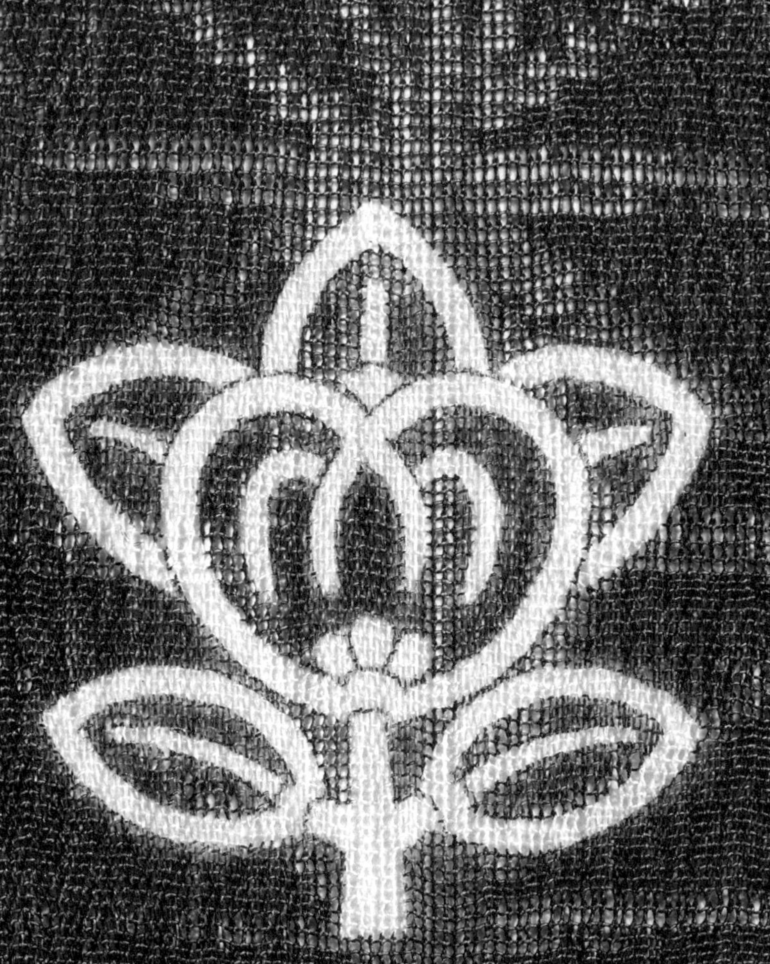

CHAPTER FIVE

Beyond Inclusion and Accessibility: On the Meaning of "Tactile Exhibitions" in Museum Spaces

BY KŌJIRŌ HIROSE
TRANSLATION BY BRIAN BERGSTROM

Why "Grand Exposition"?

From September to November 2021, the National Museum of Ethnology in Osaka held a special exhibition called *Universal Museum: Exploring the New Field of Tactile Sensation* (the direct translation of the original Japanese title is *Universal Museum: Touch! A Grand Exposition of Touch*). As a person with complete loss of sight, I have worked at the Museum since 2001 and was the Chair of the exhibition's executive committee. The recent experience of the COVID-19 pandemic had unexpectedly put the loss of touch at the forefront of everyone's minds, which allowed this "tactile exhibition" to become a prime opportunity to explore, through trial and error, the possibilities of new modes of display.

During the planning process, I found myself preoccupied with the exhibition's subtitle, which in Japanese uses the word *dai-hakurankai*—that is, "Grand Exposition." All around the world, the cultural institutions now known as museums have developed a system of well-established rules for how exhibitions are to be presented and framed for the public. By using the expression "Grand Exposition," I wanted to evoke the various ways exhibitions were put on in the era before museums, returning to a moment when the encounter between people and objects took place in diverse ways that were yet to be fully regulated (and were sometimes quite chaotic!). Additionally, I wanted to present to a world audience the Japanese-born concept of the Universal Museum—a museum that anyone can enjoy.

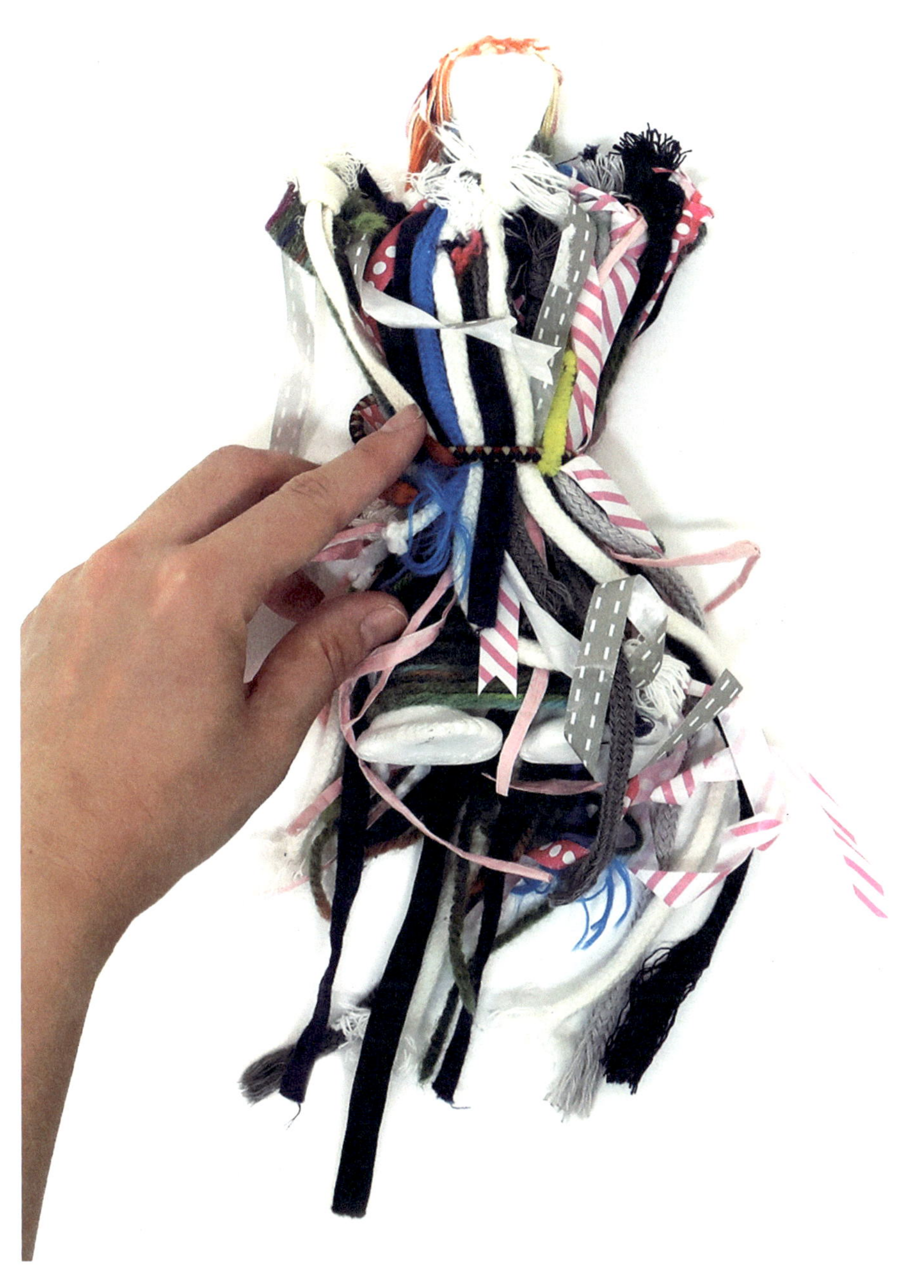

Detail, *Putting Clothes on Clay Figures*

Translating this subtitle into English presented another problem, but in the end, I decided to go with "Exploring the New Field of Tactile Sensation." I wanted to slip the bonds of the "visual exhibition" and emphasize encounters with the tactility of objects and art pieces using other senses. The phrase "New Field" thus expresses my wish that this realization could inform the creation of the museum of tomorrow.

As museums established themselves as modern cultural institutions, it has been taken for granted that exhibits are objects never to be touched. Recent exhibitions incorporating information and communication technologies can be very effective in using a variety of methods to convey information to a diverse population of visitors. But as the use of terms like "online," "remote," and the like indicate, we must be mindful of how these technologies can also create distance between people, or between people and objects, and thus end up obstructing direct communication.

Museums have recently begun to promote social inclusion in their operations, and institutions around the world have made it their goal to improve accessibility. Japanese museums have been a part of this, planning events meant to welcome people with diverse impairments to enjoy exhibitions, including increasing numbers of tactile exhibitions. These are people who have historically found accessing exhibitions difficult and have found themselves, either consciously or unconsciously, forgotten by museums. So it is wonderful for this minority population to be able to easily access and enjoy the museum. "Accessibility" and "inclusion" are no doubt key terms for humanity to use to overcome the contradictions of modernity.

Yet these key terms also make me personally uneasy. The inclusion of the minority by the majority. The creation of ways to allow the minority access to the culture made by the majority. These viewpoints have become so typical of museums in the 21st century—but is there not something missing here?

The mass media gave positive coverage to my special exhibition, characterizing it as a bold move in the midst of the COVID-19 crisis. How could a tactile exhibition take place amid a world of pre-existing visual exhibitions? This way of framing the issue stems from using "accessibility" and "inclusion" as starting points. But in this special exhibition, the Universal Museum was a space in which everything on display was meant to be touched. Its originality lay not in the fact that visitors were *allowed* to touch objects but rather in that they *had* to touch them to enjoy the exhibition properly.

The *Universal Museum* space was crowded with artworks like sculptures and paintings but also reproductions of archaeological artifacts, including Buddhist sculptures, masks, musical instruments, and toys. Visitors were able to enjoy a wide variety of materials and textures, including wood, stone, cloth, paper, resin, pottery, and metal. One of the exhibition's biggest successes was demonstrating that, with the thorough observation of safety protocols (ventilation, masking, and hand sanitization), a tactile exhibition could indeed be held even in the midst of a crisis like the COVID-19 pandemic.

That said, the number of visitors was unfortunately lower than projected, partly due to the stay-at-home order and other restrictions. Further, avoiding having objects become broken or dirty will be a challenge that cannot be overlooked to make tactile exhibitions a consistent, ongoing part of the museum's operation. The latter half of the exhibition's run saw a marked increase in visits by groups of elementary school children, an increase that corresponded with a rise in the number of objects that ended up broken or soiled. *Please touch gently and with respect.* Behind every object on display are the people who made it, used it, and passed it along. How we touch objects is linked to how we touch each other. One might even say that educating the public on precisely the "manners" involved in touch was one of the Universal Museum's main objectives.

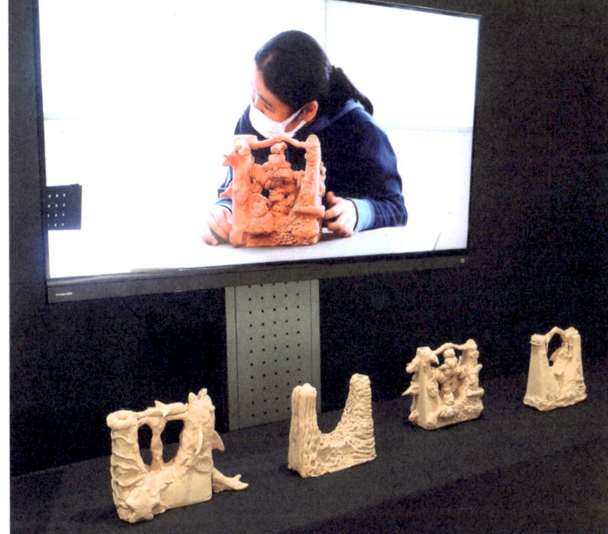

Fig. 5.1
Installation view of the *Universal Museum* exhibition in Okayama, 2023.

Photo: Chiaki Kuwata

(pp. 114–15)
Detail of objects on display at the *Universal Museum* exhibition in Okayama, 2023.

Photo: Chiaki Kuwata

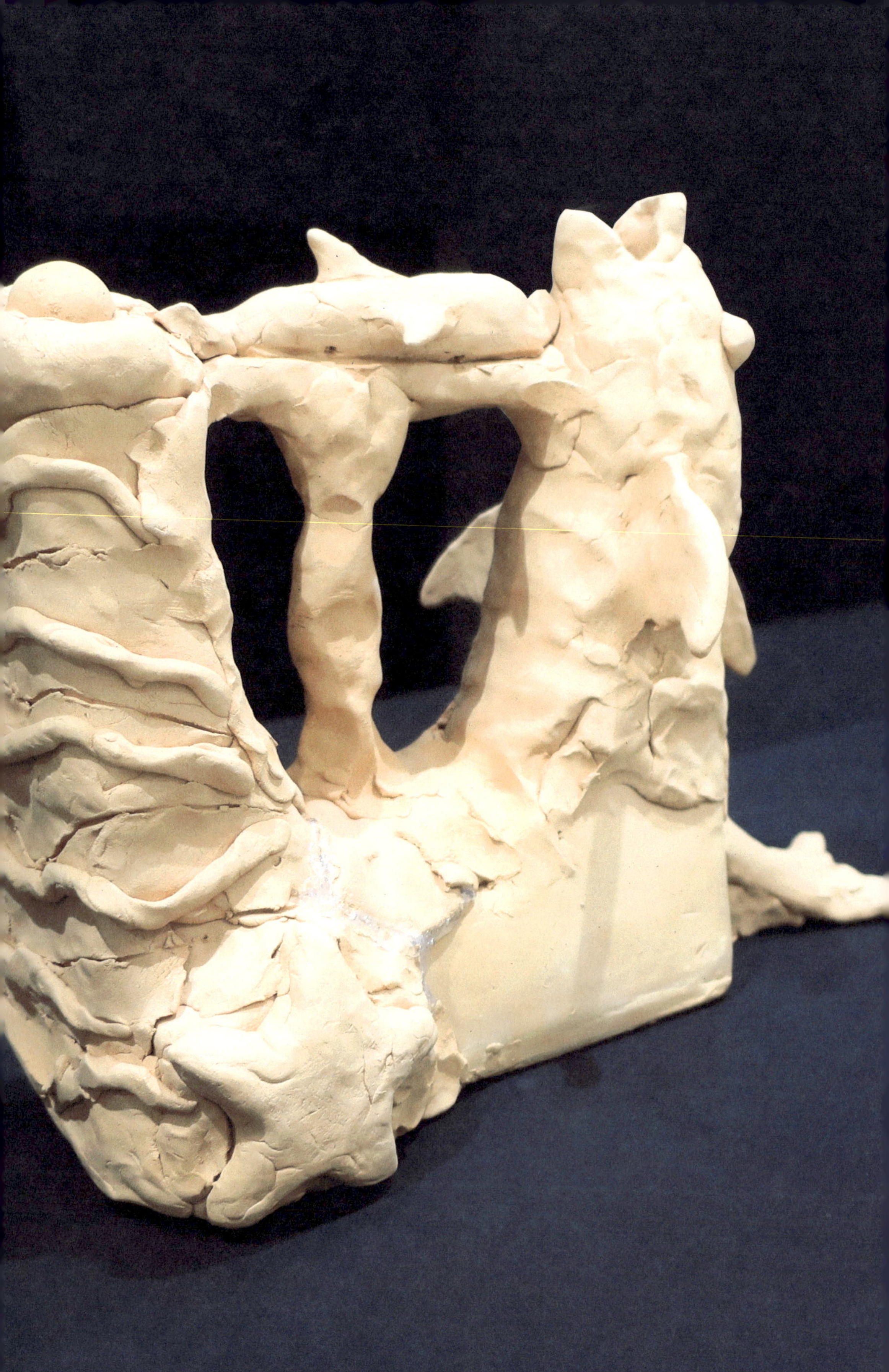

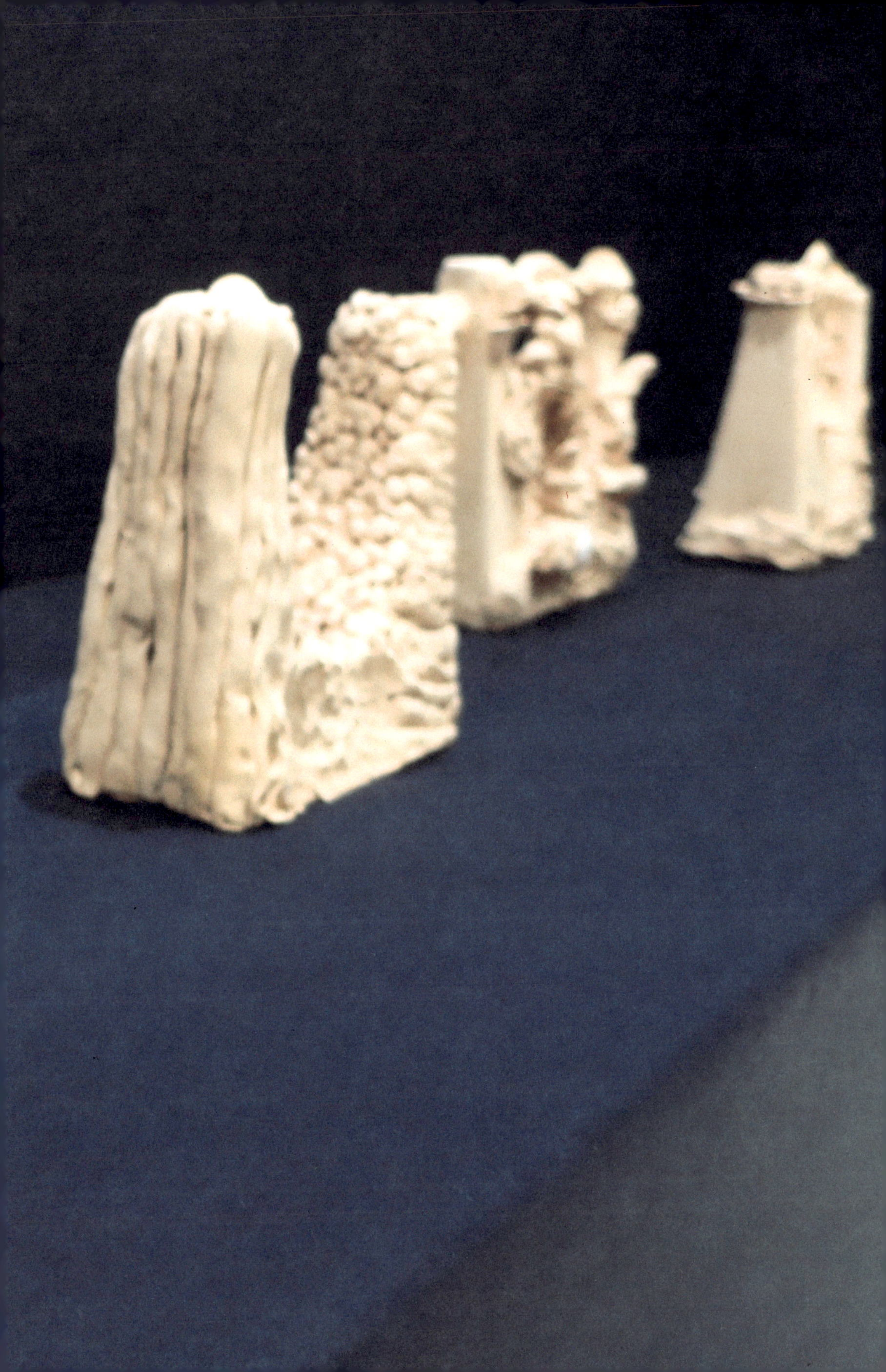

Happily, the *Universal Museum* exhibition has been able to tour various other locations starting in 2023. As of January 2025, the tour schedule has been as follows:

- Okayama, Okayama prefecture (April–May 2023)
- Ōmi-Hachiman, Shiga prefecture (October–December 2023)
- Noogata, Fukuoka prefecture (July–September 2024)
- Ōita, Ōita prefecture (October–November 2024)
- Beppu, Ōita prefecture (November 2024)

We have made a conscious effort, as the exhibition travels, to incorporate some local materials into the show and make it more welcoming to everyone. In Okayama, we added an explanatory video in sign language, while at Ōmi-Hachiman, we added panels in simple Japanese to aid comprehension by foreign visitors and visitors with developmental disabilities (Fig. 5.1 and 5.2). In Beppu, we strove to modify the layout and height of the display tables to allow visitors in wheelchairs to see and touch the objects more easily, though work remains to be done in this area. In Noogata and Ōita, we actively solicited the participation of local artists and students in exhibiting their works and taking part in the events related to the exhibition (Fig. 5.3, 5.4, 5.5, and 5.6). Our motto as we toured was "Let's Make the Universal Museum Deeper."

Another feature of the touring exhibition was our flexibility in adapting each part of the show to accommodate the capacities and features of each exhibition space. The version of the show that took place in Noogata in the summer of 2024, for example, took advantage of the space there by grouping the pieces on display into the following sections:

- Feeling—*to touch with the hand*
- Connecting—*to touch with the body*
- Seeing—*to touch with the eye*
- Broadening—*to touch with the ear*
- Deepening—*to touch with the heart*

As the names of these sections attest, the Universal Museum draws attention to how the sense of touch resides in every part of the human body. Broadly speaking, each of the five senses are included or implicated in the sense of touch. Let me briefly expand on this idea. Conventionally, "viewing" is thought of as the gathering of information by seeing—that is, using the eyes. But the viewing indicated in the show—viewing as *touching*—is communication that engages with objects using the whole body, exploring touch as a way to know the world beyond that which can be seen by the eye. Another important aspect of the sense of touch is its ability to provide an experience of "broadening" (receptivity) and "deepening" (proactivity).

Unlike other major touring shows, the *Universal Museum* exhibition lacks a stable source of backing and a reliable place for storing the artwork and other exhibits. Individuals interested in the exhibition and institutions that want to host it voluntarily bring it to their cities. This kind of grassroots network has served as the basis for the tour, which seems appropriate for a show founded on the concept that anyone should be able to enjoy it. To present touch as a universal aspect of culture, something common to all humanity and thus beyond the limits of "accessibility" and "inclusion," concepts that have the power imbalance placing the majority over the minority baked into them—this is direction in which I hope the Universal Museum continues to move, ever deepening the realization of this ideal.

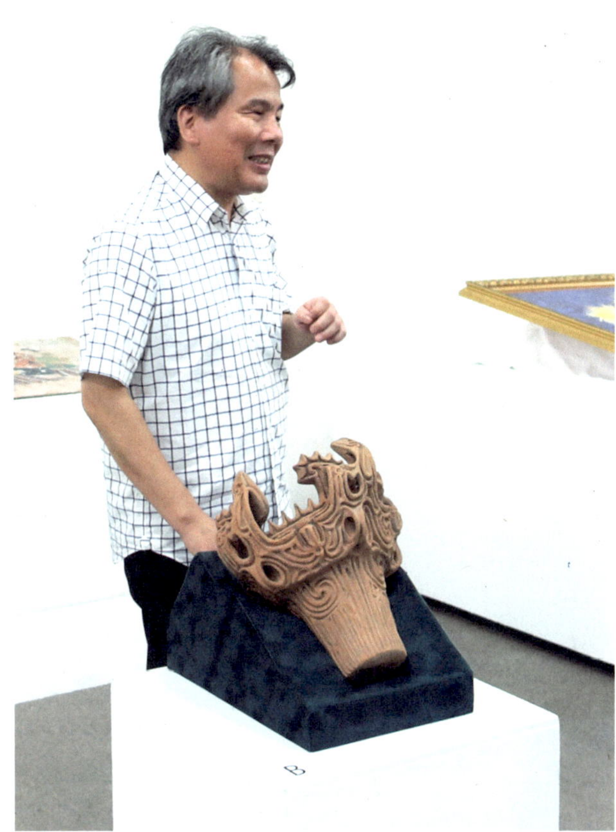

Fig. 5.2
Professor Hirose touching an exhibit at the *Universal Museum* exhibition in Noogata, 2024.

Photo: Chiaki Kuwata

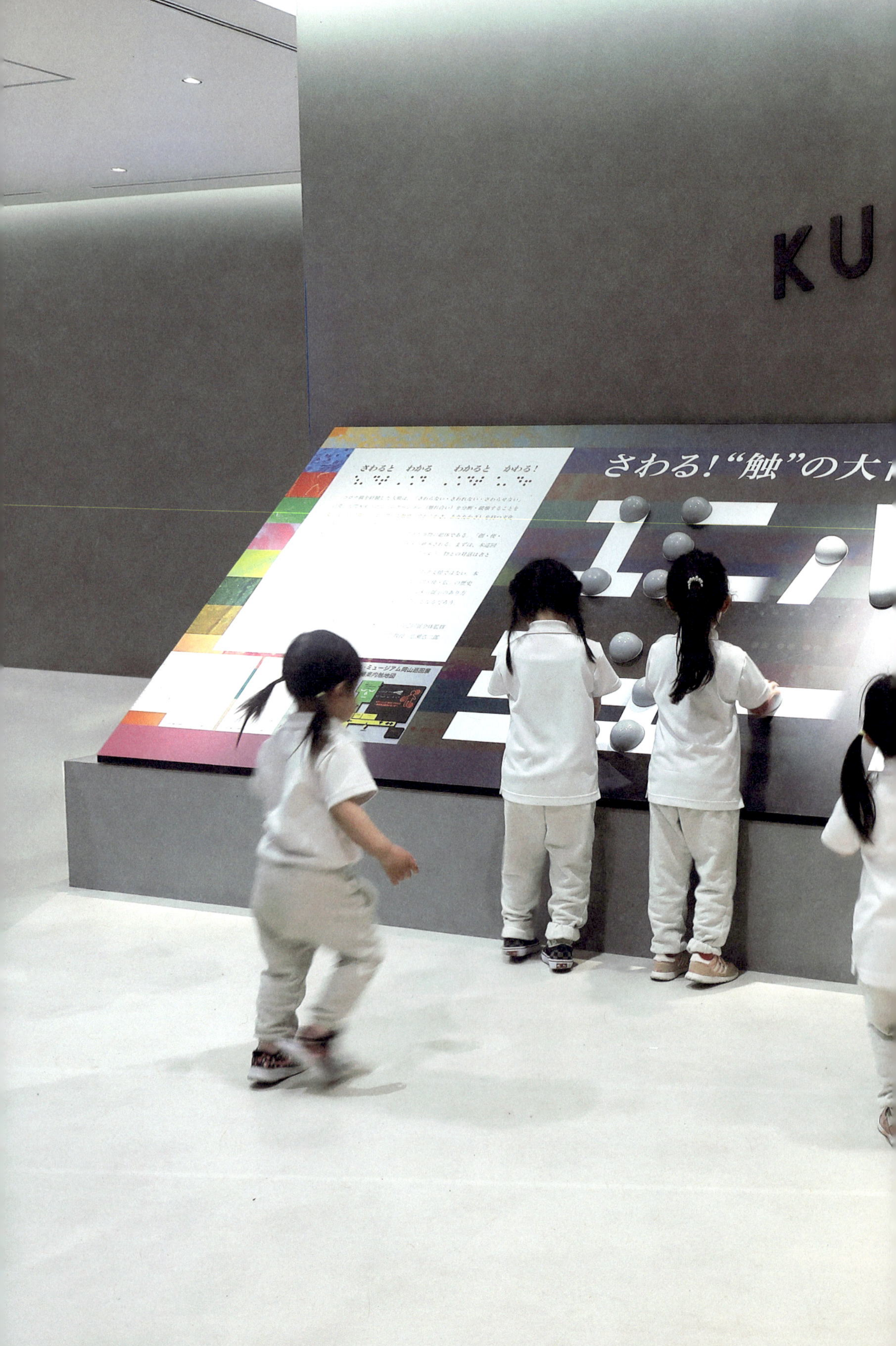
KU
さわる！“触”の大
さわると　わかる　　わかると　かわる！

UN
HALL
覧会　岡山巡回展2023
特別協賛：NTT 西日本
主催　OHK岡山放送

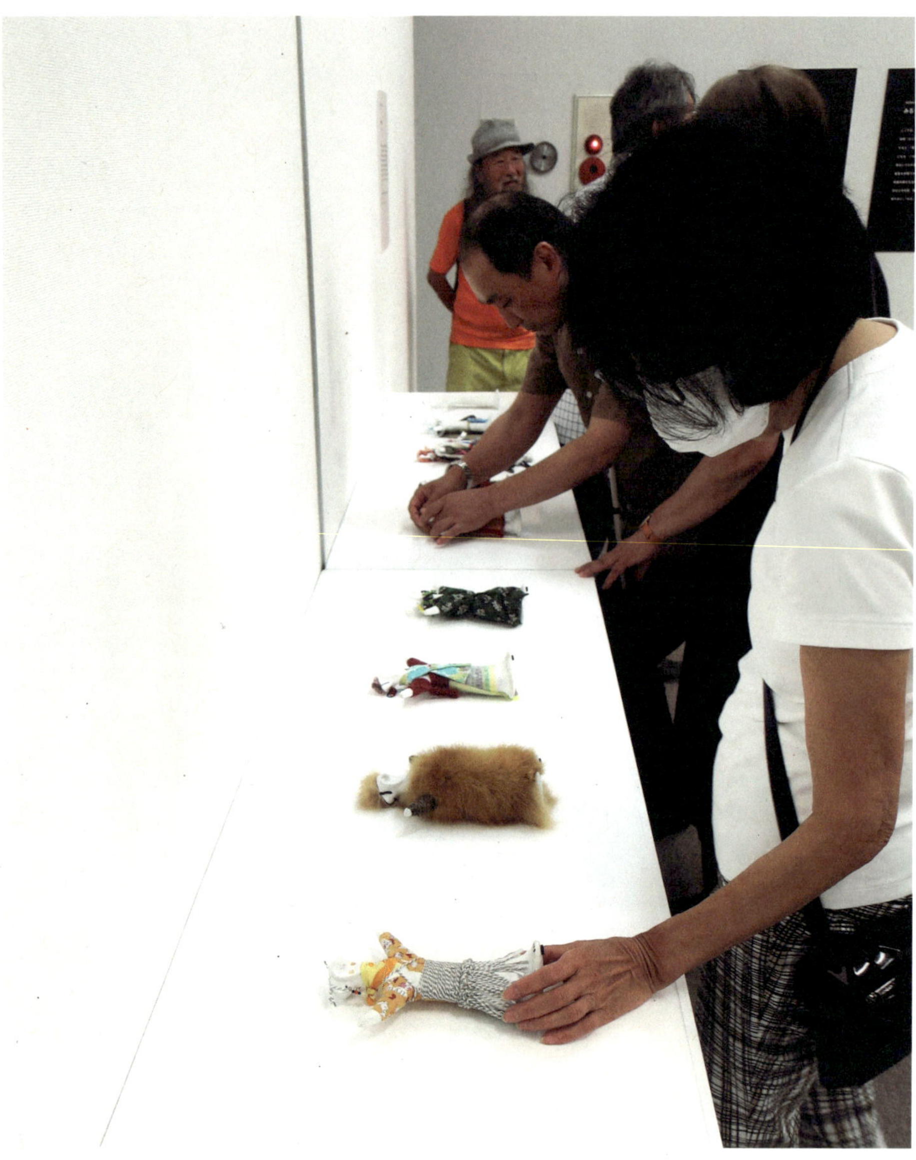

Fig. 5.4
Installation view of *Putting Clothes on Clay Figures* by Takeshi Horie at the *Universal Museum* exhibition in Noogata, 2024.

Photo: Chiaki Kuwata

Drawing Inspiration from *Ainu Spirits Singing*

I was first stimulated to start thinking about the concept of the Universal Museum when I encountered the book *Ainu Shin'yōshū* (translated into English as *Ainu Spirits Singing*), published in 1923. I will quote now from its introduction:

> In a twinkling the natural landscape as it had been since the ancient past has vanished; what has become of the folk who joyfully made their living in its fields and mountains? The few of us fellow kinspeople who remain simply stare wide-eyed, astonished by the state of the world as it continues to advance. Moreover, from those eyes has faded the beautiful sparkle of the spirit of the people of the past whose every action was informed by religious feeling. Our eyes are filled with anxiety, burn with discontent, and are so dimmed that they cannot make out the way ahead. We are compelled to rely upon the compassion of others. We are a pitiful sight. A dying people ... That is our name. What a sad name we bear![1]

The book is by Chiri Yukie (1903–22), who, working with famed Ainu studies scholar Kindaichi Kyōsuke (1882–1971), recorded the orally transmitted culture of Ainu tales and songs in written form. The *Ainu Shin'yōshū* is lauded for being the first book written in the Ainu language by an Ainu person. Ainu culture is presented not simply as something on the verge of "vanishing," something to be "promoted." Rather, it is a *natural way of being* that should be consciously reclaimed. In the same way, the tactile exhibition is our way of effectively making people re-evaluate and rethink the very essence of communication as it takes place between people, as well as between people and objects.

Yukie goes on in her introduction, saying:

> Time flows ceaselessly and the world goes on progressing endlessly. If sometime two or three strong ones should emerge from among those of us who now expose for all to see the ugliness resulting from our defeat in the arena of fierce competition, then the day will soon come when we will keep pace with the advancing world. That is our earnest hope, and what we pray for day and night ...
>
> I who was born an Ainu and grew up with the Ainu language have written down with my halting brush just one or two very short pieces from among the sundry tales that our ancestors enjoyed relating on rainy evenings and snowy nights, whenever they had time to get together.

> If the many of you who know us could kindly read them, I, together with the ancestors of my people, would consider it a source of supreme happiness, of boundless joy.[2]

Yukie's younger brother, Chiri Mashiho (1909–61), took up his sister's vision, devoting his life to the academic study of the Ainu language. You could say it was a lifelong project of resistance to Japanese attempts to quash the Ainu tongue—a struggle that used words as its battlefield. Mashiho fought passionately to promote the study of the Ainu language as a legitimate field of academic inquiry, breaking apart the ossified notion that the Ainu were an unenlightened, primitive, unlearned, and illiterate people. Along the way, he would frequently expose the discriminatory views about Ainu held by senior scholars, including his mentor Kindaichi Kyōsuke. In this sense, Mashiho became the exact kind of "strong one" his sister Yukie longed to see.

What Mashiho aimed for was a "study of Ainu language from the inside." He asserted that "within the words of primitive people, there resides the primitive soul." He decried previous research into Ainu linguistics for ignoring the "spirit of language."[3] One could say that the Ainu wisdom underlying the Ainu language is this very spirit. Clearly, Mashiho's scholarship was informed and supported by his real-life experience living as an Ainu person himself.

So the question arises: Who will lead the practical research of how to put on tactile exhibitions and concretely create a future of Universal Museums filled with rich tactile experiences? It goes without saying that the tactile exhibition is something that should be enjoyable for anyone, and therefore, any kind of person should be able to lead its creation. Hints for how to conceptualize such an exhibition are to be found throughout the Japanese traditional arts and in the skills cultivated through handiwork undertaken by artisans of all kinds. If these hints were to be properly categorized and systematized, Japanese museums would surely establish a unique position for themselves on the international stage in this field.

In addition to this, though, much in the same way that Yukie and Mashiho were "born … Ainu and grew up with the Ainu language" and were thus able to set an example for how to conduct research "from the inside," I expect people with vision impairment to play a key role in this endeavour. It is not too much to say that the enshrinement of the visual exhibition at the centre of the modern museum has placed people with impaired vision the farthest from being able to access it.

Recently, museums around the world have put in place accessibility programs to include various minorities, such as foreign people, older people, and people with disabilities.

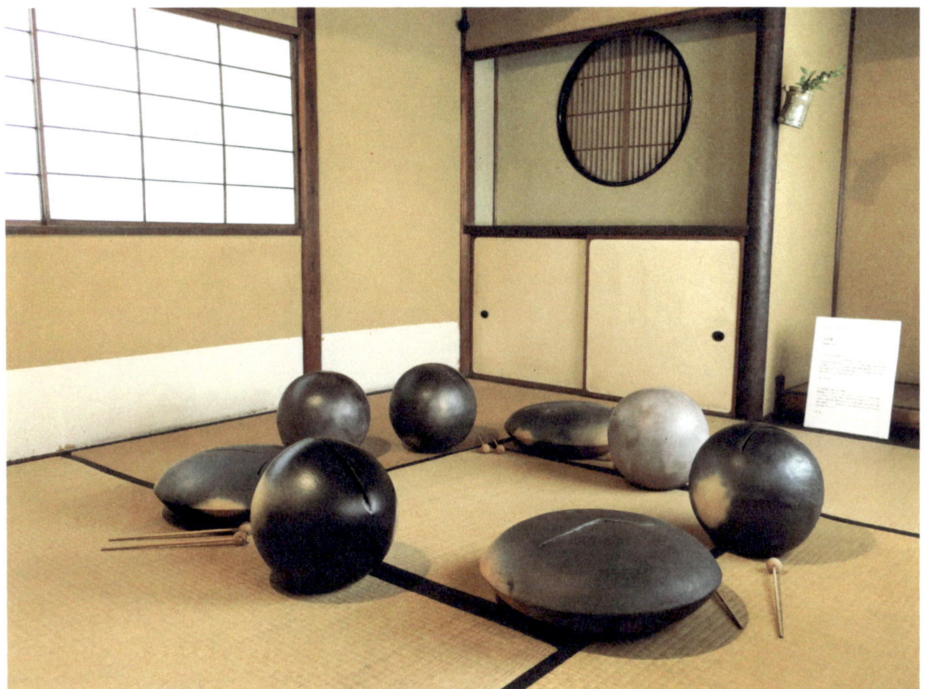

Fig. 5.5 and 5.6 (pp. 124–25)
Installation views of *The Beat of the Ground* by Yasuyuki Watanabe at the *Universal Museum* exhibition in Noogata, 2024.

Photo: Chiaki Kuwata

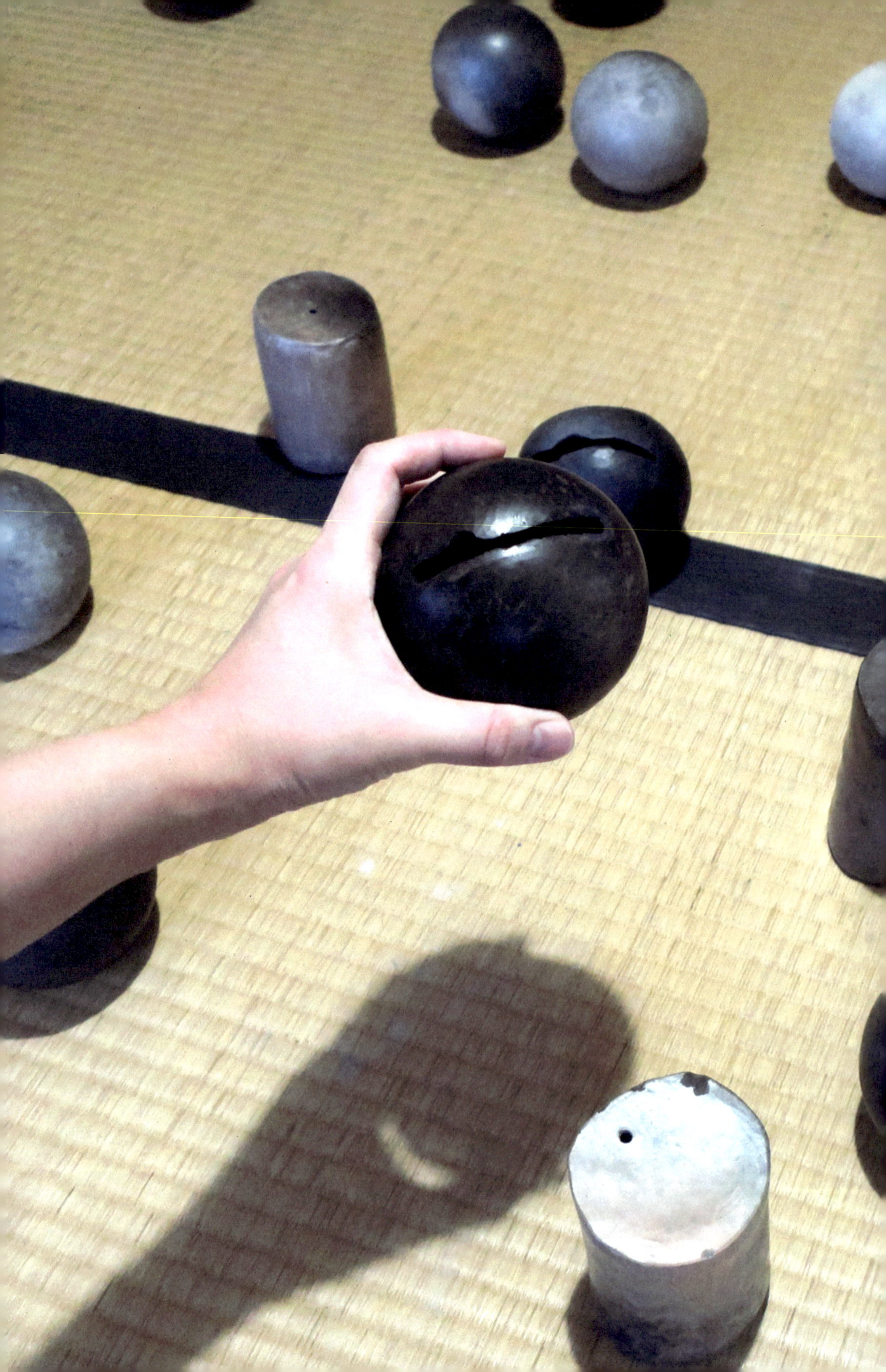

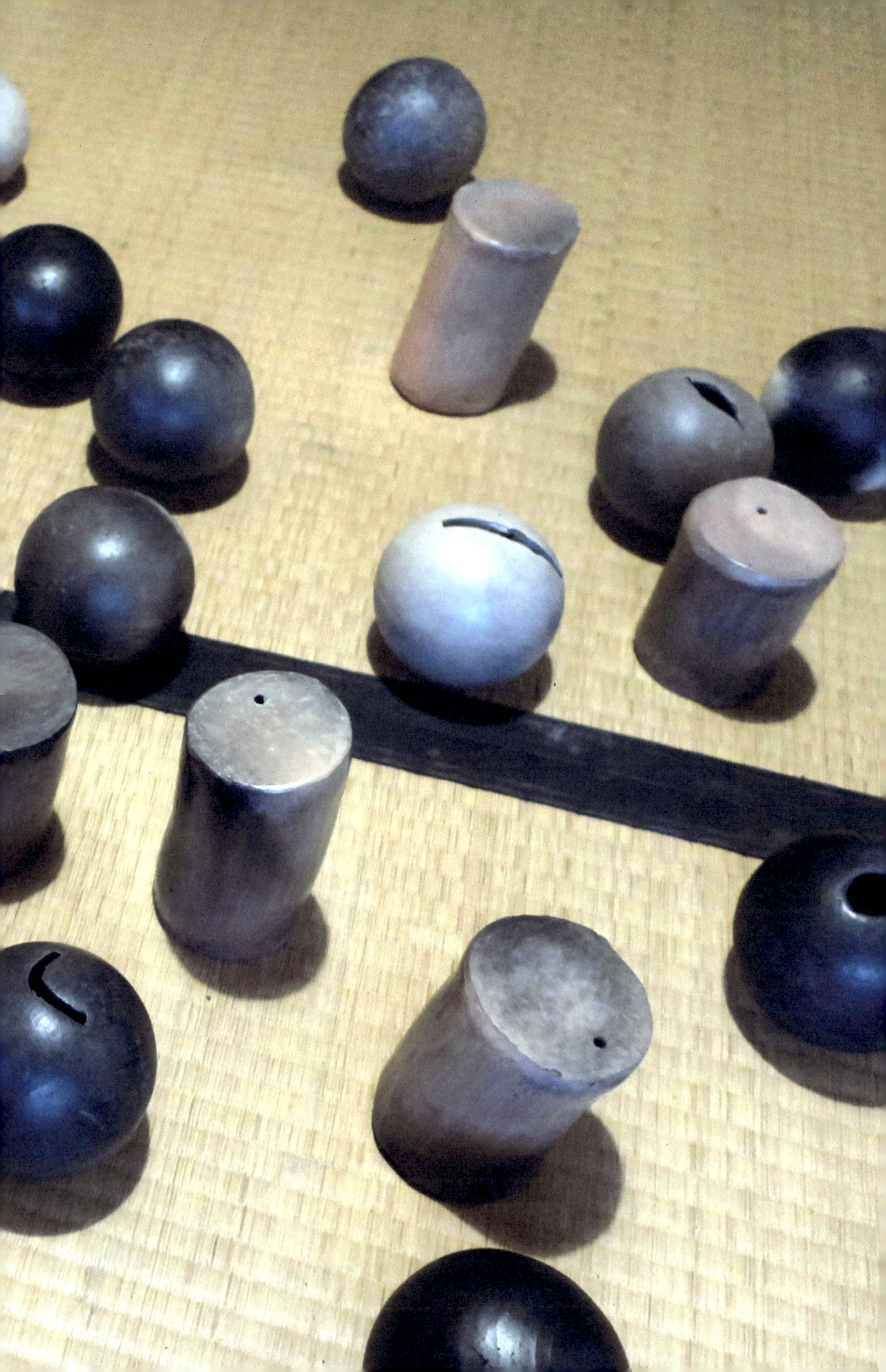

This rising trend has allowed people with impaired vision, whose existence was formerly invisible or at least difficult to discern, to emerge as one of these minorities. Today, museums are taking pains to become "user-friendly" cultural institutions and strive to include the vision-impaired in their audience (though it should not be overlooked how the assumed subject of the user-friendly concept is still a member of the able-bodied majority).

Here, I urge the vision-impaired to overcome their position as people "to be included" and instead become the strong ones pushing museums toward true universality. Just as the Chiri siblings were able to have an immense impact on the Japanese through scholarship conducted from the inside, I would like the vision-impaired to take it upon themselves to lead the planning of future tactile exhibitions. Even internationally, only a limited number of people with vision impairment are working as museum curators. Curation is still commonly assumed to be, by definition, work performed with the eye. Changing this kind of hidebound view may necessitate the reactivation of the spiritual landscape of Japan, which is rich in examples of religious and artistic groups of unsighted people, including the itinerant *biwa* players and female shamisen musicians active in premodern times.[4]

Chiri Mashiho claimed that when he was writing his most famous work, *An Introduction to the Ainu Language* (1956), his aim was to "put the study of the Ainu on the right path."[5] The tactile exhibition is not something that should be the sole province of people with vision impairment. But at the same time, the vision-impaired, whose daily lives are so rich in touch, possess a particular aptitude and responsibility to put the tactile exhibitions of the future on the right path.

Let us thus make the tactile exhibitions of the Universal Museum the start of creating a new "spirits singing" for the 21st century!

---

1 Translator's note: Translated by Sarah M. Strong, in *Ainu Spirits Singing: The Living World of Chiri Yukie's* Ainu Shin'yōshū (Honolulu: University of Hawai'i Press, 2011), 195.

2 Strong, *Ainu Spirits Singing*, 196.

3 For the achievements of Chiri Mashiho, see Hideo Fujimoto, *Chiri Mashiho no Shogai: Ainu-go Fukken no Tatakai* [The life of Chiri Mashiho: The battle to reinstate the Ainu language] (Chiba: Sofukan, 1994); and Center for Northern Humanities, Hokkaido University, ed., *Chiri Mashiho: Hito to Gakumon* [Chiri Mashiho: His life and work] (Sapporo: Hokkaido University Press, 2010).

4 Translator's note: This is a reference to premodern Japan, when blind performers travelled the countryside telling tales through song, accompanied by music, as a form of begging. One example is the *biwa hōshi*, a typically male storyteller and musician who played the lute-like biwa and dressed like a monk. Another is the *goze*, the biwa hōshi's female counterpart, who typically played the shamisen, another stringed instrument that resembles a sitar.

5 Mashiho Chiri, *Ainu-go Nyūmon: Toku ni Chimei Kenkyū-sha no tame ni* [An introduction to the Ainu language: Especially for scholars researching place-names] (Hyogo: Nire Shobō, 1956). See also Note 3 for reference.

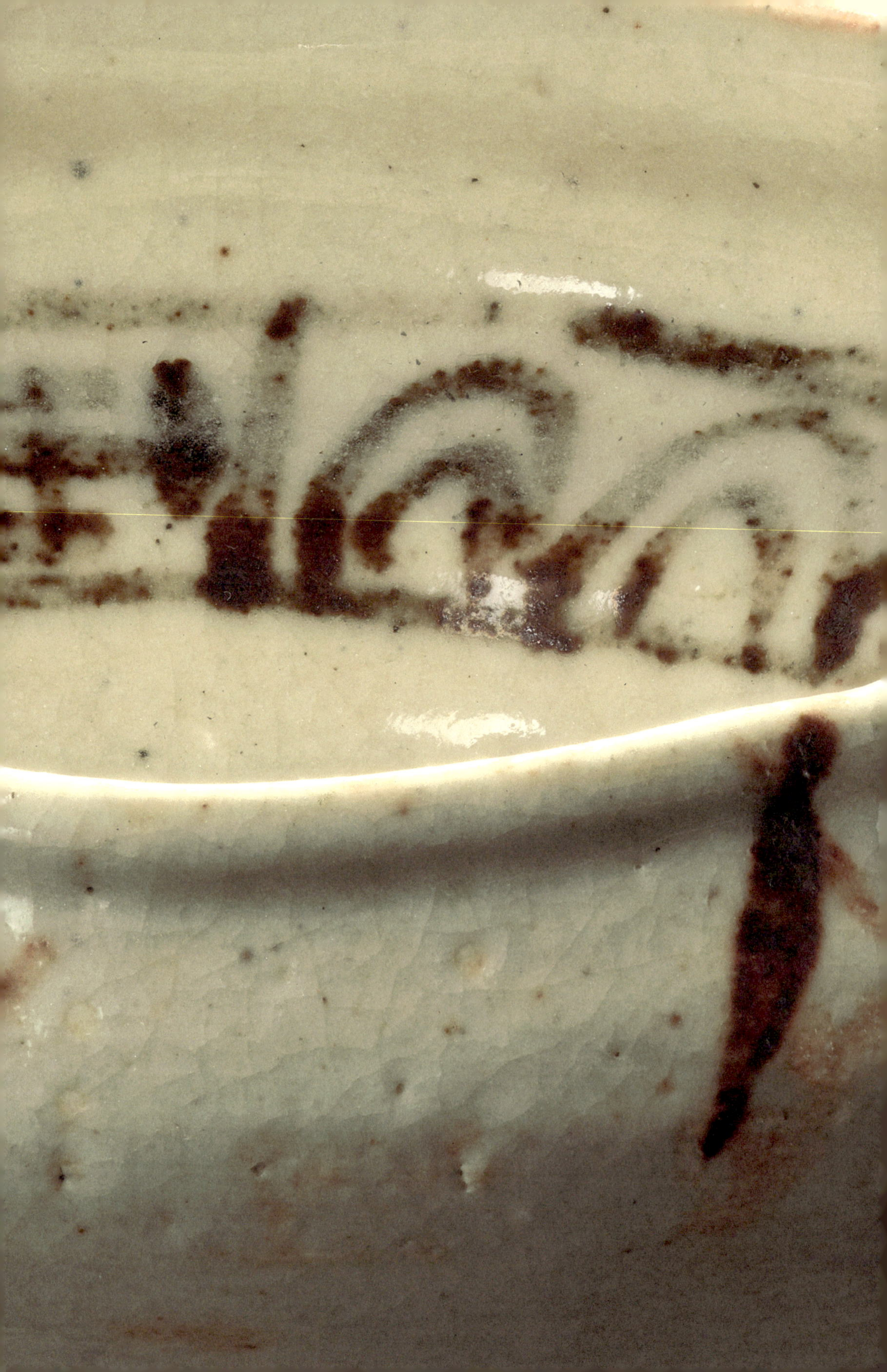

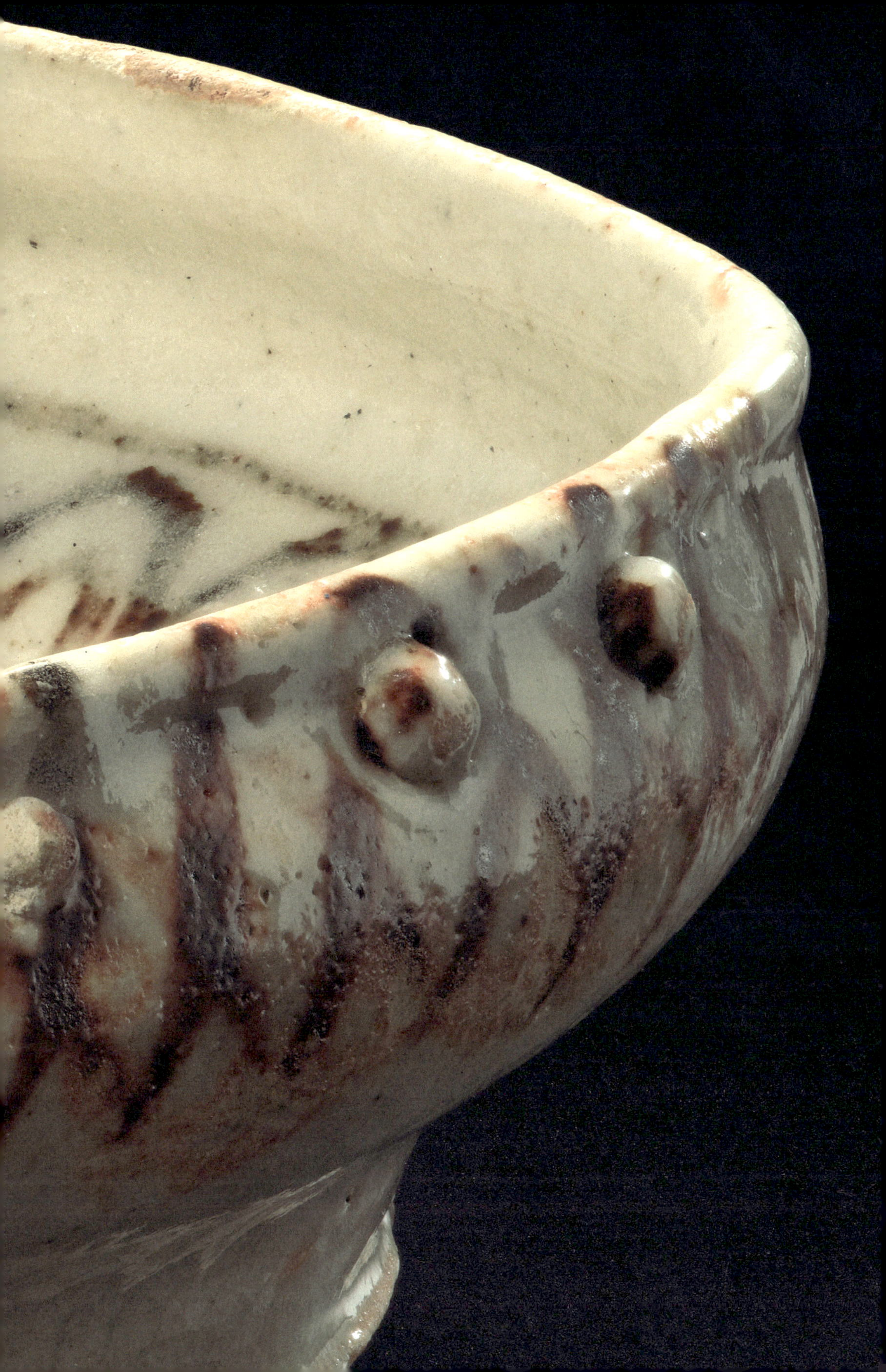

Contributors

AKIKO TAKESUE

Bishop White Committee Associate Curator of Japanese Art & Culture at the Royal Ontario Museum.

Takesue's major research interests lie in the reception and representation of Japanese art outside Japan from the 19th century to date and in the process where an object's meaning shifts as it moves through space and time.

DAVID HOWES

Professor in the Department of Sociology and Anthropology and Co-Director of the Centre for Sensory Studies at Concordia University and an Adjunct Professor in the Faculty of Law at McGill University.

Howes is best known as a pioneer of the anthropology of the senses and theorist of the interdisciplinary field of sensory studies.

KŌSUKE IKEDA

Artist, writer, and Adjunct Instructor at the Kyoto University of Education.

Ikeda's works of various media explore the existence of matter and energy surrounding human beings. His latest publications include *In Search of the Lost Thing: The Age of Uncertainty and Art* (in Japanese, *Seki Shobo*, 2019).

NATSU OYOBE

Curator of Asian Art, University of Michigan Museum of Art.

Oyobe's recent exhibitions include *Clay as Soft Power: Shigaraki Ware in Postwar America and Japan* (2022-23). She co-edited *Great Waves and Mountains: Perspectives and Discoveries in Collecting the Arts of Japan* with Allysa Payton (University of Florida Press, 2022).

KŌJIRŌ HIROSE

Associate Professor and Curator, the National Museum of Ethnology, Osaka.

Hirose's research interests include anthropological study on handicapped culture and historical study on new religions in modern Japan. As a visually impaired scholar, he is also developing a Universal Museum, where everyone can enjoy and learn through tactile exhibits.

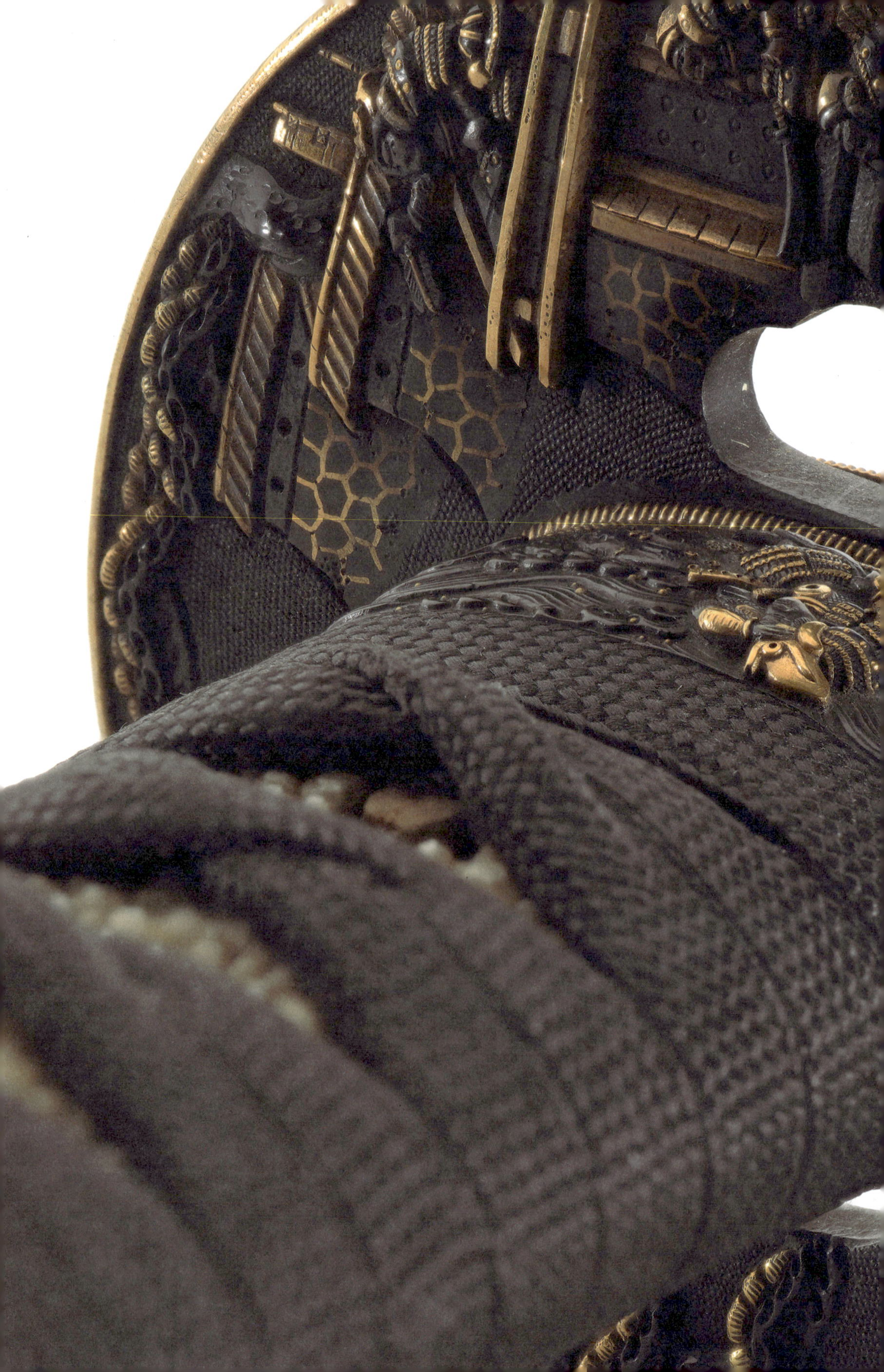

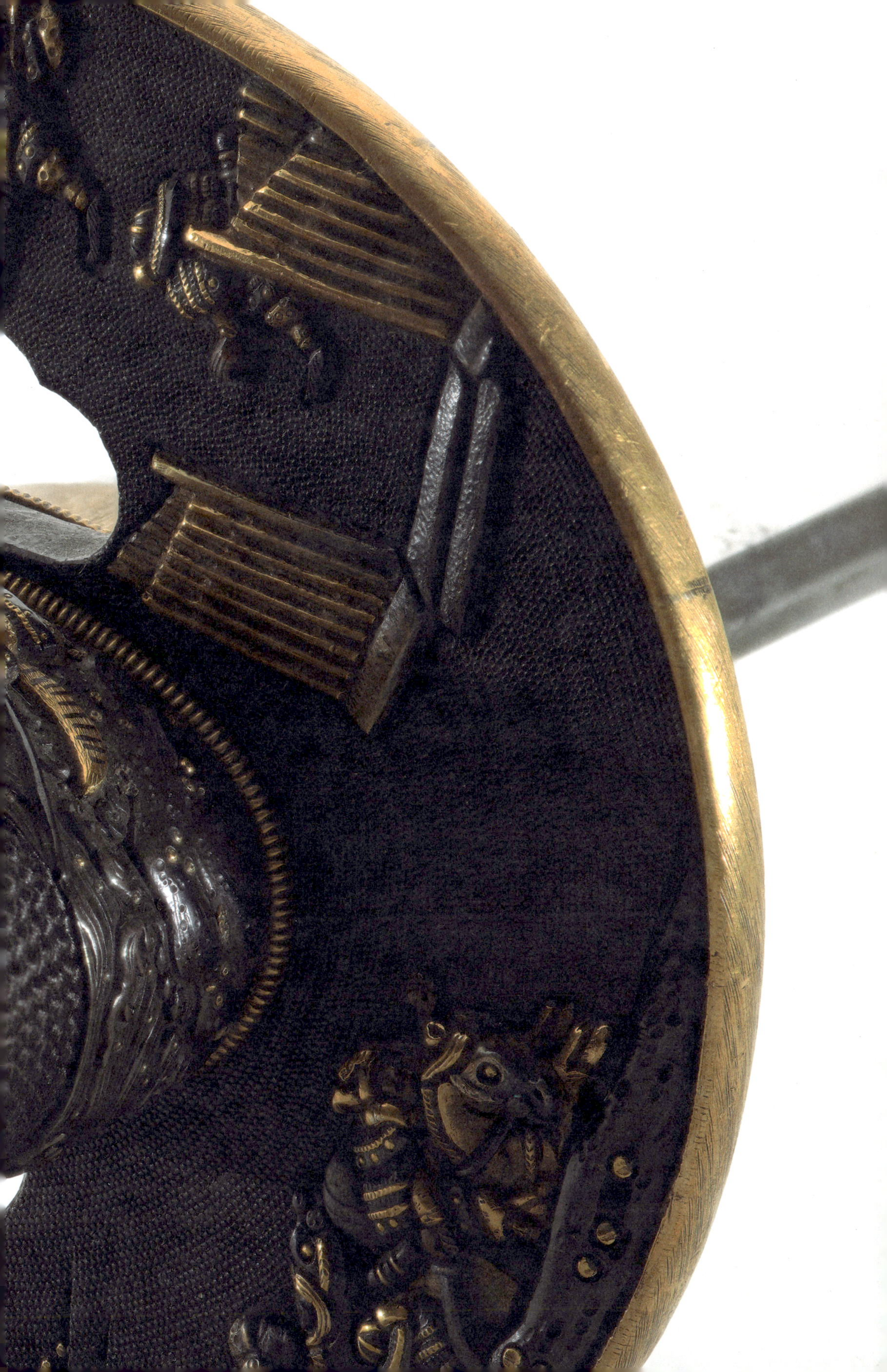

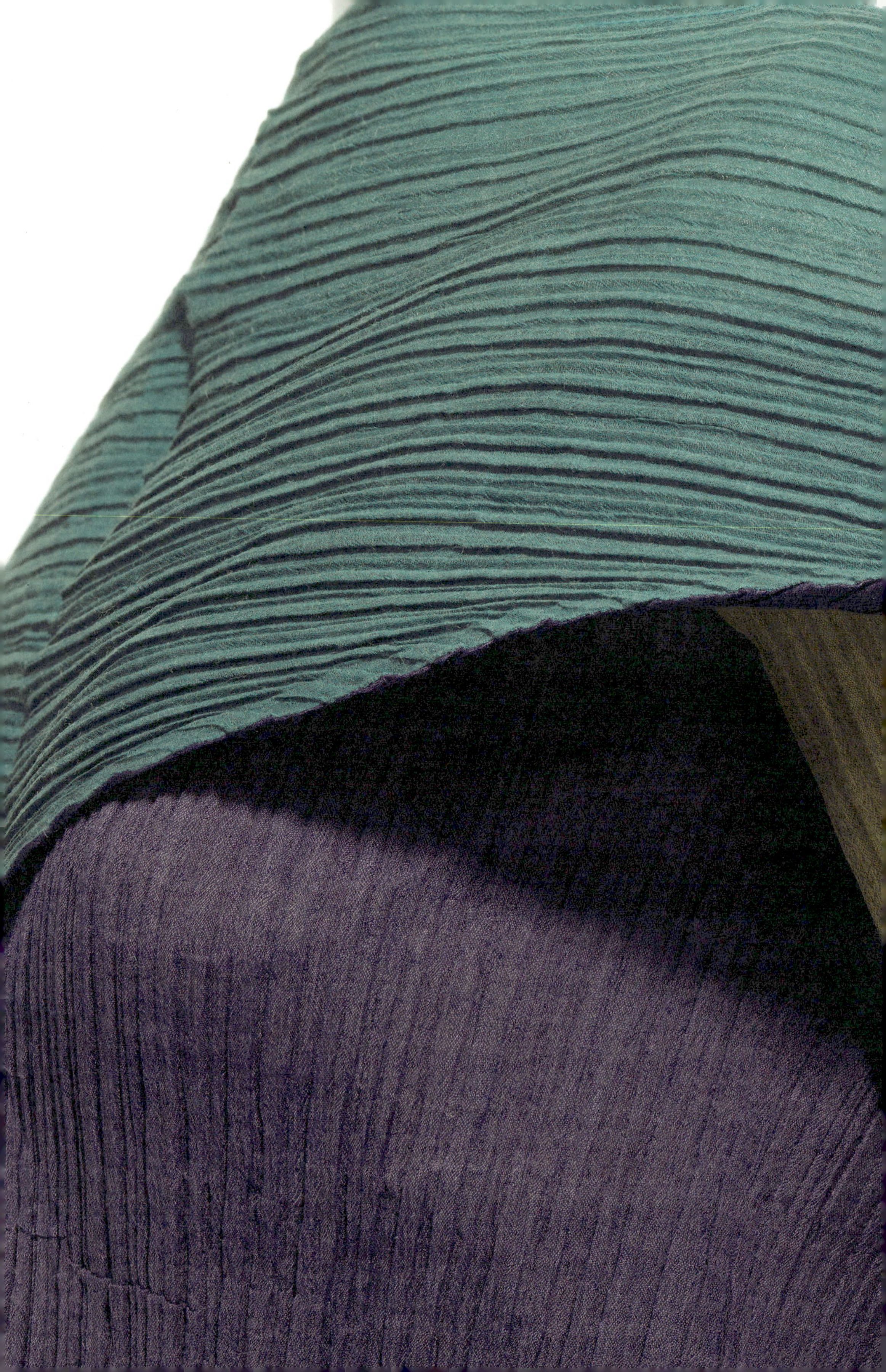

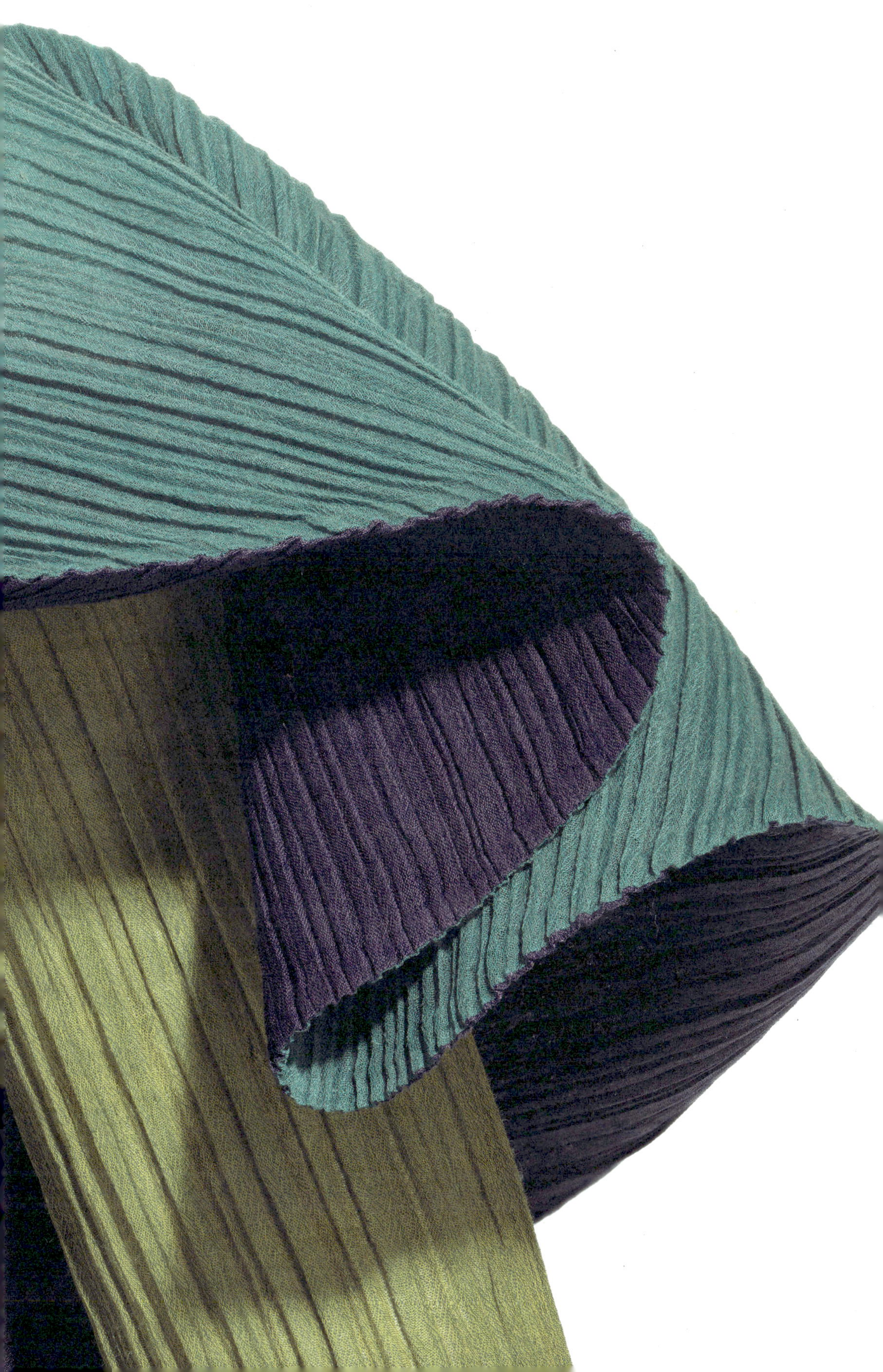

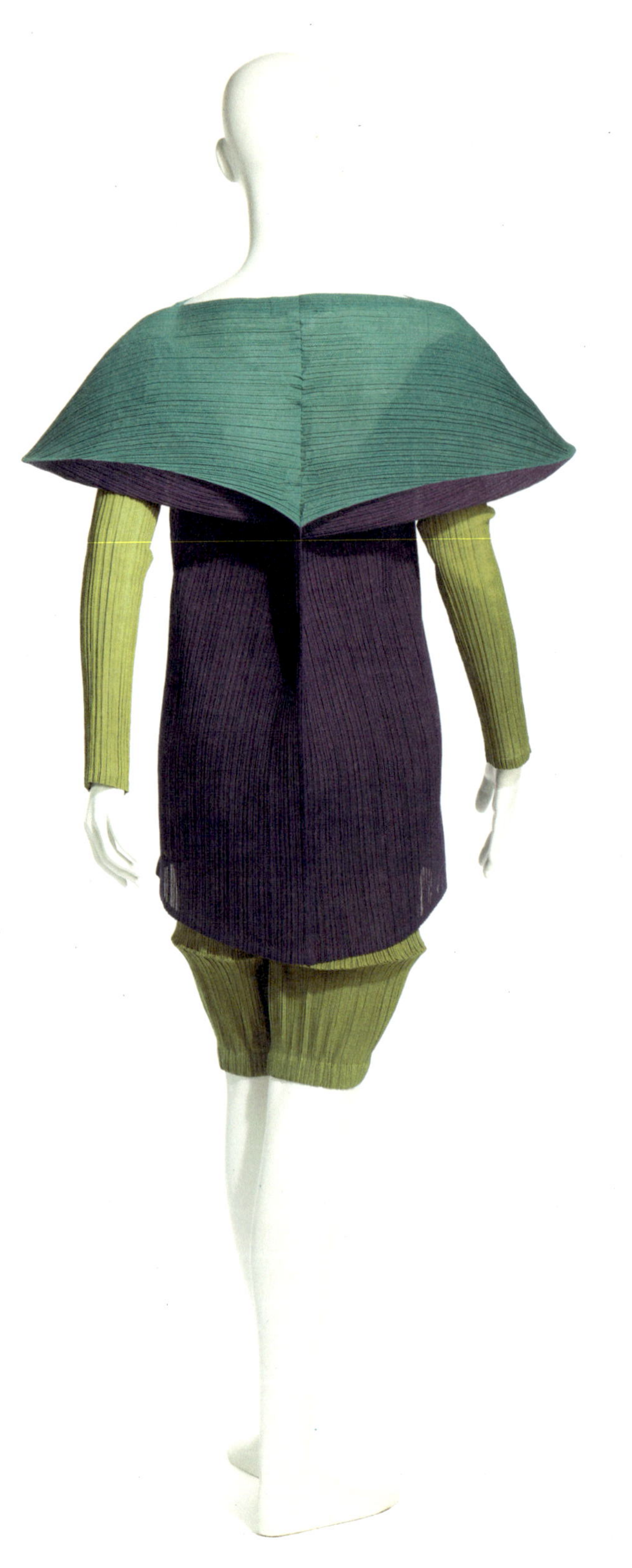